MW00571028

ST. JAMES-ASSINIBOIA SCHOOL DIVISION No. 2
## LINCOLN SCHOOL
GR.  RM. N.  G.  F.  NAME

| 20___ | Andrew Renker | 6-11 |
| 20___ | Victoria | 612 |
| 20___ | | |
| 20___ | | |
| 20___ | | |

# Canada, A Country of Change

## 1867 to Present

# Canada, A Country of Change

## 1867 to Present

*Graham Broad
& Matthew Rankin*

PORTAGE & MAIN PRESS

© 2008 by Portage & Main Press

Portage & Main Press acknowledges the financial support of the Government of Canada through the
Book Publishing Industry Development Program (BPIDP).

All rights reserved. Except as noted, no part of this publication may be reproduced or transmitted in any form
or by any means – graphic, electronic, or otherwise – without the prior written permission of the publisher.

Printed and bound in Canada by Friesens

ISBN: 978-1-55379-121-8

Project coordination and editing: Portage & Main Press
Additional editing: Richard Wood, Douglas Whiteway
Additional writing: James Chliboyko, Linda McDowell, William Neville, Richard Wood
Photo research: Robert Barrow, Susan Turner
Additional photography: Robert Barrow
Cartography: Douglas Fast
Illustration: Jess Dixon
Book & cover design: Terry Corrigan and Suzanne Braun of Relish Design Studio

This book has been published for the Manitoba Grade 6 Social Studies curriculum.  The publisher wishes to acknowledge
the following reviewers from Manitoba Education, Citizenship and Youth:

Wanda Barker, Aboriginal Languages Consultant
Al Friesen, Social Studies Consultant
Lorrie Kirk, Learning Resources Consultant
Linda Mlodzinski, Social Studies Consultant
Greg Pruden, Aboriginal Perspectives Consultant

The publisher would like to thank the following people for additional review of the content and their invaluable advice:

Carla Divinsky, Holocaust Education Coordinator, Jewish Heritage Centre of Western Canada
David Leochko, Grade 6 teacher, Victoria-Albert School
Linda McDowell, Faculty of Education, University of Winnipeg
William Neville, Senior Scholar and former Head, Department of Political Studies, University of Manitoba
Tom Rossi, Principal, Robert H. Smith School
Hart Schwartz, Director, Legal Services Branch, Ontario Human Rights Commission

**On the cover:** Satellite/Canadian Space Agency; Timber trestle, Pic River, Ontario, 1885/Canadian Pacific Archives
NS.14886, C. W. Spencer Collection; *Buffalo Hunt*, by George Catlin/Library and Archives Canada, Acc. No. 1960-50-2.6.

## PORTAGE & MAIN PRESS

100-318 McDermot Avenue
Winnipeg, MB Canada R3A 0A2
Tel. 204-987-3500 • Toll free: 1-800-667-9673
Toll-free fax: 1-866-734-8477
E-mail: books@pandmpress.com
www.pandmpress.com

**Mixed Sources**
Product group from well-managed
forests, and recycled wood or fibre
www.fsc.org  Cert no. SW-COC-1271
© 1996 Forest Stewardship Council

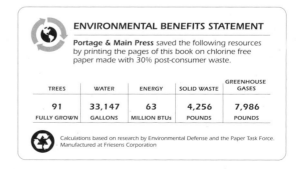

**ENVIRONMENTAL BENEFITS STATEMENT**

**Portage & Main Press** saved the following resources
by printing the pages of this book on chlorine free
paper made with 30% post-consumer waste.

| TREES | WATER | ENERGY | SOLID WASTE | GREENHOUSE GASES |
|---|---|---|---|---|
| 91 | 33,147 | 63 | 4,256 | 7,986 |
| FULLY GROWN | GALLONS | MILLION BTUs | POUNDS | POUNDS |

Calculations based on research by Environmental Defense and the Paper Task Force.
Manufactured at Friesens Corporation

*All students should be lucky enough to have teachers like Margaret Martin, Keith Watson, and Donna Goodman. This textbook is our own effort to pass on the spirit of their teachings, and the authors dedicate it to them with gratitude.*

# Contents

# About this Book

Last year, you learned about people and stories in Canada from very early times until 1867. This year, you will continue to learn the story of Canada, starting at Confederation and continuing through to modern times. In this book, you will read about new people, new provinces and territories, and the changes that have taken place in Canada since it became a country in 1867. You will learn about events such as wars and depressions, strikes, and the battles for citizenship rights. You will learn about changes in everyday life. This book tells about famous people – like Mistahimaskwa (Big Bear), Emily Stowe, and Wilfrid Laurier – and everyday people like you, your friends, and members of your family. Some of the big events in this book are recent enough that there are still some people alive who remember them and can tell us about them.

## Where to Find History

Do you have a box or an album where you keep souvenirs of special events in your life – things like programs, tickets, photos, birthday cards, and videos? Some people call these their *memory boxes*. Individual boxes may not seem very important, but when many people donate their memory boxes to museums and archives, they all add up to big collections of information about the past. When historians want to find out about the past, they can go to archives and museums to see what was important to people at the time.

What do they find there?

**Oral history.** Oral, or spoken, history is the oldest way of recording stories of people and events. Long before writing was invented, people kept track of their history by telling stories. Sometimes people memorized the history of their family or group and passed it on to the next generation. Some museums and archives now ask people to make tapes of their traditional stories and memories of earlier times so that the information will not be lost.

**Visual history.** Visual history includes images – photos, paintings, drawings, cartoons, maps, charts, movies, and videos – that were made at a particular time. In very early times, some people painted pictures in caves or on rocks (called *pictographs*). In later times, artists painted pictures of important people and events. However, until the invention of the camera, very few images of ordinary people and everyday events were made.

Once the camera was invented, photographs (and, later, movies and videos) of family events and celebrations, such as graduations or weddings, became common. There are many photographs of the historical events in this book because the camera had been invented by the time they happened.

**Written history.** Historians use written records from governments and businesses to learn about the big events of the past, such as wars and elections. Newspapers also tell about those events. These records of the past are usually found in archives and museums. Many important people, such as premiers or prime ministers, donate all of their papers and letters to archives.

Historians also read diaries, letters, and cards to learn about the lives of ordinary people. Newspaper ads, receipts, and bills provide helpful information about everyday life, including what people bought and what those items cost. Today, many of us write our letters by e-mail. Do you think historians of the future will be able to find these and use them?

**Artifacts.** Historians study things that people from the past made and used. These things are called *artifacts*. People called *archaeologists* study objects from the past to learn about life in other times.

**Places.** Historians look for information in places where important events have occurred, including national parks and historic sites. In Manitoba, The Forks and Lower Fort Garry are historic sites. Many communities have local museums. Almost every community in Canada has a war memorial listing the people who died in the world wars. Homes such as King House in Virden and Dalnavert in Winnipeg have been preserved to show us how people lived at a certain time.

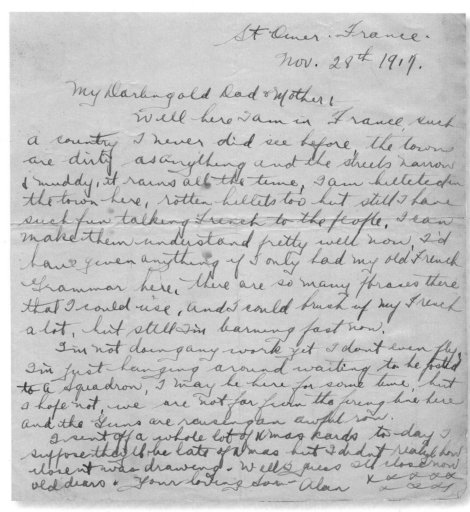

**Figure 1** Historians look at things like letters, old bills, and newspapers to tell them about the past. This letter, from Alan Arnett Macleod to his parents, tells about life in France for a young soldier (read more about Macleod on p. 96).

# Why Study History?

Where did your ancestors come from? Why did certain groups come to Canada? How did people of long ago live? We study Canadian history to find out the answers to these questions and to understand who we are.

Why do we have the laws that we do? Who decided them? Who decided what kind of government we should have? We study Canadian history to find out how and why people decided what laws we would have and how our country would be governed. The more you know about the history of government and law in Canada, the better you will be able to decide what should be changed and what should be kept.

History is not only about the past. By learning history, you will find it easier to understand what is happening today and what might happen in the future. History is *your* story, too.

## Historians as Detectives

If you like reading mysteries you will know that detectives always look for clues or evidence. First, they have to establish the facts: Who? What? When? Where? Why? and How? They also have to ask the witnesses many questions to find out what they saw or heard. Detectives have to remember that every person has her or his own point of view. They know that some witnesses might have a reason to make someone look guilty or innocent. Detectives have to be careful to check the story that each person tells. There is one important question that detectives always have to remember: Who benefits, or gets something, from this crime?

When historians write about events that happened a long time ago, they have to look at many different versions of the story and check the evidence, just as detectives do. The historian's job is even harder, because witnesses are often dead. Historians look at *primary* and *secondary*

sources. Primary sources are records of an event documented by someone who was there. These include such things as letters, photos, and videos. Secondary sources are writings or pictures by someone who has only heard or read about an event second- or even third hand. Which kind of source do you think is most useful?

To be a good history student, you must learn to ask many questions about what you read. You must learn to be a good researcher and to go to many different sources for your information. Although this textbook has been carefully researched and written, it is still a secondary source. If you want to learn from primary sources, you will need to look at those objects in memory boxes at museums and archives (or those pictured in this book). You can also talk to people who were at a historical event. Learn to be **skeptical** and question the ideas in your history books.

## Getting to Know Your Book

Whenever you start using a new book, it helps to spend a few minutes turning the pages, looking at the names, places, pictures, and maps.

You will find many illustrations and photographs in this book. There are also newspaper pictures that were created by someone who was alive when an event happened. Illustrations can give you useful information and help you to remember what you have learned.

You will also find many maps in this book. They show you where the events you are reading about took place. They show you how the land we now call Canada was divided at different times. Many of the maps in this book will show you new provinces and territories that were added to Canada after 1867. Provinces also changed size. Manitoba was called the "postage stamp province" when it joined Canada in 1870. If you look at a modern map you will see that Manitoba is now a much larger province.

## Start at the front of the book

Turn back to the cover of this textbook. What is its title? The title is *Canada, A Country of Change*. Judging by the title, what do you think you are going to read about in this book? Now look at the pictures and design on the book cover. Have you ever seen pictures of these things before?

Turn to the title page. Who wrote the textbook? Turn the page over. When and where was the book written? Since this book is about Canada, you will want to know whether it was written in Canada or somewhere else. The date it was published tells you how recent the information is. You may think that a history book does not have to be recent, because all history is old, anyway. That might be true, but historians, archaeologists, and other scholars are constantly finding new information about history. Sometimes they find out that old information is wrong.

Now turn to the contents page. This page lists 15 chapters in the book and gives you the page number where each chapter starts. The names of the chapters and of the five sections let you know what you are going to read about. You can tell from the chapter names in this book that you will be reading about topics such as Manitoba becoming a province, Aboriginal peoples in the new country, World Wars I and II, and our government.

## Go to the back of the book

On the contents page, you will see the words glossary, *index,* and *appendix*.

The glossary (p. 203) is a mini-dictionary that explains the meanings of words that you may not know. Words that are in the glossary are in **bold** type. When a word has more than one meaning, you will learn about the meaning used in this book. For example, if you want to find out what **alliances** are, you can look it up in the glossary.

> **alliance** organization of nations or other groups who join together to achieve certain aims

The index (p. 213) is an alphabetical list of major topics and names that are mentioned in the textbook. If you want to read about Elizabeth McDougall, for example, go to the index and look up the name *McDougall, Elizabeth*. The index gives you the page or pages where you can find the information you are looking for.

At the back of the book you will also find the appendixes. An appendix gives you additional useful information. This book has two appendixes. The first is a timeline of Canadian events from the time period covered in this book.

The second appendix lists all of Canada's prime ministers with the dates of their terms of office. When people write about Canadian history they often organize events by saying that they happened during a particular prime minister's term. For example, we might say that the Charter of Rights was developed during Prime Minister Trudeau's term.

Now that you have found out what is in your book, use it to help you to learn about Canadian history.

# Reading Your Book

## Reading the section introductions

In this book, the chapters are organized into sections. The title of the section is on the left page. Below it there are some paragraphs that introduce the section and tell you about what will be discussed in the following chapters. Each section includes interesting pictures of artifacts you might find in your grandmother's trunk or in someone's memory box from that time period. These pictures are called an

*advance organizer*. They will help you predict the events you will read about. The pictures are numbered, and information about them is keyed to the numbers.

## Reading the chapters

In this book, each chapter begins with a story. In the first few paragraphs you will usually find the answers to the questions *who, what, when,* and *where*? Later paragraphs will give you more information.

As you read the chapters, you will find lots of maps, pictures, and coloured boxes. Using the book will be easier if you know about the information in these special sections of the book:

**"As you read, think about" boxes.** This is a blue and gold box, with a notebook and pencil, found at the beginning of each chapter. The information in the box will help you find the main ideas in the chapter.

> **AS YOU READ, THINK ABOUT**
> - what Canada was like at the tim Confederation
> - how the British North America A the new country's government
> - the differences between Canadi and today

**"Did you know?" boxes.** These green boxes, with the heading "Did you know?" appear in different places in each chapter. They contain interesting and funny facts about people and things in the text.

> **DID YOU KNOW?** John A. Mac son, Hugh John Macdonald, repres of Winnipeg City in Canada's Parlia He later led the Conservative Party In 1900, for a short time, he was Ma before returning to federal politics

**Information boxes.** These boxes are gold with a blue bar across the top. They contain extra information about the main text you are reading. White titles in the blue bar tell you what is inside the box.

> **Social reform movements**
> There were new problems as Canada ch and grew. People in cities faced overcro poverty. There was unemployment, crin pollution. In the late 19th century, socia movements were formed to fight these One such movement was called the Soc

Some information boxes have a label with the letters *PM* in them. These boxes tell about a prime minister, such as John A. Macdonald or R.B. Bennett.

> (1815–1891) **PM**
> was not born in me from Glasgow, n, Upper Canada,

## Aboriginal names and terms

*Aboriginal peoples* is the term used to describe the original people of Canada and their descendants. There are three groups of Aboriginal peoples in Canada: First Nations, Métis, and Inuit.

Many of the names for Aboriginal peoples that are used in reports and historical documents are not the names that the people used themselves. There are many reasons for this. Explorers and early fur traders did not know Aboriginal languages very well, and sometimes misunderstood the words. Often, they copied down the translators' words incorrectly. In some cases, an unfriendly neighbouring group told the Europeans the wrong name on purpose. Sometimes, Europeans made up their own names for groups. For centuries, European versions of Aboriginal peoples' names have appeared in reports, documents and on maps.

Aboriginal peoples have always had their own names for themselves. For example, the members of the five Iroquois nations refer to themselves as the *Haudenosaunee* (meaning "the people of the longhouse"). The Cree call themselves *Nehiyaw*. In this book, you will find Aboriginal names with the European names in parentheses beside them.

**Quotations.** These blue boxes contain the words that real people said or wrote. When you read them, you

> THE NAME OF THE COUNTRY is already writ in all hearts, that of Red River. Fancy d that of 'Manitoba,' but the situation se demand that of 'North-West.' Friends o government are pleased with that of As [but] it is not generally enough liked t

will understand what the speakers or writers thought about the people they met or the times they lived in.

Pictures, maps, charts, and diagrams provide information that are not in words. They have titles or captions that tell you what they are about.

Enjoy reading this book.

# Introduction
## Citizenship in a Country of Change

When Canada became a country in 1867, it had four provinces and was part of Great Britain. Canada has grown and changed a great deal since Confederation. Today, it is an **independent** country of ten provinces and three territories. It has many different cultures and peoples. The events that you will read about in this book all played a role in what it means to be a Canadian citizen in the 21st century.

Citizenship is more than just saying you are Canadian. Citizenship is about how people work together and help each other. Citizenship cannot be owned – it is something that is shared with others. It involves taking care of and showing respect to Canada's many different cultures and peoples.

You will also read about how Canadian citizenship has changed over time. You will meet people – famous and not so famous – who have helped shape Canada into the country you now live in. As well, you will read about Canadians whose actions have changed the world.

### World citizenship

Canadian citizenship has meaning outside our own country. Canadians play a part in being citizens of the world.

Organizations such as the Canadian International Development Agency (CIDA) send

**Figure i.1** Between 1996 and 2001, girls in Afghanistan were not allowed to go to school. Since a new government lifted the ban, the Canadian International Development Agency (CIDA) has built and operated schools for girls in the country.

Canadians to help poor countries. CIDA volunteers build hospitals and schools and help improve peoples' lives.

Many Canadians speak out about the problems that the world faces. In 1997, for example, Canada helped get nations around the world to agree to ban land mines (see p. 9).

These are just some of the ways in which Canadians have been world citizens.

### Citizenship and you

There is an Aboriginal teaching that says: "We do not inherit the Earth from our ancestors; we borrow it from our grandchildren."

**Figure i.2** These students spent 30 hours without food. Not only did they raise money to reduce poverty, they raised awareness of hunger and poverty in the world.

This means that the choices people make today affect the world of tomorrow. Right now, governments in Canada and around the world decide on things that will affect peoples' lives, their country, and the world. They decide what will happen to the environment, what rights people should and should not have, and whether or not to go to war.

There are many ways for citizens to be part of Canada's future. They can join a political party or write a letter to their member of Parliament. They can take part in programs to learn a second official language or to find out more about their country.

One important idea of Canadian citizenship is **democracy.** In a democracy, the people of a country choose who will speak for them. The prime minister, premiers, members of Parliament, and mayors, for example, are all chosen by the people. These politicians must respect and consider different views, just as citizens must listen to and respect the ideas of others.

In the early 1990s, a girl named Severn Cullis-Suzuki showed that young people have an important role to play in Canada and the world.

Severn was only 12 years old when she and some friends formed a group called the Environmental Children's Organization (ECO).

The members of ECO thought adults were making a mess of the environment. They said changes had to be made. Severn learned that world governments were meeting in Rio de Janeiro, Brazil, in 1992 to talk about these problems at the United Nations Earth Summit. She thought ECO should be there, too.

To raise the money for the trip, the members of ECO baked cupcakes, made jewellery, collected donations, and held several fundraisers. Before long, they had raised $13 000. ECO was off to the summit.

To a room full of world leaders, Severn delivered a powerful speech. She said:

> I'm only a child and I don't have all the solutions, but I want you to realize, neither do you!
>
> You don't know how to fix holes in our ozone layer.
>
> You don't know how to bring salmon back to a dead stream.
>
> You don't know how to bring back an animal now extinct.
>
> And you can't bring back the forests that once grew where there is now a desert.
>
> If you don't know how to fix it, please stop breaking it!

**Figure i.3** Severn Cullis-Suzuki at Earth Summit in 1992

## The Mine Ban Treaty

A land mine is an explosive that is buried underground. It explodes when someone steps on it. In times of war, land mines can be important to an army's defence. However, land mines that have not exploded are hard to find when a war is over. Millions are still buried in old battlefields around the world. Every year, thousands of innocent people are killed or wounded by land mines.

In 1997, representatives of more than a hundred countries met in Ottawa to sign an important agreement: the Mine Ban Treaty. Canada asked other countries in the United Nations (UN) to help remove land mines. More than 150 countries have now signed the Mine Ban Treaty. They have agreed to find and destroy old land mines and to stop

**Figure i.4** These explosives experts are gathering land mines so that someone does not accidentally step on one and cause it to explode.

making new ones. More than 37 million land mines have been destroyed since 1997. The Mine Ban Treaty shows what Canadians can do by working with other countries.

Many people were moved by Severn's speech. Al Gore, who would soon become vice president of the United States, told her that she made the best speech at the meeting.

Severn's story shows how any person can speak up and be heard by those in power. A person does not have to be a world leader to bring about change. All that a person needs is the desire to help others, and the drive and courage to be an active citizen.

Canadians are proud of the country they have built since 1867. Still, there is much to be done. As you read this book, think about what you can do as a citizen of Canada and the world.

**Figure i.5** Patrick, 15, fills a box with food for a person at a shelter for homeless people. As a volunteer, his duties can include everything from mopping the kitchen floor, to making beds, to handing out food.

# Putting Canada Together

**1**

On July 1, 1867, a new nation – Canada – was born. Its founders created a government that would look after the country's growing needs. When Canada acquired Rupert's Land in 1869, the Métis and First Nations people became concerned about losing their land and culture. In 1870, Manitoba, led by Louis Riel, joined Confederation with Métis rights assured. By 1904, Canada had grown from four provinces to nine. It extended from the Atlantic Ocean to the Pacific Ocean. Two northern territories met the Arctic Ocean. Soon, a railroad connected this vast country from sea to sea. It was a country of great promise. Yet all this progress was not easy.

**2**

**3**

**4**

**5**

# In the Memory Box...

**1** Crazy quilts, made from scraps of leftover fabric, were very popular in late Victorian times, and let women of the time show off their sewing skills.

**2** Cartoon by J.M. Bengough, from *Grip* magazine, entitled "Confederation. The Much Fathered Youngster.

**3** This knife belonged to John Schultz, leader of the pro-Canadian forces at the Red River settlement. It was smuggled into Fort Garry where Schultz was being held prisoner by Riel's men. With the knife, Schultz cut a buffalo robe into strips to make a rope. He tied the rope to a window ledge, then escaped by climbing down it.

**4** Poster for Brotherhood of Railroad Trainmen, 1883. The Brotherhood looked after railroad workers' welfare in the days before unemployment, life, and disability insurance. The illustrations provided a clear message for those who could not read or speak English.

**5** This dark blue cap, along with a red jacket and tan pants, made up the official uniform of the North-West Mounted Police.

**6** These scales, from about 1900, were used in a bank to weigh gold from the Klondike Gold Rush.

**7** This diagram shows the construction of a railway.

**8** Schoolchildren used small blackboards, or slates, to do their schoolwork in class.

**9** This finger-woven sash belonged to Elzéar Goulet, a member of Louis Riel's provisional government.

**10** This cabinet photograph, showing the early settlement of Winnipeg, was a souvenir from around 1880.

# 1 Canada in 1867

## Confederation

Just after midnight on July 1, 1867, a great roar of cannons was heard in Ottawa. The shots were not fired in anger. They marked the birth of a new nation: Canada. As day broke, church bells rang. People flocked into the streets. It was the first Dominion Day.

Everywhere, the summer weather was perfect for celebrating. Bands played. Town mayors gave speeches. People rejoiced under a cloudless sky. Many new Canadians met in churches to pray for their young country.

The process of uniting Canada was called *Confederation*. Only three colonies had joined: Nova Scotia, New Brunswick, and the Province of Canada (which was immediately divided into two provinces, Ontario and Quebec). No one could be sure the country would stay together. It was good that the young nation's first prime minister was one of its greatest: Sir John A. Macdonald. He spent the rest of his life working to make Confederation succeed.

### AS YOU READ, THINK ABOUT

- what Canada was like at the time of Confederation
- how the British North America Act set up the new country's government
- the differences between Canadians in 1867 and today
- what plan the country's leaders had for the country's future

Confederation almost never happened. In 1866, the people of British North America lived in the colonies of Newfoundland, Prince Edward Island, Nova Scotia, New Brunswick, and the Province of Canada. Far to the west was British Columbia.

The colonies had no great desire to unite. In Nova Scotia, a politician named Joseph Howe even said, "A more unpromising **nucleus** of a new nation could hardly be found on the face of the earth." In the Maritimes, many people agreed with Howe. They feared losing their independence to the much larger Province of Canada. They wanted a union of the Maritime colonies, leaving the Province of Canada out of it.

Why, then, did Confederation happen at all?

One reason was that the British government wanted the colonies to take greater responsibility for themselves. The way Britain and its colonies acted was much like parents with their children. British North America's move from **colony** to nation was part of "growing up."

A second reason was the American Civil War. This terrible war, which began in 1861, was fought between the northern and southern states. The British did not join the war. They did, however, help the Southerners by selling them things such as ships. When the North won the war in 1865, some Americans wanted to attack British North America in revenge. By joining together, the British colonies could better defend themselves.

A third reason was to build a strong **economy**. Supporters of Confederation saw a great nation joined together by the steel

**Figure 1.1** The Proclamation of Confederation was announced, at noon July 1, 1867, in the Market Square of Kingston, Ontario. Celebrations continued with sporting events and a night of fireworks.

of railways. Trade would flow across the country, bringing greater riches. They even saw the country growing westward, all the way to British Columbia.

Still, Confederation had not been easy. It had taken many months of planning to bring Canada together. Even then, Prince Edward Island and Newfoundland stayed out. British Columbians waited until work began on the railroad. Aboriginal peoples had not been a part of the meetings that led to Confederation. They worried about what Confederation might mean for them.

**DID YOU KNOW?** Canada became the first of Britain's dominions in 1867. Other British colonies, including Australia, New Zealand, South Africa, and Newfoundland, also became dominions in time.

## Sir John A. Macdonald (1815–1891) PM

Canada's first prime minister was not born in Canada. John A. Macdonald came from Glasgow, Scotland. He moved to Kingston, Upper Canada, with his family in 1820. He was an amazing young man. He had his own law practice by the time he was 19. In 1844, when he just 29, Macdonald was **elected** to the Parliament of Canada. He later became leader of a new political party, the Liberal-Conservatives. Then, in 1856, he became co-premier of the Province of Canada. Macdonald led the push for Confederation. He also wrote the first draft of the British North America Act (see p. 18). In 1867, after Confederation, Macdonald became the first prime minister of Canada.

Although he was a success as prime minister, Macdonald's life was marked with sadness. His first son, John, died as a baby. His first wife, Isabella, died after a long illness. A daughter from his second marriage, Mary, was mentally and physically challenged. Apart from five years (1873–1878) when he was leader of the Opposition, Macdonald was Canada's prime minister until his death in 1891.

**Figure 1.2** Sir John A. Macdonald

# Canada in 1867

John A. Macdonald became prime minister of one of the largest countries in the world. However, it had a very small population. With an area of one million square kilometres in 1867, Canada was already bigger than the United Kingdom and France combined. Canada's population, however, was just 3.5 million people. The United Kingdom had 30 million people. France and the United States each had 40 million people.

Not only that, the number of people moving to Canada had slowed to a trickle. Thousands of Canadians moved to the United States every month. One thing that made Canada different was the **diversity** of its people. People of British, French, Irish, German, and African background lived together in this new nation with the original Aboriginal peoples.

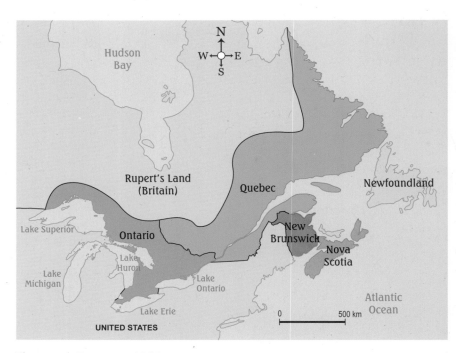

**Figure 1.3** *CANADA IN 1867*

## Going to school in the 1860s

At the beginning of the 19th century, only the children of rich families went to school. On family farms, children spent their days working with their parents. In cities, children as young as 10 sometimes worked in mills.

By the 1870s, however, most children aged 5 to 16 had some schooling. Children went to small schools. There, children from all grades learned together in a single room. Students learned to read (often from the Bible), write, and do arithmetic. They were taught Canada's history. Usually, one teacher would teach them. Most students learned by rote – memorizing, memorizing, and more memorizing. Teachers were very strict. They were allowed to hit students who misbehaved.

Children from farm families were often excused from school for the harvest. In many cases, girls went to school for fewer years than boys. This was because many girls in their teens had to stay home to help raise their younger brothers and sisters.

**Figure 1.4** A teacher at the doorway of a one-room schoolhouse rings a bell as children arrive at school. George B. Johnston, who was the teacher at Parent Creek School, made this drawing in 1865.

Only a tiny number of students went to university. Usually, only boys were allowed to go. University education was very hard. Students had to speak *five* languages – English, French, German, Latin, and Greek – by the time they finished school.

## Everyday life after Confederation

Today, it is hard for us to imagine what life was like in 1867. We live in a world of computer games, televisions, cell phones, and airplanes. In 1867, however, homes did not have electricity. There were only one or two cars in all of Canada. Most Canadians lived on farms or in very small towns. They made their living by producing **staple** products: wheat, fish, and timber.

### Population by province, 1871

| Nova Scotia | New Brunswick | Quebec | Ontario |
|---|---|---|---|
| 387 800 | 285 594 | 1 191 516 | 1 620 851 |

By today's standards, even the biggest cities in 1867, Toronto and Montreal, would seem like small towns. They had dirt roads. Their tallest buildings rose only a few storeys. People travelled from place to place by horse on muddy wagon trails. Of course, horses left manure everywhere they went – even on city streets.

Science and medicine were far less advanced than today. For instance, doctors had only just discovered that most diseases are caused by germs. Children were especially at risk from diseases. In Montreal, nearly two out of every five infants died of sickness before the age of one.

However, there were signs that things were changing. **Industrialization** was beginning. Cities were growing. **Telegraph** lines and railroads crisscrossed the nation. Canals had been built in the decades before Confederation. They allowed ships to bypass both the St. Lawrence rapids and Niagara Falls. Ships could then sail all the way from the Atlantic Ocean to the Upper Great Lakes.

Railways were very important. They allowed people to travel quickly from city to city and to faraway areas. They were seen as the only way to open the West for Canadian settlement.

## Aboriginal peoples in 1867

In 1608, Samuel de Champlain first set foot in the land that would become Canada. At that time, there were at least 150 000 Aboriginal people living near the Great Lakes and in the St. Lawrence valley. By 1867, their population was less than 30 000 people. This was due to more than two hundred years of war, hunger, and disease that had been brought to North America by Europeans. By 1867, European Canadians outnumbered Aboriginal people by more than 100 to one.

**Figure 1.5** Mary Christianne Morris, a noted Mi'kmaq artist, and her son, Joe, in 1865

For years, both the British and French saw the First Nations as important military allies and partners in the fur trade. First Nations had helped the British save Upper Canada from American invaders in the War of 1812. With the end of the war and the fur trade slowing down, the British turned their backs on their First Nations friends. "My heart now fails me. I can hardly speak. We are now slaves and treated worse than dogs," an Anishinabe (Ojibwa) chief said after the War of 1812.

By the time of Confederation, the biggest First Nations were the Mi'kmaq in the Maritimes, the Haudenosaunee [how-di-ni-SHAW-nee] (Iroquois) in Ontario and Quebec, and the Anishinabe (Ojibwa) in Ontario.

**DID YOU KNOW?** John A. Macdonald's second son, Hugh John Macdonald, represented the riding of Winnipeg City in Canada's Parliament in 1896. He later led the Conservative Party of Manitoba. In 1900, for a short time, he was Manitoba's premier before returning to federal politics.

# Citizenship in 1867

In 1867, Canadians were not really thought of as citizens. Instead, they were British subjects. As subjects, Canadians had few rights. When Canada's first federal election was held in November 1867, only 20 percent of its population was allowed to vote. There were a number of reasons for this.

Women were not allowed to vote. Neither were Aboriginal or Asian people. Most men could not vote, either. A man had to own land to have voting rights. This meant that political power was in the hands of a small group of rich men of European background.

Today, voters cast *secret ballots*. This means that no one can see who a person votes for. In the 1860s, however, voters cast their ballots in the open for all to see. This made it easier for people to threaten voters. Gangs of thugs were hired to bully people into voting for certain **candidates**. Fights were common on election day.

Slowly, things changed. Governments made laws to stamp out **corruption** in elections. The secret ballot was adopted. By the turn of the century, most men of European background were allowed to vote, even if they did not own property. But women of European background could not vote until 1917. It would be decades before other groups could vote (see page 185).

## Race and racism

*Race* is a word that is sometimes used to describe a certain group of people. The people in the group may have similar skin colour or facial features. Sometimes, race refers to a person's **ancestry**.

Throughout history, people believed that different races had different personalities. They used this idea to say that one race was better than another. This is called *racism*.

In many countries, racism was used to help write laws. Sometimes people were prevented from voting, having jobs, and even going to school.

Scientists today know that physical appearance has nothing to do with what kind of person someone is. They have also learned that there is only one race – the human race – and we are all part of it.

# Women's Lives in the 1860s

"Woman's first and only place is in her home," a Canadian writer said in 1874. Her duty, he wrote, is to make the home a "joyful" place in a "busy, heartless world."

In the late 19th century, most Canadians – including women – agreed. They believed that a woman's job was raising children and doing the household work. They did not believe women should take part in politics or work outside the home. They thought that would only take women away from the important job of looking after their families.

This is why women were not allowed to vote or go to university. It also explains why married women did not plan to get jobs. Most women got married in their mid-20s and then had large families. Usually only young women worked for wages outside of the home. In rare cases where a married woman did work, she had to give her wages to her husband. Women who wanted equal rights were seen as strange and even dangerous.

Some brave women, however, proved that a "woman's place" was anywhere she wanted to be. Such women included the missionary Elizabeth McDougall. In the early years after Confederation, she made a dangerous trip across the Prairies with her husband and six children. The family went by wagon, dogsled, and canoe. They made it to Alberta in 1873.

Another such woman was Eliza Ritchie, of Halifax. In 1889, she became one of the first Canadian women to earn the highest university degree, a PhD. She later became a professor at Dalhousie University in Halifax. She was also a **suffragist** [*SUFF-reh-jist*], fighting for women's right to vote.

Figure 1.6 Woman campaigning for women's rights around 1900

Another important woman was Henrietta Louise Edwards. Born in Montreal, Edwards started one of the country's first women's magazines: *Working Women of Canada*. She also founded the Working Girls' Association. This group helped give young women the training they needed to enter the work force.

## Emily Stowe (1831–1903)

Emily Stowe was a woman of firsts. She was the first woman to become a school principal in Upper Canada. She was the first woman to practise medicine in Canada. She also helped to set up Canada's first medical school for women.

Figure 1.7 Emily Stowe

Emily Stowe decided to study medicine after her husband, John, fell ill in the 1860s. However, no medical school in Canada would let her be a student. It was not considered right for women to learn anatomy, which is the study of the human body. After all, this would mean looking at naked men!

When she was not allowed to study at the University of Toronto, Stowe said that she hoped the school would one day open its doors to women. "Never in my day, madam!" the president of the college replied.

Instead, Stowe went to the United States. There she became a student at the New York Medical College for Women. She graduated the year of Confederation. She began to practise medicine in Toronto, even though Canadian authorities did not grant her a medical licence until 1880. Perhaps inspired by his wife, John Stowe became a dentist after he got better. He set up practice in the same office as Emily. In 1883, Emily's daughter, Augusta Stowe, became the first woman in Canada to graduate with a medical degree. Augusta graduated from the University of Toronto – the same school that had turned her mother away in the 1860s.

Emily Stowe died in 1903. She had spent her life working tirelessly for the rights of women.

# Government in Early Canada

In 1865, the American Civil War ended after four years of fighting. Nearly 600 000 Americans had been killed. In part, the Civil War was fought because Americans could not agree about what kind of government they should have. When Canada became a nation just two years later, John A. Macdonald hoped to avoid such conflicts. He wanted Canada to have a strong central government like the one in Great Britain.

## The British North America Act

The British Parliament passed the British North America Act in 1867. It made Canada a self-governing country. It gave Canadians their first **constitution**. Today, the BNA Act is known as the Constitution Act of 1867.

The BNA Act gave different powers to federal and provincial governments. When power is divided among different levels of government, it is called **federalism**.

**Figure 1.8** The first Parliament of Canada met on November 6, 1867, at the Parliament Buildings in Ottawa.

Macdonald tried to make sure that Canada's federal government was the most powerful one in the new country. For instance, the BNA Act gave the federal government power over things like national defence, trade, and taxation. Provincial governments looked after more local matters, such as education and medical care (see chart, opposite).

The Fathers of Confederation were careful about giving each level of government different powers. They hoped this would prevent problems between them. Of course, this has never worked perfectly. Provincial governments began arguing with the federal government in Ottawa almost as soon as Confederation celebrations ended.

The BNA Act set up Canada's government to be like Britain's. Canada became a *constitutional monarchy*. This means that the British monarch (the king or queen) is officially the head of state. The king or queen can only hold the power he or she is granted in the country's constitution and laws. The king or queen's role is mostly **ceremonial** and is carried out by the governor general. The job of running the country is in the hands of the Parliament.

The BNA Act also established many of the rules for Canada's government. It said that the federal Parliament would be made up of two *houses*: the House of Commons and the Senate. The House of Commons would be elected by voters. Senators would be appointed by the governor general. For new laws to be made, both houses had to vote for them. You will read more about Canada's government in chapter 15.

Not all of the rules of Canada's government are written down. Many of them are created by

**DID YOU KNOW?** *Great Britain* is the name of the island made up of England, Wales, and Scotland. These nations have been united since 1707. In 1801, Ireland was brought into what would then be known as the *United Kingdom*. Today, the United Kingdom is made up of Great Britain and Northern Ireland.

## Balancing powers: The British North America Act

The British North America Act of 1867 set out a plan for a strong central government. That is what Canada's founders had wanted. The Act stated that the federal government had the power to create laws for "peace, order, and good government." It also had *residual powers*. This meant it was responsible for things that had not been decided on yet or that might arise in the future. For example, when the BNA Act was made, there were no such things as airplanes.

Once airplanes became common and had to be looked after, the federal government took control over them.

As noted at left, the British North America Act also set out the powers of provincial and federal governments. In general, the federal government controlled national matters. The provincial governments controlled more local concerns. Here is how some of the powers were divided:

| **Federal Government** | | **Provincial Government** | |
|---|---|---|---|
| Banking | Marriage & Divorce | Civil Law | Provincial Police |
| Census | Naturalization | Courts | Public Works |
| Copyright | Navigation & Shipping | Education | Roads & Highways |
| Criminal Law | Patents | Electricity | Trade between Provinces |
| Currency | Penitentiaries | Hospitals | |
| National Defence | Postal Service | Licences | **Shared Powers** |
| Fisheries | Taxation | Natural Resources & Forestry | Agriculture |
| First Nations | Foreign Trade | Property Rights | Immigration |
| | Weights & Measures | | Old Age Pensions |

*precedent*. That means that they are based on what has happened in the past. For instance, the BNA Act does not say that Canada must have a prime minister. Prime ministers hold office because of precedent. For many years before the BNA Act, Britain had a prime minister, who was usually the leader of the largest political party in Parliament. So Canada has a prime minister, too.

Also, the BNA Act did not make Canada fully independent of Great Britain. Canada became a British *dominion*. Canada's federal and provincial governments would take care of day-to-day matters in the new dominion. Britain, however, would continue to handle Canada's *foreign affairs*. This meant that the Canadian government was not able to make its own **treaties** with other countries. In addition, changing or *amending* the Canadian constitution required Britain's permission.

## Canadian political parties after 1867

The British North America Act does not even talk about political parties. Like prime ministers, political parties came about over time. They

Queen Victoria    Lord Monck    Sir John A. Macdonald

**Figure 1.9** In Canada, the British king or queen is the head of state. The governor general is appointed by the king or queen and is his or her representative in Canada. The king or queen and the governor general represent the state publicly but they have little power. The prime minister is the head of government. In 1867, Queen Victoria was the queen, Lord Monck was the governor general, and John A. Macdonald was prime minister.

developed to help governments work in Parliaments where people had different views about important issues. They are an important part of Canada's political system.

The party system in Canada is like the one in Britain. In Canada, however, the system exists at both federal and provincial levels. (There are no provinces in the United Kingdom.)

## Nation, country, state

A *nation* is a group of people who share common experiences, such as language, customs, and traditions.

A *country* is the geographical area in which they live.

A *state* is a group of people who are governed under a single government.

John A. Macdonald was head of the Conservative Party. The Conservatives supported ideas such as a strong central government, high **tariffs** (taxes on imported goods), and close ties with Britain.

The other political party was the Liberals. It stood for **free trade** (trade without tariffs) and for greater rights for the provinces. It also stood for a more independent role for Canada in the British Empire.

New political parties came into being in Canada in the 20th century. The Conservatives and the Liberals, however, remain Canada's most important political parties.

## Building a Free Press

On New Year's Day, 1835, the *Novascotian*, a Halifax newspaper, printed an unsigned letter to the editor. The writer said **magistrates** [*MAJ-i-strates*] who were running the local government were stealing money from the citizens of Halifax.

Two months later, on March 2, *Novascotian* editor Joseph Howe was in court. He was being tried on a charge of **libel** for publishing the letter. The judge was Brenton Halliburton. (He himself had been criticized several times by the newspaper.) He told the jury to find Howe guilty. Howe spoke for more than six hours. He begged the jury "to judge me by the principles of English law, and to leave an unshackled press as a legacy to your children." He was asking the jury to support his right to tell the truth. The jury took just 10 minutes to find Howe not guilty.

In the mid-18th century, Canada's newspapers needed government money to publish. They mainly reported government statements. By the start of the 19th century, however, newspapers started selling advertising to make money. Since they no longer needed government money, editors could write about whatever they wanted. They could do so as long as the reporting was based on facts and truth.

A free press could criticize government and its leaders. It let citizens know if their governments acted in their best interests. In British North America, newspapers became a **forum** for different political opinions. They often spoke out for democratic causes, such as **Responsible Government**. Freedom of the press let people talk about important issues. It was seen as an important part of a free country.

**Figure 1.10** Early Canadian newspapers

Most newspapers gave the opinions of their editors and the political parties they supported. Reformer William Lyon Mackenzie, for example, used the *Colonial Advocate* to criticize the **Family Compact** that ruled Upper Canada. In Quebec, Étienne Parent defended the rights of French Canadians in *Le Canadien*, then *La Gazette*. George Brown of the Toronto *Globe* was in favour of Confederation and **Representation by Population**.

At the time of Confederation, the country had 291 newspapers. All of them worked with a political party or movement.

Newspapers beyond the borders of the new country had their own ideas about Canada. The *Nor'Wester* newspaper was published between 1859 and 1869 in the Red River settlement. It promoted the idea of joining Canada.

News, especially international news, was sent by ship in the early 19th century. It could take a month or more to cross the Atlantic Ocean. When the telegraph became widely used, news could be sent within hours. Newspapers began to print more world and national news in their pages.

## Looking Ahead: National Policy

In the 1878 federal election, John A. Macdonald and his Conservative Party promised Canadians a bright future. Macdonald called his plan for prosperity the *National Policy*. It involved three things:

1. **Protective tariffs.** A protective tariff would make imported goods more expensive. This would make people want to buy Canadian-made goods, which were not taxed. The tariff would only be used on finished goods such as clothing, furniture, and tools. Most raw materials were not taxed. This was to help manufacturers buy raw materials from other countries. Then the manufacturers would make them into finished goods to sell in Canada.

   For example, Canadian manufacturers could buy cotton from the United States. In Canadian factories, the cotton would be spun into cloth and made into clothes by Canadian workers.

   All this manufacturing and selling was supposed to create a strong economy. As industries grew and people became richer, Macdonald hoped that it would help farmers, too. After all, happy and well-off factory workers would have enough money to buy a lot more food.

2. **Transcontinental railway.** Like many politicians of his day, Macdonald believed the key to Canada's future was seeing the West grow. The building of the Canadian Pacific Railway across Canada would let

**Figure 1.11** Poster for John A. Macdonald's last election campaign. He won the election on March 5, 1891, but died three months later.

materials get to eastern industries. It would also help fulfill the final part of Macdonald's plan: more people living in the West.

3. **Immigration.** A working railway would bring settlers to the Prairies and farther west. The country would become settled from coast to coast. Immigrants would be the customers of Canadian companies.

## Conclusion

In 1867, John A. Macdonald and the Fathers of Confederation realized their vision for a new country. In the years that followed, the Conservative Party used Macdonald's National Policy to make sure that Canada would keep growing into the next century. In the next chapters, you will learn that the process of growing a new country was not always easy.

# 2 Manitoba Becomes a Province

On October 11, 1869, a man named André Nault was escorting his cattle across a neighbour's land. (This was near today's LaBarriere Park just south of Winnipeg.) There he was met by a team of **land surveyors**. Nault tried to tell them that they were not allowed on the property. However, Nault did not speak English, and the surveyors did not speak French. Nault ran for help. More than a dozen men on horseback returned with him. One of the men spoke English. His name was Louis Riel.

Riel told the team to leave. The surveyors left, but not before one of the men on horseback purposely stepped on the surveyor's chain. It was a simple, but defiant act.

Today, a surveying team measuring a piece of farmland is a common sight. That was not the case, though, in 1869, near today's city of Winnipeg. The people who lived there were Métis hunters and farmers and Scottish farmers. Their families had lived on the land for many years.

The English divided their land into square-shaped lots. The French had always divided their land into long, narrow lots along the river. That is the system the people of Red River used.

**Figure 2.1** The arrival of surveyors in 1869 (above) alerted the Métis that the government wanted to take over their land and prepare it for new settlement. Under Louis Riel, the Métis began a movement to keep their traditional rights to the land.

When they saw that the land was being divided into squares, they were worried. They thought their land would be taken away from them and given to settlers from the east. People were angry.

The Macdonald government worried about the young country's growth. No one knew what would happen to the area west of Ontario.

---

**AS YOU READ, THINK ABOUT**

- what life was like among the Métis of the Red River Settlement
- the concerns of the Métis, and what they wanted for their future
- the people who helped in the founding of Manitoba
- the events leading up to the founding of Manitoba

**Figure 2.2** Métis at Red River, 1870.

The Métis are a people of European and First Nations background. French and British fur traders who settled in the West married First Nations women. Their children became known as the Métis. Between 300 000 to 500 000 people today consider themselves Métis. They live mainly in Manitoba, Saskatchewan, Alberta, Ontario, and the Northwest Territories. Some live in North Dakota and Montana.

The Métis are recognized in the Canadian constitution as one of the three Aboriginal groups in Canada. The other two are First Nations and Inuit people.

**Figure 2.3** The Métis flag is a white infinity symbol on a blue background. It was flown more than 150 years before the Canadian flag.

The United States was eyeing the land in the northwest of the continent. In the 1850s, some Americans had started moving into the area.

Prime Minister Macdonald, however, did not sit idly by. He had just come to an agreement that spring with the Hudson's Bay Company (HBC). The company agreed to sell a large area, called **Rupert's Land,** to the Canadian government.

Macdonald wanted the land for English-speaking settlers from Canada. That would stop the Americans. However, he gave no thought to the First Nations and Métis people who already lived there. Neither the Canadian government nor the Hudson's Bay Company had talked to the Métis about taking over the land.

When the surveyors came, they went on people's land without asking. They did not speak French. They never told the local people what they were doing.

The Métis did not know what the future would hold for them. Within months, the act of a simple survey team led to a chain of events and series of conflicts between the government in Ottawa and the Red River settlers, led by Louis Riel.

# Arrival of "The King"

William McDougall (1822–1905) was a Father of Confederation, John A. Macdonald chose him as lieutenant governor of the North-West Territories. When McDougall left Ontario, he told Macdonald that he now considered himself "King of the Northwest."

McDougall was to begin his new job in the Red River settlement on December 1, 1869.

**Figure 2.4** Cover of the *Canadian Illustrated News*, January 29, 1870, shows "Miss Winnie Peg ... in doubt [about] which way to go."

**Figure 2.5** As a journalist and politician in Upper Canada (Ontario), William McDougall believed strongly in democracy, scientific progress, and the importance of land reform. As a commissioner of Crown lands in Ontario, he had granted Crown and reserve lands to be used for farming. He was a strong supporter of Canada taking over Rupert's Land.

The settlement was far away and hard to reach. McDougall and his staff had to go through the United States to get to Red River from Ontario. In Minnesota, he got a letter from Chief Surveyor Colonel Dennis. The letter warned McDougall there could be violence when he arrived. Others he met along the way also told him to expect trouble. In fact, Métis spies were tailing McDougall, watching his every move.

At the same time, Louis Riel began to organize the people of Red River. He formed the Métis National Committee. They would present their demands to McDougall, who represented the Canadian government. The Métis people wanted to make sure they kept their rights. They had lived along the Red River for years and had set up most of the communities there.

## People of Red River

In 1870, when Rupert's Land was taken over by the Canadian government, there were many different groups of people living in the Red River Settlement. These included

- French-speaking Métis. These people were the children and grandchildren of French-Canadian fur traders from the North West Company and their First Nations wives. They were mostly Roman Catholic. They lived by farming, through the bison hunt each year, and as traders and freighters.

- Country-born Métis. These people were the children and grandchildren of English-speaking fur traders of the Hudson's Bay Company and their First Nations wives. They were Protestants, and mostly farmers, craftsmen, guides, and interpreters.

- Descendants of the Selkirk Settlers, originally from Scotland, who were farmers.

- Land **speculators** from Ontario and the United States, who had started arriving in the 1860s.

- First Nations peoples. These were the original people of the region.

When McDougall arrived in Pembina, North Dakota, on November 2, he was met by two representatives of the Métis. They gave him a letter from Louis Riel. In the letter, Riel told McDougall that he would not be allowed to enter the settlement. He would only be allowed in by Riel's new committee.

McDougall's party was forced to stay overnight in Pembina. In the morning, they made their way to the first Hudson's Bay Company post on the Canadian side of the border. Fifty men, led by Ambroise Lepine, a member of the Métis National Committee, met the party at the tiny post. They sent McDougall and his men away.

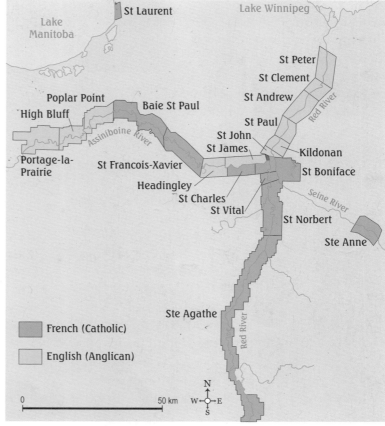

Figure 2.6 *RED RIVER SETTLEMENT, C. 1870*

### Population of Red River, 1870
[Total: 11 963 people]

**By background**

5757 French-speaking Métis

4083 English-speaking Métis

1565 European or European-Canadian

558 First Nations

**By religion**

6247 Roman Catholic

5716 Protestant

# Resistance

Within days of turning away McDougall at the border, Riel and his men took over Upper Fort Garry. (The fort was located near the forks of the Red and Assiniboine rivers.) There was a rumour that a man named John Schultz and his Canadian Party wanted to capture the fort and take all its guns. But Riel and his 100 men beat them to it. The Red River Resistance had begun.

Next, the Métis made a **proclamation**. They went through the settlement to tell all the people of Red River about their plans. They asked people from both **francophone** and **anglophone** communities

Figure 2.8 Louis Riel (centre) and some members of his council, 1869–1870. Riel, who had returned in 1868 from studying in Montreal, was an educated, well-liked leader.

to form a council. Every community in the settlement sent a person to speak for them, even though John Schultz tried to stop them. In fact, most long-time anglophone residents of Red River supported Riel.

On December 1, 1869, McDougall crossed the border into Canada. He read aloud from a document. It said that Rupert's Land was now officially part of Canada.

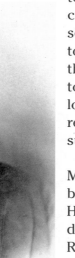

Figure 2.7 John Schultz (1840–1896) arrived at the Red River settlement in 1860 from Ontario. He became a doctor and businessman. As part owner of the *Nor' Wester* newspaper, he spoke out against the Hudson's Bay Company. He promoted joining with Canada. As leader of the Canadian Party, Schultz led a movement to overthrow Riel's provisional government. Schultz later served in the Canadian Parliament and Senate, where he remained a controversial figure.

McDougall did not know that Prime Minister Macdonald had postponed the transfer of land to Canada until the tensions had died down. McDougall had actually **forged** the document.

Colonel John Dennis, the surveyor, called on supporters to stop the Métis. A group of about 400 men set up their own headquarters at the Stone Fort (another name for Lower Fort Garry, located on the Red River 40 kilometres north of Upper Fort Garry). Most of the men were new to the Prairies. They supported the Canadian government. They thought it would be a good idea to settle the land with anglophone Protestants from Ontario.

Meanwhile, John Schultz turned his own home into a fort for his pro-Canadian force. On December 7, Riel had his men and their cannons surround Schultz's house. Local storekeeper A.G. Bannatyne came to talk to both groups. Riel ordered Schultz's group to give up. Schultz and his followers were imprisoned in Upper Fort Garry. On December 8, Riel said that his **provisional** [*pro-VIZH-eh-nel*] **government** was taking over the unstable settlement, which at the time had no official government. McDougall soon returned to Ottawa.

Riel, as president of the provisional government, set up a public meeting for January 19, 1870. Donald Smith, a special commissioner and longtime Hudson's Bay Company man, was sent by Prime Minister Macdonald to speak on behalf of the Canadian government. Smith told the people about the government's plans for the land.

Then Riel spoke. He called on the crowd to set up a council. It would be made up of 20 francophone and 20 anglophone people. They could talk with the government in Ottawa. Shortly afterward, the council, known as the Convention of Forty, was formed. It wrote a list of rights for the territory. Smith agreed to take the demands to the Canadian government.

**Figure 2.9** On November 2, 1869, Riel's provisional government took control of Upper Fort Garry from the Hudson's Bay Company. It set up its headquarters there. Today, all that remains of the fort is its front gate.

## Métis list of rights

The list of rights, below, was written by the provisional government at Red River. The document set out the terms for an agreement with the Canadian government to become a new province. Some key points of the agreement were

- the new province would be represented in Parliament and the Senate

- the provincial government would control all public lands

- French and English languages would be used in both government and the courts, as well as in any laws and official documents

- an **amnesty** would be granted to Riel and members of his provisional government

- the lieutenant governor and head of the Supreme Court would be bilingual

- a steamboat route would be set up between Lake Superior and Fort Garry

- the federal government would take on all debt of the territory and pay for all new public works, such as buildings and roads

Another point was later added that required separate French and English schools, modelled on the Quebec school system.

The document was the basis of the Manitoba Act (1870) that created the province of Manitoba. Most of the terms were agreed to. However, the federal government did not give the new province control over public lands. Amnesty was promised but was never fulfilled.

**Figure 2.10** The list of rights

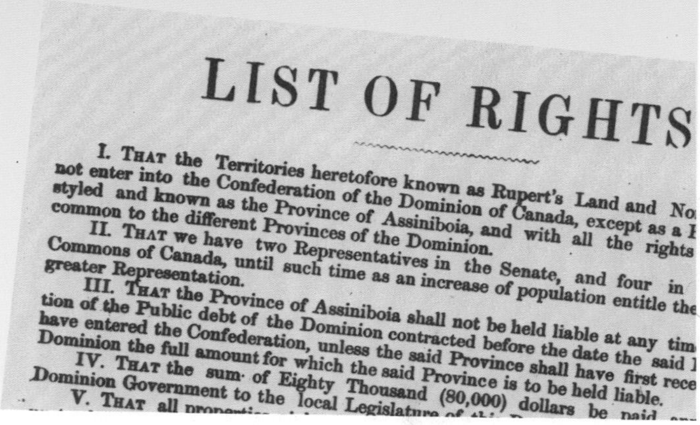

## LIST OF RIGHTS

I. THAT the Territories heretofore known as Rupert's Land and No. not enter into the Confederation of the Dominion of Canada, except as a styled and known as the Province of Assiniboia, and with all the rights common to the different Provinces of the Dominion.

II. THAT we have two Representatives in the Senate, and four in Commons of Canada, until such time as an increase of population entitle the greater Representation.

III. THAT the Province of Assiniboia shall not be held liable at any tim tion of the Public debt of the Dominion contracted before the date the said have entered the Confederation, unless the said Province shall have first rece Dominion the full amount for which the said Province is to be held liable.

IV. THAT the sum of Eighty Thousand (80,000) dollars be paid Dominion Government to the local Legislature of this

V. THAT all prope

# Confrontation

Seven of the men arrested at John Schultz's house escaped from jail in early January 1870. Among them was Thomas Scott, an unpopular hooligan. Schultz broke out of the fort a few weeks later. He used a knife that his wife smuggled to him in a pudding. The rest of the prisoners were let go in February. They joined the groups of anti-Riel forces ready to march on Riel's headquarters at Upper Fort Garry. There, they planned to drive out the provisional government. The groups came from Portage la Prairie, from the Stone Fort of Lower Fort Garry, and from St. Norbert.

The Portage la Prairie group marched eastward to meet Schultz's group. On their way, they came across a Métis woodcutter named Norbert Parisien. They arrested him as a spy. Parisien soon escaped, stealing a gun. When a man rode up to him, Parisien, who was mentally challenged, wrongly believed the man was after him. He shot the man, who later died. The man Parisien shot, Hugh Sutherland, knew that it was an accident. He asked the nearby mob, including Thomas Scott, to spare Parisien. They did not. They beat Parisien so badly, he later died.

After learning what happened, Riel called for calm. The mob broke up, but some of the men were jailed as they passed Fort Garry.

In prison, Thomas Scott made nasty remarks to the guards about their race and Catholic religion. He even upset his fellow prisoners. Finally, Scott tried to break out of his cell by overpowering the guards.

## Alexandre-Antonin Taché (1823–1894)

As archbishop of St. Boniface, Alexandre-Antonin Taché was both a spiritual and political leader to the French-Catholic community in the Red River settlement. Throughout the 1860s, he became concerned about English-speaking Protestant people from Ontario moving to the area. He wanted to make sure that the language and religious rights of the community would be respected. When the Canadian government sent its survey crews without talking to the people of Red River, he made a trip to Ottawa (on his way to Rome). There he spoke to members of the federal government about his concerns.

In December 1869, the Canadian government asked Taché to return from Rome. They wanted him to act as an **emissary** to the people of Red River. The government told Taché that the demands of the provisional government would be met. He was also told that amnesty would be granted to all who were part of the resistance. When Taché returned to Red River, he convinced Riel to send a group to Ottawa to make a deal with the Canadian government. Unfortunately, because Thomas Scott had been killed, amnesty was taken away. Taché felt that he had been lied to by the government. He continued to fight for amnesty.

**Figure 2.11** Alexandre-Antonin Taché

Riel's supporters wanted to make an example of Scott. Scott was charged with **treason** against the provisional government. On March 3, 1870, a six-man jury voted four to two for the death penalty. On March 4, Scott was killed by a firing squad in front of the fort. His last words were, "This is horrible. This is cold-blooded murder."

## A New Province

Prime Minister Macdonald and his representatives finally began to talk with the people of Red River. Archbishop Taché of St. Boniface, a supporter of Riel and the people of Red River, had been talking to the federal government about the colony's future. The provisional government was invited to send people to Ottawa.

On March 23, 1870, Father Joseph-Nöel Ritchot, Judge John Black, and Alfred Henry Scott went to Ottawa. They went to hammer out the terms of entry into Confederation based on the Métis' list of rights (see p. 27). The two sides finally reached an agreement. Manitoba would become a province. French and English would be official languages. Religious rights would be protected. The Métis would receive title to their lands, as well as a land grant of about 570 000 hectares for future generations. The Manitoba Act was passed on May 12, 1870. It came into effect July 15, 1870. Canada's fifth province was born.

At the same time as these talks were going on, John Schultz and his **cohort** Charles Mair were going throughout Ontario, stirring up hatred for Riel and the provisional government. Many people in Ontario were furious about the death of Thomas Scott. They demanded that justice be done.

### Manitobah

In 1867, before Manitoba was a province, the town of Portage la Prairie became the centre of the Republic of Manitobah. A man named Thomas Spence, concerned because the area had no government, wanted to transform it into a recognized part of Canada. In January 1868, the settlers formed a council for the new republic. Spence tried to raise money for Manitobah by taxing imports. However, few of the town's businesses, including the Hudson's Bay Company, would pay. Things got worse when a shoemaker named McPherson suggested that the collected tax money was being spent on liquor for members of the council. McPherson was charged with treason, but his trial, in a log cabin, turned into a brawl. The Republic soon collapsed.

Spence himself soldiered on. At one time, he had been the editor of John Schultz's *Nor'Wester* newspaper. A few years later, he became editor of Louis Riel's *New Nation*.

**Figure 2.12** The Manitoba Act promised a large amount of land to the Métis at Red River. However, instead of land, each Métis person was given *scrip*. This was a paper certificate that could be traded for land or money. This plan did not work well. Many Métis never got money or the land they were promised.

## The Wolseley Expedition

In June 1870, Prime Minister Macdonald sent 1100 hearty troops west on "a friendly expedition." They went to make sure that power was transferred peacefully from the provisional government to the federal government. Many of the soldiers had read the anti-Riel newspaper articles. They agreed with the hateful message of Schultz and his men. Riel had sent guides to help the expedition. They listened to the fireside chat of the soldiers. They reported that the troops were set on revenge.

The force was led by Colonel Garnet Wolseley. It arrived at Red River in late August 1870 after a difficult trip. Riel feared that the soldiers wanted to kill him. Just hours before they arrived, Riel escaped to the south.

> THE NAME OF THE COUNTRY is already written in all hearts, that of Red River. Fancy delights in that of 'Manitoba,' but the situation seems to demand that of 'North-West.' Friends of the old government are pleased with that of Assiniboia [but] it is not generally enough liked to be kept. Choose one of the two names 'Manitoba' or 'North-West.' —*A letter from Louis Riel to Father Ritchot on April 19, 1870*

Wolseley's soldiers settled in for a long stay. It soon became clear that many in the force were not there to protect anyone. They were there to punish the settlement for the resistance and for Scott's execution. Many soldiers beat and looted their way across the settlement. André Nault, the

**Figure 2.13** *Red River Expedition, Colonel Wolseley's Camp, Prince Arthur Landing on Lake Superior*, by W. Armstrong

man who had spotted the surveying party the year before, was beaten and left for dead. Nault lived, but a number of people were killed. These included a man who was on Scott's jury, one who was in Scott's execution party, and the owner of a well-known saloon in the town.

The takeover of Manitoba, which the residents had so feared, had begun. But the people did have a province, with their historic rights guaranteed.

## After the Red River Resistance

Even though he was living in exile in the United States, Riel was elected to the Canadian Parliament to represent the **riding** of Provencher in 1873. However, Riel was a wanted man. Charged with Scott's murder, he never took his **seat** as a **member of Parliament**. Still, he is considered by many Canadians as the founder of Manitoba. You will read more about Louis Riel in chapter 4.

## Conclusion

Life began to change for the Métis after Manitoba became a province in 1870. New people came. They soon gained power in the province. The Métis had trouble proving ownership of their land. Their ways of life were disappearing just as the bison herds were dying out. Many of the Métis moved farther west to the North-West Territories or to the American states just south of the border.

**DID YOU KNOW?** In 2007, the Manitoba government announced a new holiday, Louis Riel Day, to fall on the third Monday of February. The holiday honours Riel as the founder of the province of Manitoba.

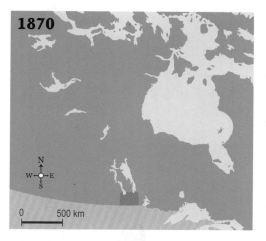

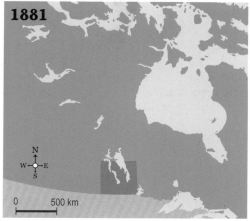

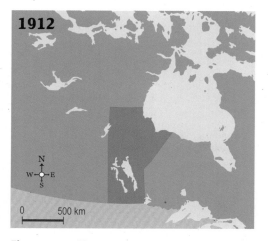

**Figure 2.14** *MANITOBA IN 1870, 1881, AND 1912*
The Postage Stamp province was Manitoba's nickname when it became a province in 1870. It was roughly square in shape. Compared to its size today, it was also very small. It was only 209 by 177 kilometres – around 37 000 square kilometres or about 1/18th of the province's present size. Manitoba's boundaries were extended twice: once in 1881, then north to the 60th parallel in 1912.

# 3 From Sea to Sea
## Adding Provinces and Territories

## Heading West

> May 1. Went to the 'New' Fort, Toronto, with the intention of enlisting in the North-West Mounted Police [NWMP].... Colonel George Arthur French, the Commissioner of the Force, and my father had served together in the … Army, and the Colonel at once informed my father in downtown Toronto of my action and whereabouts. Father lost no time in coming post haste to interview the Colonel, with the view of preventing my enlistment, but after a rather stormy argument between us, he arranged with the Colonel to take me on as Trumpeter for a period of not more than six months. And so I am now a member of the NWMP at the age of fifteen years.

A teenager named Frederick Augustus Bagley wrote the above words in 1874. Bagley was one of many Canadians who looked forward to adventure in the Canadian West. He joined the new police force being formed in the North-West Territories.

Prime Minister Macdonald and the Fathers of Confederation dreamed of a country that would stretch from sea to sea. However, many things had to change before those dreams could come true.

First, the Canadian government had to negotiate with the First Nations who lived on the Prairies. The government wanted their land for settlement.

Second, the government wanted to end the illegal whisky trade that had sprung up there.

Third, the government wanted to drive out the American hunters and traders who roamed the Prairies. Many people worried that the United States still had its eyes on Canada's land.

In May 1873, something terrible happened in Cypress Hills, Saskatchewan. Thirty-six Nakota (Assiniboine) men, women, and children were murdered by American whisky traders who wanted to hunt in the Nakota territory. Macdonald knew that he could not wait any longer

**Figure 3.1** Frederick Bagley joined the North-West Mounted Police in 1874 at the age of 15. He planned to be with the force only six months. Instead, he served close to 25 years. He retired in 1898.

**AS YOU READ, THINK ABOUT**

- the role the North-West Mounted Police played in the North-West Territories
- the changes that came about when gold was found in British Columbia
- how the railway was built, and how it changed the country
- how Canada became a country from sea to sea

to bring law and order to the West. On May 23, 1873, Parliament passed the act that created the North-West Mounted Police.

From the fall of 1873 to the spring of 1874, 300 men trained as police officers at Fort Garry. In July 1874, they left from Fort Dufferin, south of Fort Garry, to begin their journey west to the area around the Cypress Hills. In Ottawa, the Liberals, led by Alexander Mackenzie, had defeated Sir John A. Macdonald's government. The new police force would begin under Prime Minister Mackenzie.

**Figure 3.2** The start of the police march from Fort Dufferin, Manitoba, by Henri Julien. Julien was an artist for the *Canadian Illustrated News*. He was invited by the NWMP commander G.A. French to record what he saw on the March West.

## Alexander Mackenzie (1822–1892) **PM**

Alexander Mackenzie was born in Perthshire, Scotland. He went to Canada at age 20. He soon found work as a stonemason and building contractor in Canada West (Ontario). Mackenzie had always liked politics. He was a strong believer in a society where people were equal, and not separated by class. By 1852, Mackenzie was the editor of a newspaper that called for reform. In 1861, he was elected to the Provincial Assembly of Canada West. In 1867, he was elected to the House of Commons. Mackenzie was a member of both the provincial and federal governments until 1872. At that time, he gave up his Ontario seat.

In April 1873, when Prime Minister Macdonald resigned because of the Pacific Scandal (see p. 38), Mackenzie became prime minister as leader of the Liberal party.

Mackenzie was not seen as a strong leader, possibly because the country fell into an economic decline during his term. However, while Mackenzie was in office, from 1873 to 1878, the Supreme Court of Canada was created. The Royal Military College was set up in Kingston, Ontario. Thousands of square kilometres of land were cleared for the transcontinental railway. More than 19 000 kilometres of the railway were surveyed. Mackenzie's government also passed the Dominion Elections Act, 1874. This made secret ballots the law.

**Figure 3.3** Alexander Mackenzie

John A. Macdonald was re-elected prime minister in 1878. Alexander Mackenzie stayed on as a member of Parliament until his death in 1892.

## The North-West Mounted Police

In 1874, Frederick Bagley came under the command of Colonel George Arthur French, the force's first commissioner. Bagley wrote:

> In a speech to the men during General Parade, P.M. Colonel French pointed out that hardships, starvation, thirst and possible death awaited us in the West, and if any man feared for the future he was at perfect liberty to leave the Force immediately, and no attempt would be made to stop or arrest him. Fifteen men deserted during the past two nights. Supper of wet and dry [*dry toast and tea*].

As a trumpeter, young Bagley had to give the orders to the rest of the outfit. The trumpeter was the unit's alarm clock, waking everyone up in the morning. If the unit had to attack, he was the one to sound the charge. When the men were to hit the trail after a meal, he played "Boot & Saddle." In between, he did what he was ordered to do and played any song that he was ordered to play.

**Figure 3.5** The Great March West ended just north of Sweetgrass Hills, Montana.

## The Great March West

On July 4, 1874, 300 men of the North-West Mounted Police left Fort Dufferin, Manitoba, on horseback, dressed in bright red jackets. They took livestock and wagons full of supplies with them on their 1500-kilometre trek. Half the men headed to Fort Whoop-up, just north of the Montana border. That was where the whisky-trading bandits were hiding out. The rest headed north.

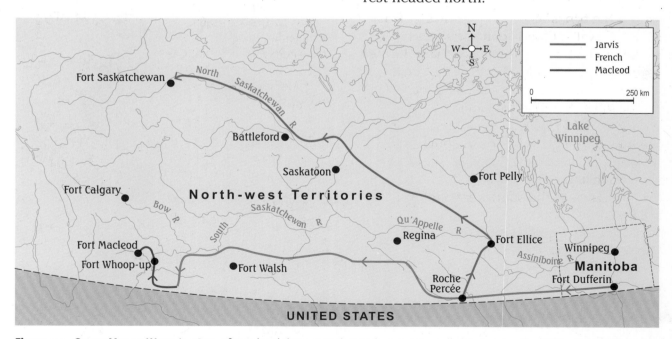

**Figure 3.4** *GREAT MARCH WEST.* In 1874, after a hard three-month march, one group of about 150 police led by Colonel James Macleod went after the whisky traders near the Cypress Hills. Other members of the force led by Inspector W.D. Jarvis set up other posts, such as Fort Ellice and Fort Saskatchewan. Fort Calgary and Fort Walsh were built the following summer.

## Jerry Potts (1840–1896)

Jerry Potts was the son of a Kainai (Blood) mother and a Scottish-American father. He was hired away from the whisky trade by the North-West Mounted Police. On the March West, he guided the force to Fort Whoop-up. He seemed to know every bit of land. He also knew the ways of the peoples living on the Prairies. He was a very useful guide and interpreter. Potts helped the police and First Nations make peace with each other. He worked the last 22 years of his life as a NWMP scout.

**Figure 3.6** Jerry Potts

During the trip, some men became sick from drinking bad water. Clouds of mosquitoes and severe thunderstorms made the trip hard. Horses grew weak from lack of food and water, and many died. When the force arrived at its destination in early October, the whisky traders had fled.

Over the next few years, the Mounties, as the police force came to be known, built forts throughout the Northwest. These posts became their headquarters:

- Fort Macleod, in the southwest corner of what is now Alberta
- Fort Calgary, on the Bow River
- Fort Walsh, in the Cypress Hills
- Fort Saskatchewan, on the North Saskatchewan River near present-day Edmonton.

## Establishing law and order

When we think about police today, we think about men and women who catch criminals and keep us safe. When the North-West Mounted

**DID YOU KNOW?** The North-West Mounted Police became the Royal North-West Mounted Police in 1904. The British government gave it the new name after several men from the force served with honour in the Boer War (see p. 80). When the force **merged** with the Dominion Police in 1920, it was renamed the Royal Canadian Mounted Police (RCMP).

Police was formed, its most important duties were to form good relations with First Nations and to get rid of the whisky traders. The police did far more, however. They

- provided medicine
- gave out food to First Nations people when supplies were low
- delivered mail
- took the census
- acted as justices of the peace
- kept track of agricultural conditions
- settled fights

## Sam Steele (1851–1919)

Sam Steele was born in Orillia in Upper Canada. As a young man, he travelled west with Colonel Wolseley's force to the Red River settlement (see p. 30). He was the third officer signed on to the North-West Mounted Police.

Steele was known for his great strength. He was hired to train the men to ride horses on the March West. With the harsh conditions, horses often fell down from weakness. Steele had to keep them going to get to the next rest stop.

**Figure 3.7** Sam Steele

In 1897, Steele was ordered north to become NWMP commander in the Yukon (see p. 41). He also fought in the Boer War and the First World War. In 1919, while in England, he died from the flu. He is buried in St. John's Cemetery in Winnipeg.

# British Columbia Joins Canada

"There is no doubt of the richness of the diggings, men being able to make from five to twelve dollars a day easily, and that, too, with the rudest implements," read one California newspaper about the new gold discoveries in British Columbia.

The promise of gold brought many adventurers to the West Coast. In 1849, gold fever had spread among men hoping to strike it rich overnight in the hills near San Francisco. In 1857, word spread of a new discovery on the Fraser River of British Columbia. Many of the gold-hungry men turned their sights northward. They flocked to British Columbia. Often they abandoned their California lives in a matter of hours.

Within months, the orderly little town of Victoria (population 700) was surrounded by a huge ring of grey canvas tents. By the end of the year, 30 000 **prospectors** had made their way through Victoria to stake gold **claims** along the Fraser River.

The governor of Vancouver Island, James Douglas, watched as American gold seekers flooded the area. He became concerned that the United States was about to invade. He was also worried about gold seekers trespassing on Aboriginal land. He worried they would violate First Nations' own rights to the gold there – gold they had been mining for years. The First Nations of British Columbia shared that worry.

To avoid any trouble, Douglas made the miners take out licences. He demanded they follow the law. Judge Matthew Begbie was charged with keeping the peace. The newcomers learned to behave.

**Figure 3.8** Sir James Douglas, governor of British Columbia

**Figure 3.9** *The New Eldorado – A Complete View of the Newly Discovered Goldfields in BNA with Vancouver Island and the Whole of the Seaboard from Cape Flattery to Prince of Wales Island.* This print, published in 1858 in London, shows the British Columbia goldfields.

## Amor de Cosmos (1825–1897)

Among those who joined the Fraser Valley gold rush was a man with an unusual name. In 1852, Bill Smith left his native Nova Scotia for the goldfields of California. There, he found his own kind of gold. It was in the new business of photography. This is how he made his living. He also decided to change his name to Amor de Cosmos (meaning "lover of the universe").

Figure 3.10 Amor de Cosmos

While de Cosmos seemed interested in gold rushes, he did not do any real prospecting. He came to the Fraser Valley because he liked the energy of the gold rush itself. In 1858, he followed his brother to Vancouver Island. There, he started his own newspaper, still published today as the Victoria *Times-Colonist*. As its editor, he was a reformer who wanted change. He spoke out against the government of James Douglas and his upper-class friends. He considered them undemocratic. He became a strong **advocate** for Confederation and Responsible Government in the new province.

De Cosmos became premier of the province between 1872 and 1874. He also became a member of Parliament. He left politics in 1882 after losing his seat in the federal election. As he got older, his **eccentricities**, which included fist-fighting, public temper tantrums, and crying, became more serious. He was labelled "of unsound mind."

The Fraser Valley gold rush did not last much beyond the end of 1857. Many disappointed miners returned home. But others thought that the gold must be coming down the river from somewhere. They pushed farther north in search of its source. In 1861, a miner named Billy Barker found gold in the Cariboo district. This discovery sparked another gold rush. Between 1862 and 1870, more than 10 000

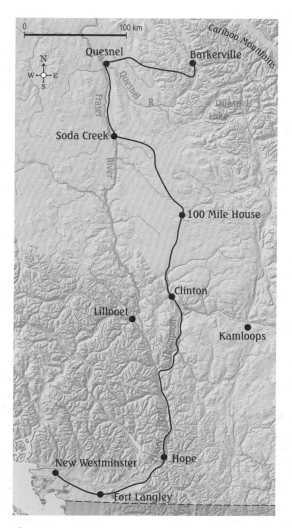

Figure 3.11 *GOLD RUSHES OF THE FRASER VALLEY AND CARIBOO*

fortune seekers went to the goldfields near Barkerville, British Columbia.

The 1858 gold rush brought many Americans to the area. This led the British government to strengthen its power in the region. It proclaimed the mainland the Crown colony of British Columbia. New Westminster was its capital.

Vancouver Island had been its own colony since 1849. The two colonies joined together in 1866. In 1871, the new province of British Columbia joined Confederation, based on the promise of a transcontinental railway joining it to the rest of Canada.

# Railway!

The big black locomotive chugged its way westward. The number 374 was painted on its front. A photograph of Queen Victoria hung above it. The train had made its way from Montreal. It travelled over the rugged Canadian Shield, across the flat Prairies, and through the breathtaking mountains of British Columbia. On May 23, 1887, as the train came to a stop, a band struck up the song "See, The Conquering Hero Comes." The new city of Vancouver was now officially open for business.

**Figure 3.12** Locomotive 374 arrives in Vancouver in 1887.

The building of the railway had taken several years, cost millions of dollars, and taken the lives of many people. It had forced Prime Minister Macdonald from power for four years. It took the will of many people to complete the railway. However, when it was finished, the railway helped change the face of Canadian society by bringing new people to Western Canada.

## The Pacific Scandal

Hugh Allan was the richest man in Canada in the 1870s. He was an **industrialist** who owned his own steamship line. He heard about plans to build a railway from sea to sea, and made up his mind to be the one to build it. However, Allan knew that to win the contract, he would need something the other bidders did not have.

Meanwhile, Prime Minister Macdonald was getting ready for his second election in 1872. He was losing support in Ottawa and Quebec. He needed money to pay for his **campaign**.

Macdonald needed money. Allan needed a favour. After Macdonald won the 1872 election, it was learned that he had accepted $360 000 from Allan to help pay for his election campaign. In return, Allan and his company had been promised the railway contract. There was a huge public outcry. The affair became known as the *Pacific Scandal*. Macdonald and his government resigned in October 1873. Alexander Mackenzie's Liberals became the next government. Allan's company lost the contract.

## A new start

Macdonald returned to power in 1878. By then, the Liberal government had completed 4000 kilometres of railway. Macdonald's Conservatives wanted to see it finished. They hired a **syndicate** of Canadian businessmen and European bankers to complete the project. The new firm was called the Canadian Pacific Railway Company. An American railway engineer named William Van Horne (1843–1915) was hired to oversee the construction. Under Van Horne, 19 000 kilometres of new rail line were to be built between Ontario and British Columbia. It was to meet up with another line that was being built from Port Moody on the Pacific Coast to Kamloops in British Columbia's interior.

People came from the United States, Eastern Europe, Scandinavia, Italy, and Germany, eager to work on the railway and start a new life in Canada. Survey crews staked out the route for the new railway. Construction crews followed. The men who built the railway worked long, hard days. They laid track through swamps, across rivers, and over mountains. They used dynamite to build tunnels through rock. They built huge **trestle** bridges to raise the track across deep canyons and raging rivers.

Figure 3.13 Construction crew at Rat Portage (Kenora) building a trestle bridge over muskeg (1881–1882). Trestle bridges were made from braced frameworks of wood. They were designed to go over obstacles, such as swampy land, ravines, and through mountains.

Figure 3.15 Chinese railway workers in British Columbia. Sir John A. Macdonald said that "without the great effort of Chinese labourers, the CPR could not have been finished."

It was very hard to build the rail line from the Pacific Coast to the interior of British Columbia. This was because it passed through mountains and around steep, rocky cliffs. Although that section of the railway was only 615 kilometres long, it took seven years and 15 000 men to build. Close to 9000 of the workers were Chinese.

An American contractor was in charge of this section of the line. To save costs, he had the workers use a cheaper but more dangerous explosive than dynamite to blast the rock along the route. More than 700 men, mostly Chinese, died building this dangerous stretch of railway.

On November 7, 1885, company partner Donald A. Smith drove in the last spike of the Canadian Pacific Railway at Craigellachie, British Columbia. The railway from the Atlantic to Pacific was complete.

Figure 3.14 Donald A. Smith drives the last spike of the Canadian Pacific Railway at Craigellachie on November 7, 1885. Peeking out from behind Smith is young Edward Mallandaine. He had run a pony express service to the construction crews. Edward grew up to be an architect and land developer. He was also cofounder of the city of Creston, British Columbia.

# The Klondike

To Whom It May Concern,

I do, this day, locate and claim, by right of discovery, five hundred feet, running up stream from this notice. Located this 17th day of August, 1896. —G.W. Carmack.

One August day in 1896, George Carmack, his wife Kate, Kate's brother Skookum Jim Mason, and a friend, Tagish Charlie, were looking for gold at a place named Rabbit Creek, Yukon. History is not clear on what exactly happened there. Carmack claimed he saw a huge gold nugget and pulled it from the ground. Jim and Charlie said that Carmack was asleep and that Jim found the nugget while washing dishes in the creek. Nevertheless, the find was worth about four dollars, and there was promise of more.

There *was* more. Over the next few days, the men made claims along the site. Soon they had many small gold nuggets. The find brought people from all over the continent. Rabbit Creek was renamed Bonanza Creek.

**Figure 3.17** George Carmack

About 100 000 prospectors made the dangerous and expensive trip to the Klondike goldfields.

**Figure 3.16** Two miners and their dog stand beside a gold rocker. The miners poured gravel and water into the top, then rocked the box back and forth. Water and sand washed out, leaving the gold in the bottom. When they had access to a lot of water, miners used a sluice box, like the long trough shown in the background. They shovelled gravel into the trough, which was tilted downward. Then they poured water in to wash away the dirt and gravel. The gold remained in ridges on the bottom. Rockers and sluices were two of the basic tools used in this kind of mining.

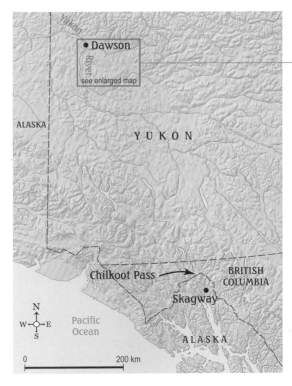

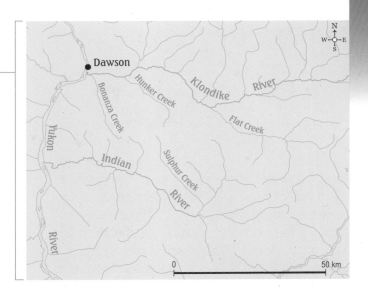

**Figure 3.18** *The Klondike Gold Region*

A new city arose where the Klondike and Yukon rivers meet. It was called Dawson City. It soon had a population of 40 000. The North-West Mounted Police were sent to keep things in order. Sam Steele was in charge of the busy Yukon force. The usual problems, such as gambling and drinking, were allowed, but watched closely.

Many men struck it rich. However, the end of the 19th century was also the end of the Klondike gold rush. In 1899, thousands of the men left the Yukon and headed back south. Within five years, Dawson City's population was down to 5000.

## Faith Fenton (1857–1936)

In the 1880s, Faith Fenton was one of Canada's leading female journalists. Although journalists were not always liked, thousands read Fenton's column in Toronto's *Empire* newspaper. She often wrote about famous people whom she met.

During this same period of time, Alice Freeman worked as a schoolteacher. Only Freeman's closest friends knew that she was leading a double life. Alice Freeman, the teacher, was also Faith Fenton, the journalist.

In 1894, a year after her real identity was discovered, Freeman gave up teaching to write full-time. In 1897, Freeman went to the Yukon along the same trails as the prospectors searching for gold. She wrote several stories about the dangerous journey for the *Globe* newspaper.

**Figure 3.19** Faith Fenton

**Figure 3.20** Prospectors who came to the Klondike from Skagway, Alaska, had to trek across the Chilkoot Trail to the Yukon. To be allowed into Canada, miners needed to bring a year's supply of food with them. They also needed to bring clothes and other supplies. They would make a series of trips over many months. Once at the top, 939 metres above sea level, they could travel down the other side on toboggan-like pieces of wood. The march continued 24 hours a day. Those who dropped out to rest often had to wait many hours to get back in line.

## Robert Service (1874–1958)

Robert Service, more than any other writer of his time, captured the spirit of the Klondike gold rush:

> *Men from the sands of the Sunland;*
> *men from the woods of the West;*
>
> *Men from the farms and the cities,*
> *into the Northland we pressed.*
>
> *Graybeards and striplings and women,*
> *good men and bad men and bold,*
>
> *Leaving our homes and our loved ones,*
> *crying exultantly – "Gold!"*

– from *The Trail of Ninety-Eight*

Service was born in England and raised in Scotland. He moved to British Columbia in 1896. He arrived in the Yukon in 1905. It was long after the gold rush had ended. As a bank clerk, he met the prospectors, gamblers, and others who had stayed in the town. He listened to their stories and turned them into poems that became popular around the world.

**Figure 3.21** Robert Service at his Yukon home

# More Provinces and Territories

## Prince Edward Island

The leaders of Prince Edward Island had chosen not to join Confederation in 1867. They worried that the small colony's concerns would be ignored in such a large country. They also thought they would have to pay higher taxes. They were happy to remain a colony of Britain.

At first, Prime Minister Macdonald accepted Prince Edward Island's decision. Within a year, however, Macdonald became worried that there was too much trade with the United States. In 1869, he again tried to get the island to join Canada. He offered money, trade, and communication links to the mainland. However, the people still refused.

THE NEW IDEA OF CONFEDERATION.

**Figure 3.23** This cartoon appeared in August 1879 in *Grip* magazine. What do you think the cartoonist was trying to say?

By 1873, however, the people of Prince Edward Island were tired of railway debts and British landlords who did not live on the island. The

**Figure 3.22** Celebrations in Edmonton, as Alberta joins Canada, 1905

island colony decided to join Canada, because it was promised a steamship service to the mainland. It was also promised six representatives in Parliament. As well, each person would receive $50. On July 1, 1873, Prince Edward Island became Canada's seventh province.

## Yukon

At the end of the 19th century, thousands of people travelled to the Yukon in search of gold. In 1898, the Canadian government made the Yukon a separate territory with its own council. That way, it could better control the growth of the area. Dawson City became its capital. In 1952, Yukon's capital moved to Whitehorse.

## Alberta and Saskatchewan

The beginning of the 20th century was an exciting time for Canada. The economy was strong. The population was growing. Between 1870 and 1890, many farmers from eastern Canada, then people from Europe, moved to the West (see chapter 5). With the population growing so quickly, the federal government decided to make a province in the North-West Territories. This would allow roads, schools, and other services that the provinces were responsible for to be built. In 1905, the territory was divided into *two* new provinces: Alberta and Saskatchewan. Once again the map of Canada changed.

## Newfoundland

Newfoundland had been asked to join the new nation in 1867. Some Newfoundlanders were excited by the idea. Others were not. Roman-Catholics worried they might become victims of anti-Catholic laws. Merchants did not want to pay higher taxes. In the end, the people of Newfoundland decided they wanted to control their own economy. They decided not to join Canada.

From 1916 on, however, Newfoundland had great economic losses. It had huge debts from being part of the First World War. Then, in the 1930s, the price of fish dropped. This sank the colony into an economic **depression.** In the 1940s,

**Figure 3.24** Joey Smallwood signs the agreement bringing Newfoundland into Confederation. Newfoundland officially became a province on March 31, 1949.

newly built American and Canadian military bases provided jobs, but the economy still suffered.

In 1946, the government of Newfoundland held a national convention to talk about the colony's future. A journalist named Joseph (Joey) Smallwood was a delegate at the convention. He led the campaign for Confederation. In 1948, the people of Newfoundland voted to join Canada. They won by a very small margin. In 1949, Newfoundland became the tenth province. Joey Smallwood became its first premier. In December 2001, the province's official name became *Newfoundland and Labrador*.

## Northwest Territories

As Canada grew in size, the North-West Territories got smaller. Before 1870, it was the name for all the land that lay northwest of central Canada. It belonged to the Hudson's Bay Company. In 1870, the Hudson's Bay Company sold all this land to Canada. Over the years, new provinces and territories were carved out of this huge piece of land. These include Alberta, Saskatchewan, and Yukon Territory. Older provinces – Ontario, Quebec, and Manitoba – expanded their boundaries into the territory. In 1999, the Northwest Territories (its name since 1906) was divided into two parts. The eastern part became Nunavut. The western part is today's Northwest Territories.

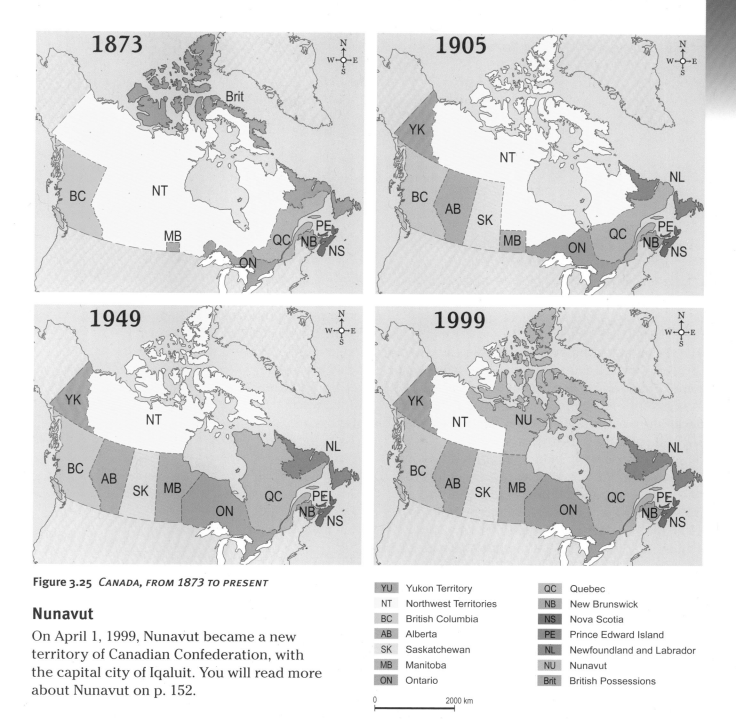

**Figure 3.25** *CANADA, FROM 1873 TO PRESENT*

**Legend:**

| | | | |
|---|---|---|---|
| YU | Yukon Territory | QC | Quebec |
| NT | Northwest Territories | NB | New Brunswick |
| BC | British Columbia | NS | Nova Scotia |
| AB | Alberta | PE | Prince Edward Island |
| SK | Saskatchewan | NL | Newfoundland and Labrador |
| MB | Manitoba | NU | Nunavut |
| ON | Ontario | Brit | British Possessions |

0 ———— 2000 km

## Nunavut

On April 1, 1999, Nunavut became a new territory of Canadian Confederation, with the capital city of Iqaluit. You will read more about Nunavut on p. 152.

## Conclusion

In the years since Frederick Bagley, the trumpeter, walked to the North-West Territories, the land has not changed very much. But its boundaries on the map certainly have.

**DID YOU KNOW?** With the creation of Nunavut, Canada now has a "four corners." Manitoba, Saskatchewan, the Northwest Territories, and Nunavut all meet at 60°00 N, 102°00 W.

# Challenges for a New Country

**A**s Canada moved westward, it had its share of growing pains. The First Nations people of the Northwest faced starvation, illness, and loss of their land. The Métis people struggled to protect their identity and unique way of life. Soon settlers from many other countries brought their own distinct cultures, filling the West. They faced floods, cold, and rocky soil as they learned how to survive in a foreign land.

The French and English clashed over language and religion. They were also divided over Canada's role in the British Empire, as Canadian soldiers fought in Britain's Boer War. New inventions changed the way Canadians lived. Cities grew. With that growth came poverty and crime – and reformers who wanted to fix these new problems.

*I have devoted my life to my country. If it is necessary for the happiness of my country that I should now soon cease to live, I leave it to the Providence of my God.*

*Louis Riel.*

**2**

**3**

**5**

**4**

## In the Memory Box...

**1** This treaty medal was presented to Chief Nanaojakaba of Manitoba's White Mud Band in 1876. It shows the government treaty commissioner shaking hands with a chief.

**2** Louis Riel's final statement before his execution in 1885.

**3** A Boer war soldier with his beloved horse, Baron, around 1900.

**4** This embroidered moose-hide hat belonged to Chief Pitikwahanapiwiyin (Poundmaker), an important leader of the Northwest Resistance in 1885.

**5** This advertisement from 1886 shows a farmer with a horse-drawn "Wild Irishman" plough tilling his land.

**6** Advertisement from a 1900 *Canadian Magazine* shows modern conveniences of the time.

**7** Formed in 1912, the Norwegian Glee Club was a choir of Norwegian immigrants. This banner reflects the old country and the new. One side has the flag and fishnets of the fishing economy of Norway. The other shows a bison of Manitoba and the lyre, representing music.

**8** Application for passage to Canada by steamship in the late 1860s. Immigrants came for the promise of free farmland in Canada, available for a $10 registration fee.

**9** Frederick Phillips, immigrated to Canada from England in 1880. His illustrated letters to his fiancée Marian show shipboard scenes and ranch life in Manitoba.

# 4 Aboriginal Peoples in the New Country of Canada

On September 24, 1907, a very important meeting was held at St. Peter's **reserve** near Selkirk, Manitoba. The Canadian government was offering $90 to any landowner who would sell his land and move to a new location. Now, the owners were voting on the government's offer, but the meeting did not go smoothly. Government officials who attended spoke only English. Many of the voters spoke only Cree or Ojibwa. Although there was a translator, not everyone could hear or understand what was being said. When the government officials counted the vote, they said that 107 owners wanted to sell their land and 97 did not. An ex-chief named William Asham did not agree. He said that more owners had voted against selling their land. He believed that the vote had been unfair. The government bought the land anyway.

The people of St. Peter's had lived on the reserve since 1871, when they signed a treaty (see p. 50) called *Treaty One*. Treaties were meant to move First Nations people to reserves

**Figure 4.1** This shirt from the 1840s belonged to a Siksika (Blackfoot) warrior. It shows warrior traditions that would end with the arrival of the Europeans

where they could learn to farm. The people of St. Peter's settled in well. By 1907, they were growing crops on hundreds of hectares of fine farmland. In spite of this, they lost their land.

The St. Peter's residents were moved to a new reserve (now named Peguis) two hundred kilometres away. When they arrived at the reserve, they found only swampy, rocky land. It was not good for farming.

The St. Peter's people were not the only ones whose lives changed so much in so short a time. In the 1850s, about 35 000 First Nations and Métis peoples lived in the West. For many of them, their troubles began in 1857. That year, the British government hired an Irish explorer named John Palliser to survey the Canadian

**AS YOU READ, THINK ABOUT**

- the problems that Aboriginal peoples faced as Canada expanded westward
- what the numbered treaties were and how they changed the lives of Aboriginal peoples
- what caused the Northwest Resistance
- the people and events of the Northwest Resistance
- how life changed for Aboriginal peoples after the Northwest Resistance

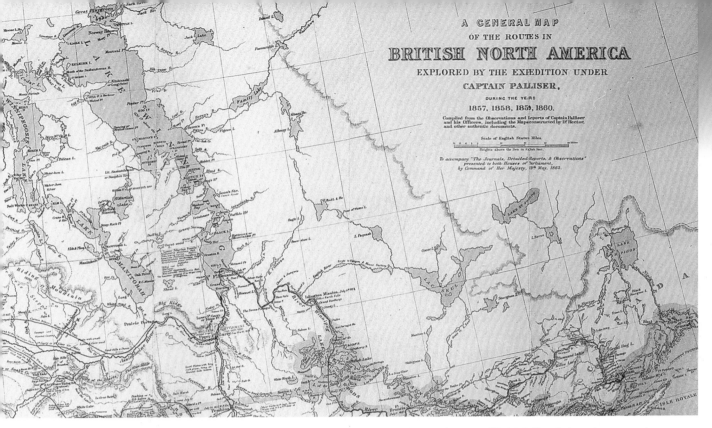

**Figure 4.2** A detail of John Palliser's map (above) shows the eastern and central parts of British North America.

West. The government wanted to know if the Prairies were good for farming. In the days before the railroad, crossing the West was difficult and dangerous.

Palliser and his team travelled west of Lake Superior along old fur-trade routes. They crossed the Prairies and found passes through the Rocky Mountains. They ended their journey three years later in British Columbia's Okanagan Valley. During that time, they met many Aboriginal peoples. Palliser found that much of the Prairies was ideal for farming. He learned that people had been living in the huge stretch of land between Red River and British Columbia for a very long time. He also found that there were minerals in the West that could be mined.

Palliser's trip paved the way for people to come west. In 1872, Parliament passed the *Dominion Lands Act.* This act was meant to bring people to the West by offering land to settlers at a very low cost. Within a few years, a trickle of settlers became a flood. These people called themselves *homesteaders*. Many Aboriginal peoples moved farther west as the homesteaders

arrived. In the 1880s, the new Canadian Pacific Railway (see p. 38) crossed thousands of kilometres of Aboriginal land. It carried even greater numbers of people westward.

Homesteaders and the railroad were not the only things that caused problems for Aboriginal peoples. By the middle of the 1800s, fashions had changed. The fur trade was coming to an end. Animals had been overhunted. Fur farms, where animals valued for their pelts were raised, began to appear. As the fur trade dropped off, a way of life for thousands of Métis and First Nations peoples also disappeared.

Even worse, almost all the bison herds had disappeared because of overhunting (see p 53). Many Aboriginal peoples of the Prairies needed the bison so they could live. As they competed for fewer and fewer resources, fighting even broke out among the Siksika (Blackfoot), Nehiyaw (Cree), Nakota (Assiniboine), and Métis. For the Aboriginal peoples, these were hard times. They had to find ways to adjust to the changes in their lives.

# Making Treaties

A treaty is a legal agreement made between nations. Nations make treaties to trade goods, settle differences, end wars, and decide land ownership. Aboriginal nations had been making treaties with one another for centuries before the Europeans arrived. One such treaty led to the creation of the Iroquois Confederacy.

Following the Seven Years' War (1756–1763), King George set out a plan for organizing Britain's new lands. The Royal Proclamation of 1763 said that large parts of the West would be *reserved* for Aboriginal peoples. The Proclamation became the basis for treaties between Britain and the First Nations in its North American territories.

After the Canadian government bought Rupert's Land from the Hudson's Bay Company, thousands of people headed to the region. Aboriginal peoples who lived there worried they would lose everything to the new settlers. Some thought that treaties with the Canadian government would protect some of their land.

Canada's government was interested in the West, too. It wanted to build railroads, telegraph lines, mines, canals, and even fisheries on Aboriginal lands. Prime ministers John A. Macdonald and Alexander Mackenzie wanted to bargain with Aboriginal peoples. They did not like the policy of the

Figure 4.3 Chief Robert Fiddler of the Deer Lake First Nation, after signing Treaty 5 on June 9, 1910. Chief Fiddler is draped with the Union Jack and is wearing a treaty medal on his chest. Between 1875 and 1910, more than 35 First Nations signed Treaty 5. This treaty covered much of central Manitoba. It also covered bordering parts of Ontario and Saskatchewan.

Figure 4.4 In this 1876 drawing by Henri Julien, the artist compares the way Americans treated Aboriginal peoples (above) with the way Canadians did (below).

United States government. The Americans had the army force Aboriginal peoples from their land.

Between 1871 and 1921, the government of Canada signed 11 treaties with Aboriginal peoples of the West. These are called the *numbered treaties*. Seven of them were made in the 1870s. Through these treaties, the government agreed to provide First Nations with land reserves, services, and supplies. In return, the First Nations would sign over much of their land to the government.

To Aboriginal peoples, the idea that people could "buy" and "own" the land was very strange. They saw themselves as the land's caretakers rather than its owners. People of European background believed that land could be bought and sold. This difference led to misunderstandings when treaties were made. Many Aboriginal peoples thought that their traditional hunting grounds were still theirs to use after signing the treaties. The Canadian government thought differently.

The treaties were often unfair. Aboriginal peoples gave up huge territories for much smaller reserves. Many First Nations, especially the Nehiyaw (Cree), did not sign the treaties at first. Once they knew the treaties were happening anyway, some of them asked for such things as schools for their young. They also asked for farm supplies and equipment.

Some people, such as the Anishinabe (Ojibwa), tried to find work in the railway, telegraph, and mining industries. All of them did what they could to cope with a changing world without letting their traditions die. Still,

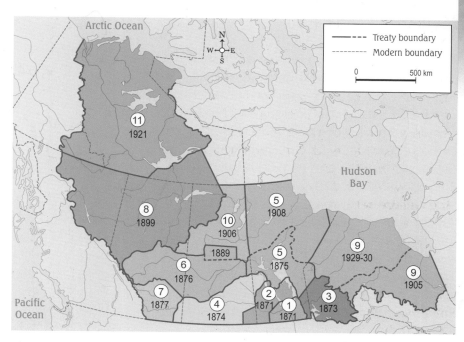

**Figure 4.5** *THE NUMBERED TREATIES, 1871–1921.* Between 1871 to 1921, there were 11 numbered treaties between First Nations peoples and the government of Canada. The map above shows how much of the land was given up in return for reserve lands and other benefits. It also shows the years in which the original treaties were signed.

the Canadian government wanted the country to grow and develop. It was very slow to keep its end of the bargain. Sometimes, it did not keep it at all. Expansion was the government's major concern. Justice for Aboriginal peoples was not.

## Treaty 6

Treaty 6 was one of the most important of the numbered treaties. It changed the lives of thousands of First Nations peoples. Treaty 6 came at a time of great hardship for these nations. Hunger and disease were a risk to survival. Canada's negotiator, Alexander Morris, wrote that the Aboriginal peoples feared for "the future of their children."

When First Nations signed the treaty in 1876, they did so reluctantly. First Nations people gave away huge areas of land in Saskatchewan and Alberta (and, later, parts of Manitoba). In return, they got reserves with one-half of a square kilometre of land for each person. They were also promised farming supplies and yearly help of five dollars per person from the government. Treaty 6 also promised that a medicine chest would

be kept on each reserve to help fight outbreaks of sickness and disease.

Some Nehiyaw, including those led by chiefs Pitikwahanapiwiyin (Poundmaker) and Mistahimaskwa (Big Bear), refused to sign the treaty. "We want none of the Queen's presents," Mistahimaskwa said to the Canadian negotiators. Pitikwahanapiwiyin said, "This is our land! It isn't a piece of **pemmican** to be cut off and given in little pieces back to us."

In time, their suffering forced nearly all of the Nehiyaw to sign. They hoped that, under the treaty, the government would give them the resources they needed and life would improve for them. For most, it did not.

# Reserves

First Nations peoples signed the numbered treaties out of **desperation**. Their old way of life was dying out. Europeans were settling the West. The bison herds were nearly gone. First Nations peoples across the West hoped that life would be better for them after the treaties were signed.

First Nations peoples handed over huge amounts of land to the government through the numbered treaties. For example, under Treaty 6, they gave up more than 300 000 square kilometres of land. Treaty 8, signed in 1899, involved nearly 850 000 square kilometres. This is an area larger than the entire country of France. In return, the First Nations were given small reserves of land – about half a square kilometre per person.

The government wanted First Nations peoples to become farmers. There were reasons that farming on the reserves proved to be hard. Most First Nations had never farmed before. Most of the farms that families were given were too small to farm. The land was often barren and rocky. To make matters worse, the government was often late sending the equipment, seeds, supplies, and animals it had promised in the treaties.

> I AM STRIVING TO WORK ON MY FARM that my children may benefit, but I am not accustomed to work on a farm and am short of implements. I mean the same thing used by the white man. A reaper, a mower, that is what we want. … We cannot work in winter. It is cold and we are naked. There is much sickness on my reserve and I would like a doctor there.
> —*Chief Pitikwahanapiwiyin*

The government also wanted to build railways and roads on the land. Soon, the government tried to convince many First Nations people to sell parts of their reserves. Many people on the reserves were poor, and they gave in to the pressure to sell. Many other people were forced to give up the land.

## Isapo-muxika (Crowfoot, 1830–1890)

Isapo-muxika (Crowfoot) was a chief of the Siksika (Blackfoot). He lived in southern Alberta. As a young warrior, he was known for his great cunning and skill. Isapo-muxika fought in many battles – including one against a grizzly bear. He survived many wounds. He was once shot in the back. For the rest of his life, he lived with a musket ball lodged in his body. As an older and wiser man, Isapo-muxika looked for peaceful solutions to problems. He helped to negotiate Treaty 7 in 1877. He also stayed out of the Northwest Resistance in 1885 (see p. 54). Later he travelled to Ottawa where he met Prime Minister John A. Macdonald.

**Figure 4.7** Isapo-muxika (Crowfoot)

In many ways, however, Isapo-muxika's life was a sad one. Many of his children died before him. More and more, he believed that the Canadian government was treating his people unfairly. In his last years, he grew very ill with a lung disease called tuberculosis [*too-BUR-cue-LOW-sis*]. Life, he said, "is like the flash of the firefly in the night." He died in 1890.

**Figure 4.6** Cree farmers from the File Hills farming colony, 1910

## The disappearance of the bison

For thousands of years, huge herds of bison grazed on the Prairies. These large animals were hunted by the First Nations peoples of the West. Later they were hunted by the Métis. Nations such as the Nehiyaw (Cree) relied on the bison for much of their food.

In the late 19th century, however, few bison roamed the Prairies. Hunters with rifles had killed almost all of them. When the bison were hunted for only their hides, they were often killed with poisoned bait. When this happened, Aboriginal people could not eat the meat. The poison could also kill the dogs that the Aboriginal peoples used to help them hunt.

As the bison herds disappeared, **famine** gripped entire First Nations. Some were forced to eat prairie dogs. Some even ate rodents to survive. Famine was

**Figure 4.8** *Assiniboine Hunting Buffalo*, by Paul Kane, c. 1851–1856.

one reason so many First Nations finally agreed to sign treaties and settle on reserves.

By 1900, there were only 400 to 500 bison left on the Prairies. Their numbers have increased over the past 100 years however. They no longer face extinction.

In many ways, Canada's federal and provincial governments dealt with Aboriginal peoples undemocratically. Those who lived on reserves were not allowed to vote. In the West, the government created the *pass system*. First Nations peoples needed permission from government officials if they wanted to leave the reserve for any length of time. This system lasted until the 1940s. Status **Indians** were not given the right to vote in federal elections until 1960. Those who worked for fair treatment were often treated as dangerous troublemakers by the authorities.

Over time, there have been disputes about the reserve boundaries. These disputes have led to what are called **specific land claims** cases. A land claim is a legal process. In a claim, Aboriginal peoples and the government try to agree about who controls certain pieces of land. In some instances, it has taken many years for the government to settle these disputes. One case, involving Ontario's Manitoulin Island, took nearly 130 years to settle.

There are more than 2400 reserves in Canada today. About 500 000 people live on the reserves. That is nearly half of the Aboriginal population of Canada. Many of these reserves were created by treaties signed in the late 19th and early 20th centuries.

Some Canadians think Aboriginal peoples should give up the reserves and all of their traditions. However, this would be like asking non-Aboriginal Canadians to give up their homes and their traditions. For many First Nations peoples, the reserves are more than just homes. They are communities. There, people can live by their traditions. On reserves, they have some control over the ways in which they live and the ways they earn their living.

# The Northwest Resistance

"History repeats itself," a famous saying goes. At first, the Northwest Resistance seemed like it would be a repeat of the Red River Resistance. It certainly must have seemed that way to Prime Minister John A. Macdonald. Louis Riel was back as leader of the Métis. In Batoche (near present-day Saskatoon), he formed a provisional government, just as he had at Red River in 1870. Once again, Riel demanded that the Canadian government deal with the Métis.

## Origins of the Northwest Resistance

By the 1880s, the Nehiyaw (Cree), Siksika (Blackfoot), and other peoples living on the Prairies fell on the hardest times they had ever known. The bison herds were almost gone. Many Plains people turned to farming. However, bad weather led to years of crop failure. The First Nations peoples lived on the edge of starvation, but the Canadian government did little to help them. John A. Macdonald's government took advantage of their situation by forcing First Nations to sign unfair treaties.

The Métis of the Saskatchewan River valley, many of whom had come from Red River, were not much better off. As the railway moved ever closer, they feared losing their farms to newcomers. For years, the Canadian government would not agree to the Métis' land claims. Looking for help, the Métis turned to their former leader, Louis Riel.

**Figure 4.9** Soon after this portrait was taken in 1884, Louis Riel returned to Canada. He set up a provisional government at Batoche, the centre of Métis culture in the North-West Territories.

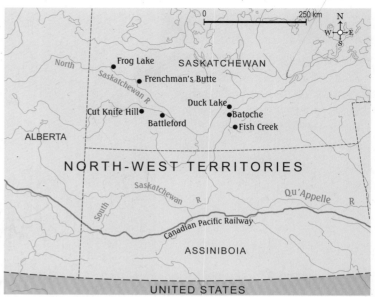

**Figure 4.10** *THE NORTH-WEST TERRITORIES, 1885*

## Louis Riel returns

Following the Red River Resistance, Louis Riel lived in different places in Canada and the United States. In 1870, Louis Riel moved to Montana. There, he married and had children. He became a schoolteacher. It seemed as if he was settling down to a normal life. Then, in 1884, a group of Métis led by Gabriel Dumont asked Riel to return to Canada. They wanted him to lead them. The group hoped Riel could do at Batoche what he had done at Red River 15 years earlier. There, Riel had reached an agreement with the Canadian government that protected the rights of the Métis.

In March 1885, Riel set up a provisional government at Batoche. He demanded that the Canadian government negotiate with the Métis. However, talks never took place. Later that month, an armed force of Métis led by Dumont defeated a force of North-West Mounted Police in a short battle at Duck Lake.

Much had changed since 1870. Even Riel was different. He now believed he had been selected by God to lead the Métis. The Métis, he believed, were God's chosen people. For his beliefs, he lost the support of the church. Riel tried to make an **alliance** with the First Nations. But the First

Nations backed away. They did not share his beliefs. Also, many of them had signed treaties with the government that they did not want to break. Even some Métis did not want to join him. They feared the power of the Canadian government. Riel had been away for years. He did not know how quickly the Canadian government could now send soldiers to the West.

## The soldiers arrive

In 1870, it took four months for troops to travel from Ottawa to Fort Garry. Now, there was a transcontinental railroad. The government was able to send 3000 troops to the Prairies in less than four weeks. Some had come

**Figure 4.11** On March 26, 1885, a battle broke out between the Métis and the North-West Mounted Police at Duck Lake. The Métis won. The incident triggered the Northwest Resistance.

from as far away as Quebec and Halifax. Less than a month after the battle at Duck Lake, this huge force of Canadian troops was ready to strike at Riel and his followers. The leader of the troops was a British officer. His name was Major General Frederick Middleton. Middleton had a simple plan. He decided to move in force on Batoche and crush Riel's provisional government.

However, a group of Nehiyaw and Nakoda (Stoney) people had taken control of Battleford, the territorial capital. Now Middleton had two wars to fight.

## Mistahimaskwa (Big Bear, 1825–1888)

The Nehiyaw chief Mistahimaskwa (Big Bear) was one of the last Plains chiefs to sign treaties with the Canadian government. He was among the wisest and most noble leaders of his people. He guided them through a time of great suffering. The bison were nearly gone. The Canadian government used this to try to get the people to accept unfair treaties. However, by 1882, the Nehiyaw were starving. Mistahimaskwa was sure his people would receive food if he signed a treaty with the Canadian government. He felt he had no choice. He signed.

In 1885, cheered by the Métis victory at Duck Lake, some of Mistahimaskwa's followers decided to fight to preserve their way of life. They attacked settlements at Frog Lake and Battleford.

Mistahimaskwa believed that fighting the Canadian government was hopeless. He tried to make a deal with them instead. After his followers were defeated, Mistahimaskwa was arrested. He had always wanted peace. However, he was blamed for his followers' actions. He spent two years in prison. Those two years were hard on him. His health was ruined. He died only a year after being released.

**Figure 4.12** Mistahimaskwa

# The Fighting Begins

General Middleton's army was joined by troops from the Canadian West. By mid-April 1885, Middleton had nearly 5000 soldiers. In addition, his troops had powerful new weapons – quick-firing rifles. They even had a hand-cranked machine gun called a Gatling gun.

Still, Middleton was cautious. He had good reason to be. In 1876, in Montana, a regiment of United States Cavalry had been defeated, with a loss of 210 men, by the Lakota (Sioux) and Tsitsista (Cheyenne). This was at the Battle of Little Bighorn. In 1879, in distant southern Africa, a British army was defeated by the spear-carrying warriors of the African Zulu nation.

**Figure 4.14** This painting is called *The Capture of Batoche*. It shows Canadian soldiers surrounding the Métis and Nehiyaw fighters at Batoche. With the new railway rushing Canadian troops to the Plains, the Métis were soon outnumbered. By the last day of the battle, the Métis were out of bullets. By May 12, the Canadians had won. It was the last battle of the Resistance.

**Figure 4.13** A Gatling gun

Middleton had heard about these battles. He knew that better weapons did not always lead to victory. Overconfident invaders could be defeated by people defending their homes. When he began his attack, Middleton wanted to make sure he made no mistakes. First, he sent a powerful force led by Lieutenant-Colonel William Otter to fight the Nehiyaw (Cree) at Battleford. He sent a second force to defend Calgary. On April 23, 1885, Middleton marched with the rest of his troops toward Batoche.

At the Battle of Fish Creek, Gabriel Dumont and a force of Métis ambushed Middleton's army. Middleton was forced to retreat. Two weeks later, in early May, the Nehiyaw war chief Fine Day defeated Colonel Otter at the Battle of Cut Knife Creek. Still, the Métis and First Nations who chose to fight were badly outnumbered. They could only delay the troops. They could not stop their advance.

## The Battle of Batoche

Louis Riel had many fine qualities. He was brave and intelligent. He inspired his supporters. However, he was not an experienced military leader. Gabriel Dumont was, but Middleton had more men and more guns. Dumont knew he could not beat the Canadian troops in an all-out fight. He wanted to fight a **guerrilla** [*geh-RILL-a*] war. This involves using hit-and-run and ambush **tactics**. Dumont hoped that over time he and his men could break the Canadian government's will to fight. Riel, however, believed that everything was in God's hands. He insisted that Dumont dig in and prepare to fight for Batoche.

At the Battle of Batoche (May 5–12, 1885), Riel and Dumont had only 250 men. They faced nearly 1000 troops. The Métis held off the government troops for days. However, the Métis grew tired. They finally ran out of ammunition. On May 12, Batoche was captured by the government troops. Riel fled, but he gave himself up four days later.

With Riel in custody, the troops kept fighting the Nehiyaw. Within six weeks, the Nehiyaw chiefs Pitikwahanapiwiyin and Mistahimaskwa surrendered.

**Figure 4.16** This is a monument in the Métis cemetery of Batoche, Saskatchewan. It stands in memory of the Métis who were killed there in 1885.

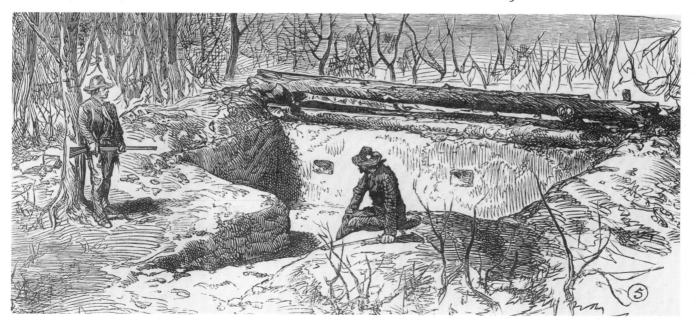

**Figure 4.15** Skilled Métis marksmen in the Battle of Batoche fired from inside rifle pits, such as the one shown above.

# The Trial of Louis Riel

In July 1885, the Canadian government charged Louis Riel with treason. He was sent to trial in Regina. That way, the authorities would be sure that no Métis, French, or Catholics would be on the jury. Riel's lawyers wanted to argue in court that he was innocent, because he was mentally ill. Riel would not let them. He did not want people to think that his efforts to help the Métis were those of an insane man.

It took the jury just one hour to find Riel guilty. Even though the jury asked the judge not to sentence Riel to death, the judge did so. In Ottawa, John A. Macdonald's advisors warned the prime minister that the Conservative Party would lose support in Quebec if Riel was hanged. "He shall hang though every dog in Quebec bark in his favour," Macdonald replied. On November 16, 1885, Louis Riel was hanged in Regina.

Riel's execution divided Canadians. In Ontario, many Protestants of British background supported his death. In Quebec, many French-Canadians were outraged over the hanging of a French-speaking Catholic. In Manitoba and Saskatchewan, the Métis were saddened by the loss of a hero who had stood up for their rights.

## Paying the price for resistance

Twenty-three Métis were killed during the Resistance. Many Aboriginal participants were later hanged or put in prison for their actions. Eight Nehiyaw (Cree), who had attacked and killed settlers at Frog Lake and Battleford, were hanged. Twenty-one Métis were put in prison. Some of them stayed there for as long as seven years. Reserves that the government thought had supported the Resistance were cut off from supplies and services. Mistahimaskwa's (Big Bear) **band** was broken up. Its members were sent to live with other bands. Many Métis people became landless and were branded as rebels. This is a label that would last a century or more.

**Figure 4.17** Louis Riel addresses the jury at his treason trial in Regina, July 20 to August 1, 1885.

WHAT WILL HE DO WITH HIM?

Figure 4.18 This cartoon was published in *Grip* magazine, May 23, 1885. Most people in Ontario wanted Riel hanged. Most people in Quebec considered him a hero.

## Gabriel Dumont (1837–1906)

Figure 4.19 Gabriel Dumont

Gabriel Dumont was Louis Riel's military leader during the Northwest Resistance. Dumont grew up hunting, riding, and canoeing. He fought his first battle, at the Grand Coteau, when he was just 13 years old. In 1884, Dumont was one of the Métis who asked Riel to come to Batoche to lead them. In the Resistance, Dumont had a personal loss. His brother, Isidore, was killed at the Battle of Duck Lake.

Dumont was a famous **marksman**. Soon after the fall of Batoche, some British militiamen caught up with him. He told them he still had plenty of ammunition left if they wanted to fight. They let him go. He escaped to Montana.

In the United States, this former leader of the Métis, who spoke six languages, ended up performing in Buffalo Bill's Wild West Show. He did not return to Batoche until 1890.

## Pitikwahanapiwiyin (Poundmaker, 1842–1886)

Figure 4.20 Pitikwahanapiwiyin

Pitikwahanapiwiyin (Poundmaker) was an important Nehiyaw chief. He spent much of his life acting as a peacemaker. Like many Plains First Nations leaders, he led his people through years of hunger and hardship in the late 1870s and early 1880s. Only reluctantly did he sign treaties and settle on a reserve. He believed that peaceful negotiation was the only choice for his people. "The whites will fill the country," he once told his followers. "It is useless to dream that we can frighten them."

Some warriors on Pitikwahanapiwiyin's reserve disagreed with him. They chose to fight in 1885. Pitikwahanapiwiyin did not join them. After the Battle of Cut Knife Creek, he convinced them not to attack Colonel Otter's retreating troops. This probably saved the lives of many of Otter's troops.

Pitikwahanapiwiyin even tried to make peace between Louis Riel and General Middleton. Nonetheless, after Riel was captured, Pitikwahanapiwiyin was forced to give himself up to Middleton. He was tried for treason. "Everything I could do was done to stop bloodshed," he told the court. The jury found him guilty. Like Mistahimaskwa, Pitikwahanapiwiyin was sentenced to three years in prison. While imprisoned, he fell very ill. He died just four months after being released.

**DID YOU KNOW?** Riel left no direct heirs. Sadly, his three children died when they were quite young. His daughter, Marie-Angélique, died from diphtheria at 13. His son Jean died at 26 from injuries he suffered in a buggy accident. Riel's infant son died shortly before Riel was hanged.

# Residential Schools

Beginning in the 1880s, the Canadian government began to build residential schools in the West. In all, 80 schools were built. Thousands of First Nations children were sent to these schools. Residential schools were sometimes called boarding schools. This is because the students *boarded* or lived at the school, away from their homes.

Residential schools were not a new idea. They had existed in New France. Later, they existed in British North America before Confederation.

In some ways, residential schools seemed like any other schools. Students studied in classrooms, and learned skills such as farming and housekeeping.

There was a much darker side to the residential schools, however. Their goal was to **assimilate** First Nations children by taking away their language and culture. The schools were often built far from the reserves. That meant that students sometimes spent years away from their families and their traditional cultures.

**Figure 4.21** Priests, nuns, and school children at a residential school, 1899. Residential schools were run jointly by the Canadian government and Christian churches. Students were not allowed to speak Aboriginal languages or follow their spiritual traditions. Instead, the schools promoted English or French, Euro-Canadian culture, and the Christian religion. Many students suffered in their adult life from the way they were treated in the residential schools. The last residential school, in Qu'Appelle, Saskatchewan, was closed in 1996.

Students were not allowed to speak their own languages. Aboriginal spiritual practices were banned. The schools received very little money from the government. This meant that the living

## The Indian Act

In 1876, Prime Minister John A. Macdonald's Conservatives passed a law called the *Indian Act*. The goal of the Indian Act was to assimilate Canada's Aboriginal peoples into the rest of society. However, most Aboriginal peoples wanted to keep their own languages and cultures. These were not important to most members of Parliament.

Under the Indian Act, First Nations peoples who lived on reserves had to register with the government as Indians. Those who registered were not allowed to vote or to drink alcohol. A First Nations woman who married a non-First Nations man lost her **Indian status**. She also lost many other rights, such as the right for her and her children to live and be buried on the reserve. Later changes to the Indian Act banned important Aboriginal rituals such as the Sun Dance and the **potlatch**. The Indian Act also set up the band council system (see p. 193).

The Indian Act has been changed several times since 1876. In many ways, the changes have been good. For example, the bans on First Nations ceremonies have been removed. In 1960, voting rights were given to First Nations peoples. By the late 1960s, residential schools were closing down. First Nations peoples began looking after their own education. Status women married to non-status men no longer lost their Indian status. Women who had lost their status had it returned. This was also true for their children.

conditions were very bad. Many children became sick and died from tuberculosis. Discipline was harsh, and students were sometimes abused.

One woman remembers being taken to a residential school at the age of eight. "The priest came to get us and told us we were going for a ride in the country. I was really happy. I'd never been in a car before." Once she arrived, "the first thing they did was cut off all our hair. Then we were given numbers." Although students were punished for speaking their language, the woman recalls that she kept her language alive by talking late at night, after dark.

Figure 4.22 In 1896, these Kainai (Blood) people prepared for a Sun Dance, an important religious ceremony. Certain parts of the Sun Dance were outlawed by various governments. However many nations continued to hold the ceremonies, which were made legal again in 1951.

## Conclusion

After Confederation, the Aboriginal peoples of the West suddenly had to deal with the Canadian government. They faced many challenges and problems. These included colonization, the construction of the railroad, and the disappearance of the bison. First Nations and Métis peoples responded in many different ways. Many bargained with the government. This led to the 11 numbered treaties and the creation of over two thousand reserves. Other groups resisted signing treaties. In the Northwest Resistance of 1885, for example, the Métis and others chose to fight.

Aboriginal peoples had many different responses to Canada's growth into the West. However, the Canadian government's approach did not change. John A. Macdonald himself once remarked that Aboriginal people "in every respect have the right to be considered equal" to other Canadians. Nevertheless, the Canadian government did not treat them that way. It thought Canada's Aboriginal population stood in the way of progress. For decades, it tried to force them to assimilate. Aboriginal people endured many years of hardship and unfair treatment. Today, hundreds of thousands of Aboriginal peoples proudly practise traditional customs while continuing to struggle for equal treatment.

# 5 The Newcomers

In the four years after Confederation, Canada grew to nearly 10 times its original size. Rupert's Land, the North-West Territories, and British Columbia joined the original four provinces of Nova Scotia, New Brunswick, Ontario, and Quebec. By 1871, Canada was 40 times bigger than Great Britain.

Immigration has always been important to Canada. In the 19th century, the Irish came to Upper and Lower Canada to escape famine in Ireland. African-Americans came north on the **Underground Railway** to escape slavery in the United States. The Fraser Valley gold rush in 1858 brought Chinese and Americans to Canada.

Still, by 1871, Canada did not have a large population. There were fewer than four million people – less than were living in the city of London, England! Of those, thousands of people were **emigrating** from Canada to the United States every month. They were looking for better jobs or a warmer climate. In fact, more people left Canada in the 1880s than were born in the country.

For that reason, Canada's government began to promote **immigration**. It sent agents overseas to raise interest in Canada, especially the Prairies. Canada opened immigration offices in Britain and in Europe.

Canada's first Immigration Act passed in 1869. It set up an *open-door* policy. This meant that there were very few limits on who could immigrate to Canada.

**Figure 5.1** In Europe, thousands of posters and pamphlets promoted Canada. The poster on the right is in Dutch. It was one of many published in foreign languages to attract immigrants from northern Europe.

---

**AS YOU READ, THINK ABOUT**

- how the Canadian government promoted settlement in Canada
- who the immigrants were, and why they wanted to come to Canada
- what immigrants found when they arrived here
- how immigrants built their homes and farmed the land

Meanwhile, the Homestead Act encouraged immigrants to settle in the West. It offered them land at very low prices. Sixty hectares of land cost only $10.

The first big wave of immigration to Canada began in the 1890s. Prime Minister Wilfrid Laurier created a new cabinet position: **minister** of immigration. Clifford Sifton, a lawyer and businessman, was Canada's first minister of immigration. He used several methods to boost immigration. His department produced posters advertising Canada. In 1902, Sifton tried a new form of promotion. He hired Canada's first filmmaker, James Freer of Brandon, Manitoba, to make films promoting Canada for audiences in Britain.

The Canadian government's efforts came at a good time. Europe was changing, and millions of people were already thinking about immigrating to Canada. In all, more than 3.5 million immigrants came to Canada between Confederation and the start of the First World War in 1914. Most arrived after 1900.

While some immigrants left Canada for the United States, those who stayed greatly changed Canadian life. By 1914, nearly half of all Canadians were either immigrants or the children of immigrants. The number of people in Canada probably would have shrunk in the years after Confederation were it not for immigration. That was because so many Canadians moved to the United States.

**DID YOU KNOW?** You emigrate *from* a country, you immigrate *to* a country.

**Figure 5.2** This wagon, full of corn, grain, and vegetables, was taken across Scotland in 1904. It advertised the rewards of immigrating to Canada. To Clifford Sifton, minister of immigration, the tough farmers of northern Scotland were the right kind of settlers for the Canadian West.

Most of Canada's new immigrants still came from Britain. However, more and more were arriving from other parts of the world. Germans, Ukrainians, Italians, Greeks, Scandinavians, Poles, Jews, and many others from across Europe immigrated to Canada. Chinese, Japanese, Koreans, and others crossed the Pacific Ocean. Canada was a multicultural country long before people called it one.

All new immigrants hoped they would find a better life in Canada. Of course, that did not always happen. The Canadian government may have wanted immigrants, but few newcomers felt welcome.

### Immigrants to Canada, 1896 to 1914

| | | | |
|---|---|---|---|
| 1896 | 16 835 | 1906 | 211 653 |
| 1897 | 21 716 | 1907 | 272 409 |
| 1898 | 31 900 | 1908 | 143 326 |
| 1899 | 44 543 | 1909 | 173 694 |
| 1900 | 41 681 | 1910 | 286 839 |
| 1901 | 55 747 | 1911 | 331 288 |
| 1902 | 89 102 | 1912 | 375 756 |
| 1903 | 138 660 | 1913 | 400 870 |
| 1904 | 131 252 | 1914 | 150 484 |
| 1905 | 141 465 | | |

# "The Last, Best West"[1]

Immigrants came to Canada from all over the world in the years after Confederation. In ports such as Montreal and Quebec City, people must have heard a dizzying number of languages every day: English, Gaelic, Dutch, German, Italian, Greek, Russian, Polish, Yiddish, and many others.

Some of the newcomers settled in the Maritimes or in eastern Canada. Others went south to the United States. Most travelled west on the Canadian Pacific Railway. Immigrants found all kinds of work. Some became doctors, teachers, lawyers, police officers, or even government officials. Many worked in mines, logging camps, factories, and on the railroads. Some became servants for the rich. Many became farmers on the Prairies.

The population of the Prairies soared as immigrants flooded in. The number of people in Manitoba grew nearly 20 times between 1871 and 1911. The number of people in Saskatchewan and Alberta grew four times between 1901 and 1911. Small towns such as Calgary, Regina, and Winnipeg grew rapidly into big cities. When Manitoba became a province in 1870, Winnipeg had just 3000 people. By 1911, it had 150 000 people. The city became known as the "gateway to the West."

The **influx** of immigrants created many problems for the Métis and First Nations peoples. Immigrants were promised land that Métis and First Nations people had lived on for generations.

## Reasons for migrating

Why did immigrants come to Canada? Many left their homelands because conditions in their own countries made it hard to stay there.

Some groups of immigrants hoped to escape poverty in their own countries. Some of their countries were overpopulated. This meant there were few jobs and not enough land to farm. This was the case for most immigrants from Britain. It was also true for many of the Italians, Germans,

## The *Empress of Ireland*

The *Empress of Ireland* was a ship that sailed between Canada and Liverpool, England. In all, the *Empress* made 96 voyages across the Atlantic Ocean. It carried more than 100 000 passengers to Canada. This included thousands of immigrants. On May 28, 1914, the *Empress* left Quebec with nearly 1500 passengers. Among them were several hundred immigrants going home to visit relatives. At 2:00 AM, in heavy fog, the *Empress* hit another ship. Heavily damaged, the *Empress* rolled over and sank, and 1012 people were drowned. It was a major disaster – just as the sinking of the *Titanic* had been in 1912.

**Figure 5.3** The *Empress of Ireland*

Ukrainians, and Poles who came to Canada before the First World War.

Some people hoped to escape religious **persecution.** These included Jews escaping the violence they faced in Russia. Doukhobors [*DOO-kuh-bores*] also left Russia. They built a community of 6000 in British Columbia. **Pacifist** Mennonites came to Canada from Russia, Germany, and even the United States so they would not have to serve in their national armies. They built **homestead**s in Ontario, Manitoba, and Saskatchewan.

Some people escaped natural disasters. Immigrants from Iceland left after ash from a volcano ruined their island.

Immigrants from China came to Canada's West Coast for one of two reasons. Some hoped to strike it rich in the gold rush. Others wanted jobs building the Canadian Pacific Railway.

When looking for new places to settle, these people found that Canada promised many of the things they were looking for.

For most immigrants, Canada's promise of cheap farmland was the main reason to leave their homelands. Those who settled in Canada's cities set up their own neighbourhoods. They started churches and newspapers and opened stores and restaurants.

---

1   The phrase "The Last, Best West" was used to market Canada to immigrants in Europe. It refers to the fact that all the best land in the western United States was already taken, but that there was still lots of good farmland in the Canadian West.

**DID YOU KNOW?** More immigrants arrived in Canada in 1913 than in any other year in Canadian history. More than 400 000 people arrived that year. That is more than in the first 10 years after Confederation put together.

**Figure 5.4** Dutch immigrants to Manitoba, 1910.

**Figure 5.5** A family of Russian Jews, around 1911, at Quebec City.

**DID YOU KNOW?** The United States was the second biggest source of immigrants arriving in Canada.

**Figure 5.6** A family from Galicia (a region now part of Ukraine and Poland) at Quebec immigration sheds

**Figure 5.7** Scottish crofters prepare to leave Britain for a new life in Canada, early 1900s.

**Figure 5.8** This cartoon appeared in an unknown newspaper in the latter part of the nineteenth century, as settlers from foreign countries flooded the prairies. Many Canadians were concerned about how the newcomers would fit in.

**Figure 5.9** Norwegian immigrants, about 1911

## The Republic of New Iceland

In 1875, the Canadian government made one of the most unusual reserves in Canadian history. It was called the Republic of New Iceland. It was created on the west shore of Lake Winnipeg for a group of about 1500 Icelanders. They had fled volcanoes and other disasters in their homeland. Their biggest settlement was the town of Gimli, named after a place in Norse mythology. In New Iceland, the settlers hoped to make a life like the one they had left behind. Unfortunately, disease and hunger nearly destroyed New Iceland. Many settlers moved to Winnipeg. In 1881, New Iceland became part of Manitoba. Today, more than 70 000 Canadians are descended from Icelanders.

**Figure 5.10** This painting, *The Landing*, by Arni Sigurdsson, shows Icelandic immigrants arriving at New Iceland on Lake Winnipeg.

# Challenges in a New Land

In 1886, 28-year-old Conrad Anderson and his wife, Jacobine, settled near Calgary. Conrad found a job in a lumber mill. Later the family bought a homestead for $10. As farmers, the family lived through **drought** and heavy snow. They even lived through an outbreak of smallpox in nearby towns. In some difficult years, there was almost nothing to eat but wild rabbits. Conrad and Jacobine's son remembers a mealtime prayer that went like this:

> For rabbit roasted and rabbit fried,
> For rabbit cooked and rabbit dried,
> For rabbit young and rabbit old,
> For rabbit hot and rabbit cold,
> For rabbit tender and rabbit tough,
> We thank thee Lord, we've had enough.

Conrad and Jacobine were immigrants from Norway, a Scandinavian country 7000 kilometres away. The Andersons were like thousands of other immigrants. They found that life on Canada's Prairies was not everything that the government had promised in its posters, pamphlets, and movies. They struggled through many hard years on their prairie homestead. At home, they spoke Norwegian.

The Anderson children went to school with classmates from many different backgrounds. In school, they learned to speak English. They were taught Canadian history. They remained proud of their Norwegian heritage. However, they became more used to their new country than their parents did. In fact, Conrad and Jacobine's youngest son became a veterinarian at the Calgary Zoo.

The Andersons settled in a place where other Scandinavians lived. Some were their relatives. Immigrants from one region or background often settled near one another. This made the move to Canada, with its different languages, laws, and customs, much easier. By living together in communities, new immigrants could keep some of their own culture. They would worship together and shop in stores owned by people they knew.

Unfortunately, many immigrants faced **discrimination.** This was especially true for those who settled in cities. They had more day-to-day contact with other Canadians. Employers were sometimes unfair. They made immigrants work long hours for less pay than other workers – and fired them if they complained. Some groups were better treated than others. Settlers from the British Isles usually had an easier time fitting in. On the other hand, African-Americans and Asian immigrants were ill treated almost everywhere they went.

Many African-Americans had come to Canada to escape slavery before the American Civil War. After slavery was ended in the United

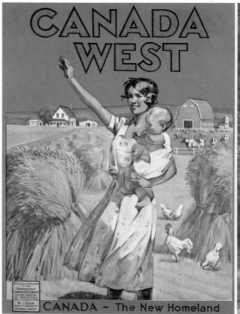

**Figure 5.11** The poster on the left was made to show that Canada was a perfect place for immigrants. The photograph on the right shows a real immigrant woman with her baby near Yorkton, Saskatchewan, in 1903. How does the photo on the right differ from the poster? How is it the same?

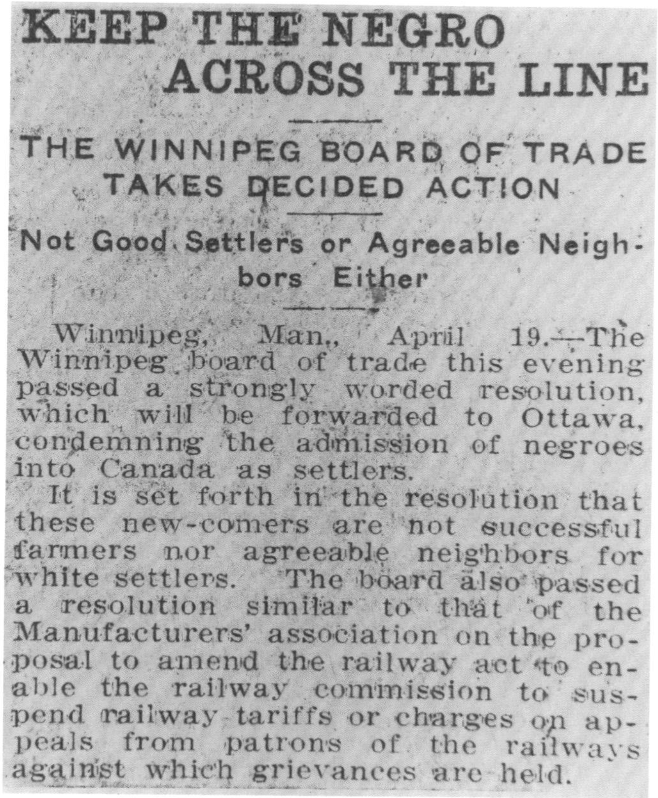

## KEEP THE NEGRO ACROSS THE LINE

### THE WINNIPEG BOARD OF TRADE TAKES DECIDED ACTION

#### Not Good Settlers or Agreeable Neighbors Either

Winnipeg, Man., April 19.—The Winnipeg board of trade this evening passed a strongly worded resolution, which will be forwarded to Ottawa, condemning the admission of negroes into Canada as settlers.

It is set forth in the resolution that these new-comers are not successful farmers nor agreeable neighbors for white settlers. The board also passed a resolution similar to that of the Manufacturers' association on the proposal to amend the railway act to enable the railway commission to suspend railway tariffs or charges on appeals from patrons of the railways against which grievances are held.

**Figure 5.12** Article in the *Albertan* newspaper, 1910

States in 1865, some freed slaves came north to start a new life. However, they were often treated badly in Canada.

Many thought African-Americans were not equal to other Canadians. Words such as *menace* and *troublesome* were used by politicians and newspaper editors to describe them. In 1911, an article in the *Manitoba Free Press* said that African-Americans could not survive long in Canada's cold climate because their ancestors had come from Africa. It was a strange thing to say. Just two years earlier, Matthew Henson, an African-American man, had become world famous for co-discovering the North Pole!

Asian settlers were also treated badly. Chinese immigrants often faced discrimination. Chinese people had been coming to Canada since the 18th century. However, large numbers did not begin to arrive until the era of the gold rush. Many Chinese prospectors came from San Francisco and eventually set up communities in British Columbia.

In the 1880s, nearly 15 000 Chinese people immigrated to Canada. Most were young men seeking work. Many found jobs building the western end of the Canadian Pacific Railway (CPR). For this dangerous work, Chinese immigrants were paid half of what other workers earned. The CPR was finished in 1885. At that time, the Canadian government decided it no longer needed Chinese immigrants. It forced Chinese immigrants to pay a *head tax* (entry tax) when they arrived. This was to keep them from coming to Canada.

**DID YOU KNOW?** To fit in, many immigrants changed the spelling or pronunciation of their names to something easier for English or French Canadians to remember. The name Schmidt, for example, was often changed to Smith.

**Figure 5.13** This family was unusual, because the government did not want Chinese men in Canada to bring their wives and families from China. They would have to pay an expensive head tax. The government wanted Chinese people as workers, but not as citizens.

# The Home Children

In the 1860s, a visitor to London, England, wrote about the city's "swarms of children" who were "dirty and barefoot." These children were a common sight in the crowded slums of 19th-century England. **Social reformers** worried about the kind of future they would have. Would they turn to crime to make a living? Some thought they should send the orphans and poor children to Canada, Australia, and other parts of the British Empire. As a poem from the time went,

> Take them away! Take them away!
> Out of the gutter, the ooze, and slime…
> They'll prove a blessing to other lands –
> Here, if they linger, a curse.

The reformers thought these children would have a better life working in Canada or Australia than living in England's slums. As one woman remembered, years after being sent to Canada, "We were so very poor. My father was slowly dying from tuberculosis from working in the coal mines." Her parents were among the thousands of poor who sent their children across the sea, hoping they would find a better life. These children became known as *home children*.

Most of the children sent to Canada were between the ages of eight and fourteen. However, some were as young as four. Some of the children were orphans. Others had to leave behind their parents and friends. "I was so frightened of leaving the only home I'd ever had, leaving my school friends, my only sisters, and of leaving my best friend," one home child recalled. Usually the children had no say in the matter. Many young children did not even know what was happening. Most never saw their parents again.

Crossing the Atlantic Ocean by steamship was often frightening for these children. For most, their arrival in Halifax or Montreal was just the start of their trip. Once they were in Canada, the children were placed in special *receiving homes*. They stayed in these homes until they were chosen by a family.

Some children were adopted by loving parents. Others became servants or farm workers. If they were lucky, these children worked for families who cared for them. Good families made sure the children attended school, and even paid them wages. Many other children, however, were treated badly.

"I would get up at 4:00 AM and go to bed at six or seven in the evening," one home child recalled. "You would work all day: harness the horses, clean out the stables, plow, cultivate, and **harrow**. The farmer wouldn't feed me. I would steal food from the barn."

One girl, whose family was very cruel, often thought about running away. "Sometimes I would go upstairs and I would sit and cry and I would pack my bag," she remembered. "Then I would sit down and think *where* am I going to run away to? And I would unpack my bag." Supervisors were supposed to make sure that the children were well treated. Often this did not happen.

Once they were 18 years old, the children could do what they wanted. Some continued to work for the families who had chosen them. Others left and made lives for themselves in Canada. A few went back to England.

Nearly 100 000 British children immigrated to Canada without their parents. Most of them arrived in the late 19th and early 20th centuries. However, children continued to arrive every year until the late 1920s.

**DID YOU KNOW?** When they grew up, many home children tried to find their families. Few were successful. It is estimated that close to four million Canadians are descended from the 100 000 home children who came to Canada.

## Dr. Barnardo's Homes

Thomas John Barnardo was born in Dublin, Ireland. In the 1850s, he went to study medicine in England. There he came across homeless orphans in London's poor East End. He soon started a charity that sent poor children to homes in countries of the British Empire. More than 30 000 of these children were sent to Canada. Perhaps Dr. Barnardo wanted to help children because he had had sadness in his own life. Of his seven children, three died from sickness at a young age.

Barnardo and other child-welfare reformers of this time thought they were doing the right thing. However, some people think that sending children away created as much misery as it prevented.

**Figure 5.14** A young boy plows a field at a farm in Russell, Manitoba. The farm was run by Dr. Barnardo's organization. It trained boys from Britain to be farm labourers.

**Figure 5.15** These are some of the 30 000 "Barnardo Children" sent to Canada from Britain between Confederation and the First World War.

# A Land of Plenty

Though life was often hard, most immigrants were glad they came to Canada. Many were still sure that Canada was a land of opportunity. Poverty and **prejudice** had been part of life in Europe and Asia, too. Often it had been much worse there. For instance:

- Throughout Europe and Asia, poor families worked for generations on farms owned by rich landowners. In Canada, they could buy a homestead of their own.
- Unlike in Canada, most poor people in Europe had no hope of sending their children to school.

- Young men in most European countries were made to serve for a time in the military. In Canada, only volunteers served in the army.
- In Europe, religious groups such as the Doukhobors, Mennonites, and Jews had often been attacked for their beliefs. Some had even been killed. In Canada, these groups found the freedom to practise their religions.
- Many immigrants had few political rights in their home countries. In Canada, many of them had the right to vote for the first time.

These are some of the reasons that many immigrants took great pride in their new country. Even today, people come to Canada

## Famous Canadian immigrants

Canada's governor general, Michaëlle Jean, was born in Haiti in 1957. In 1968, her family fled the **dictatorship** there and came to Canada. After going to university in Montreal and in Europe, she became a journalist. For many years she worked for the Canadian Broadcasting Corporation. There she made documentary films and hosted radio and television programs. In 2005, she became Canada's governor general. Michaëlle Jean has a master's degree in literature and speaks five languages.

Immigrants to Canada have become actors and athletes, painters, poets, and even prime ministers. Here are just a few immigrants who became famous in Canada and around the world:

**Figure 5.16** Michaëlle Jean, shown here around 1999, worked as a journalist before becoming governor general.

**Figure 5.17** John A. Macdonald, Canada's first prime minister, born in Scotland

**Figure 5.18** Yousuf Karsh, photographer, born in Turkey

**Figure 5.19** Michael Ondaatje, novelist and poet, born in Sri Lanka

**Figure 5.20** Adrienne Clarkson, former governor general of Canada, born in Hong Kong

**Figure 5.21** Donovan Bailey, Olympic sprinter and gold medallist, born in Jamaica

# Farming the Land

**Figure 5.22** Singers perform at Canada's National Ukrainian Festival, which is held every year in Dauphin, Manitoba. The festival celebrates Ukrainian culture in Canada. Ukrainian people began settling in Canada around 1892.

from all over the world looking for freedom and a better life.

Hardly any region of Canada is untouched by immigrants. In cities, especially, immigrants have made Canada a place of great diversity. Every year, events such as Dragon Boat races in Vancouver, the Icelandic Festival in Gimli, Caribana in Toronto, and the St. Patrick's Day Parade in Montreal celebrate immigrant cultures.

Imagine a family of settlers had arrived on the sweeping prairie in the middle of the summer. Perhaps the settlers were English or French-Canadians, attracted by the promise of a free homestead. Perhaps they were immigrants from Europe or elsewhere. They might be British, Dutch, Russians, Poles, Germans, Norwegians, or others. Suddenly they found themselves having to start a new life.

The first task was to dig a well for water. On their first nights, they would sleep in a tent or under their wagons. Then they would build a temporary place to live. Usually, these were small huts made of mud and straw. If the settlers were lucky, they already owned or could buy everything they needed to break the sod and plant a small crop for the first season. Many immigrants, however, had never tried farming. Plowing, planting, and harvesting crops were new to them. Even jobs such as yoking an ox or horse to a plow were very hard the first time they tried it.

**Figure 5.23** This painting shows life on a settler's homestead near Carberry, Manitoba, at the end of the 19th century.

**Figure 5.24** Many immigrant families lived in sod huts. The huts were made from thick prairie grass with strong matted roots known as *sod*. The sod would be cut into strips, then used as building blocks to make walls. Later, families would build more permanent homes.

One writer, E.B. Mitchell, wrote about some of the problems farmers had with livestock:

> The pig falls mysteriously ill and has to be nursed, or a calf is born in a great frost and has to be coaxed into life beside the kitchen stove, or a horse strays from the pasture … or the poultry get up a vast excitement because they see a white pigeon and think it is a new kind of hawk … day in day out, in fair or foul weather, in health or sickness, the cows must be driven from pasture and milked, the team-horses watered and fed … no holiday or change is possible.

Another problem was the cost of farming. Land was cheap; however, farm equipment was not. Nor were the materials needed to build a house to replace their temporary huts. It cost hundreds of dollars to get a farm up and running. This was money that most immigrants did not have. Instead, families

## A woman describes life on a prairie farm

In the 1920s, a woman named R.C. Phillips wrote about what life was like for women who lived on Prairie farms:

> *We find farm women getting up early in the morning, preparing breakfast for six, seven, and sometimes more people. Washing dishes, the cream separator and milk utensils, packing school lunches and speeding the children on their way; feeding and caring for the chickens … hurrying back to the house to make beds, sweep and dust … ironing, washing, baking, scrubbing, to say nothing of the family sewing … somehow time must be found for planting and caring for the garden as well as the canning and preserving of the fruit and vegetables for winter.*

Mrs. Phillips also had to prepare a hearty lunch and dinner for her hard-working family. She had worked like that every day since marrying a farmer 15 years

**Figure 5.25** A woman does the family laundry on an Alberta homestead, 1908.

earlier. Her family's farm had succeeded, she wrote, only "by gruelling labour and sacrifice." Her story was like that of thousands of women on the Prairies.

often traded their crops for things they needed. These included livestock, farm tools, cloth for making clothes, and food (such as sugar, coffee, and tea) that they could not grow themselves. In many families, the father and older sons worked for part of the year in forestry, fishing, or on the railroad to earn extra money.

## A boy's life on the Prairies

In 1903, a boy about 12 years old kept a diary. In it, he wrote about his life on a Manitoba farm. Here is what he wrote from March 16 to March 22. Notice how his daily life centred around activities such as chopping wood and visits with friends. Notice, too, that he did not go to school regularly and washed only once during the week!

*Monday, March 16*
Father took Bert to town. Washed. Ground [sharpened] *axe*

Went over to Bing Johnston's at night.

*Tuesday*
Bagged up potatoes. Cut wood down. Mrs. Jeffrey here in afternoon. Snowed.

*Wednesday*
Father, mother, Bruce and Earl took a load of potatoes to town and got $1.25 a bag. School supposed to start but teacher did not get in. Bought a rocking chair.

*Thursday*
School started. Cut wood down. Cold. 10 degrees below zero.

*Friday*
Cut wood down. Bert came home. Uncle Mack's baby died.

*Saturday*
Father and Bert sawed wood down. Snowed. Uncle Mack's baby buried.

*Sunday*
Bert and Mother and I went to church. Snowed.

Other notes in this boy's diary included "made fence posts" and "took five loads of wheat to town." This boy, like many who lived on prairie farms, seemed to have little time for things such as going to school or playing sports.

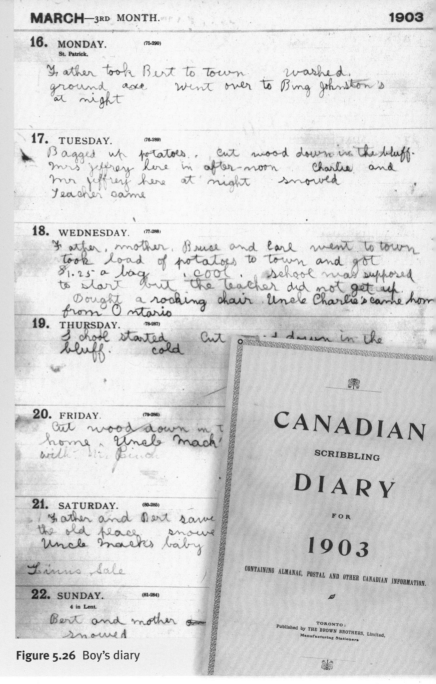

**Figure 5.26** Boy's diary

# Farming Technology

In the late 19th and early 20th centuries, new **technology** and scientific discoveries began to change farm life.

Two new machines changed farming the most. One was the mechanical thresher. Separating kernels of grain from wheat chaff took a lot of time. Then, in the mid-1800s, hand-cranked mechanical threshers started to appear. They were hard to run, but they increased by 10 times the number of **bushels** a farmer could produce. By the end of the century, the latest mechanical threshers increased output by *another* 10 times.

The second important invention was the steam-powered *traction engine*. (Soon, people started calling them *tractors*.) For hundreds of years, farmers had used horses to plow fields and haul carts. Farmers spent a lot of time feeding, stabling, and grooming their horses. And horses could not always be depended on. Cold and sickness killed many horses every year. Tractors needed to be cared for, too. However, a good one could last for many years. A tractor could also do more work than a

**Figure 5.27** Peter Soli and his threshing team in Queenstown, Alberta, 1918. With mechanical threshers, threshermen like Soli went to many farms during the harvest to separate grain. It was cheaper for farmers to pay threshermen by the bushel than to spend a lot of money buying an expensive machine.

**Figure 5.28** Tractors slowly replaced horses on prairie farms. Here, Doukhobor settlers break up soil with a steam tractor, 1912.

## Prairie inventors

Sir Charles Saunders (1867–1937) was an important inventor. His "invention" was a new kind of wheat. The wheat most often grown on the Prairies was called *Red Fife*. Red Fife was not well suited to the Prairie climate, however. It took too long to grow and was sometimes damaged by frost before it could be harvested. In 1903, Saunders started developing a type of wheat he named *Marquis* [*mar-KEE*]. Unlike Red Fife, Marquis wheat ripened quickly enough to avoid frost damage. By the early 1920s, nearly every Prairie farmer was growing Marquis wheat.

Norman Criddle (1875–1933) was born in England. He moved to Manitoba with his family in 1882. The Criddles were well educated. Norman's father had studied music in Germany. His mother, Alice, had a degree from Cambridge University in England. Norman himself became an expert in entomology [*en-tuh-MAW-luh-jee*], the study of insects. In 1902, he invented a poison that killed grasshoppers. His invention, which became known as *Criddle mixture*, saved thousands of crops. Criddle was later hired by the government of Manitoba to help farmers fight insects.

horse. By the start of the 20th century, gasoline-powered tractors began to replace the original steam-powered models.

Tractors and mechanical threshers cost a lot of money. A tractor could cost as much as 10 pairs of horses. For a long time, tractors and mechanical threshers were found only on big, profitable farms. Horses were used for much of the work on small farms until the late 1940s.

Farming would never be easy. However, technology helped farmers add to their crop **yields**. This made the Prairies the "breadbasket to the Empire." By the end of the century, people around world were buying Canadian crops, especially Canadian grains.

## Farming Cooperatives

Settlers on the prairies had many problems. Science and technology made some things easier. However, the new machines could not solve every problem. Another thing that made farming easier was old-fashioned neighbourliness. Pioneers often helped one another at planting and harvesting time. Often they worked together to raise barns and build houses.

In time, they started groups such as farmer's unions and cooperatives. As members of cooperatives, farmers shared costs of supplies and services. Cooperatives also helped farmers **market** their crops. Cooperative groups eventually ran their own grain elevators and stores.

The Saskatchewan Grain Growers Association was founded in 1906. The United Farmers of Alberta was founded in 1909. Both were run democratically. Every farmer who was a member had a vote in the way that the cooperative was run.

Canadian farming cooperatives also spoke out for Canadian farmers. They asked governments for such things as fair crop prices and fair transportation costs. They pushed for modern services, such as water and electricity, for rural communities.

Members of cooperatives shared their knowledge with one another. This helped new immigrants who did not know much about farming. Cooperatives also had an effect on the way large companies sold members' crops.

## Conclusion

In the late 19th and early 20th centuries, immigrants from Europe settled in the vast regions of Western Canada. Most came for the promise of farmland. They joined the Métis, First Nations, French, and Scottish farmers already in the West. By the early 20th century, there were more than 3000 new rural communities. Farmers grew more and better crops through technology and science. Soon, Canadian crops were feeding people the world over. The young country of Canada was taking its place among the nations of the world.

**Figure 5.29** Members of the Grain Growers Grain Company, a farming cooperative, promoted its ideals at an exhibition.

# 6 Into the 20th Century

hen John A. Macdonald died in 1891, his death marked the end of an era. For the next several years, the Conservative Party had a hard time finding another leader to take his place.

In the election of 1896, Liberal leader Wilfrid Laurier swept to power. He was the country's first French-Canadian prime minister. He would serve for the next 15 years. However, Laurier's Canada faced many challenges. It was a rapidly changing country. Canadians were divided over how it should be run.

## Imperialism and Nationalism

In 1897 Queen Victoria had **reigned** for 60 years. Her *Diamond Jubilee,* as the anniversary was known, was celebrated throughout the British Empire. Canadians held parades and rallies, the biggest since Confederation. This all took place for a woman who had never even visited Canada.

**Figure 6.1** In 1897, Diamond Jubilee celebrations throughout the British Empire marked 60 years of Queen Victoria's reign.

Such respect for a queen who lived so far away may seem strange to us today. In the 19th century and early 20th century, however, there was no difference between being Canadian and being a British subject.

"A British subject I was born, a British subject I shall die," John A. Macdonald once said. Many English speaking Canadians agreed with him. In the late 19th century, many English Canadians were **imperialists**. Imperialism was the belief that Canada should have very close ties to Great Britain and the British Empire.

---

**AS YOU READ, THINK ABOUT**

- what different groups of Canadians thought about their country as the 20th century began
- how the Boer War affected Canadians
- how technology and reform movements began to change society
- Canada's changing relationships with other countries

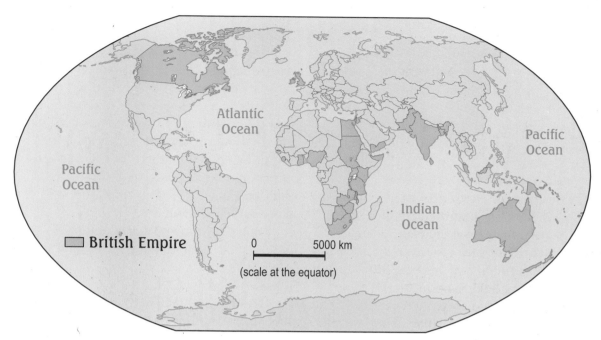

**Figure 6.2** *The British Empire, 1900*

By the 1890s, the British Empire covered nearly one-quarter of the world. Maps of the empire hung in classrooms throughout Canada. Teachers and textbooks taught students the "glorious" history of Great Britain and its empire. Children were taught that the empire worked for positive change in the world. They were taught that the British had a special duty to help people in other countries. Groups such as the Imperial Order Daughters of the Empire (IODE) worked to promote imperialism throughout Canada. The government started a new holiday, Empire Day. It even made a postage stamp to highlight the greatness of the empire.

Opposing the imperialists were people known as **nationalist**s. Most nationalists were French-Canadian. They believed that the imperialists put Britain's interests before Canada's. Nationalists did not necessarily want full independence from Britain. However, they did want Canadians to have more control over their own country. Mostly, they wanted Canada to stay out of Britain's wars unless Canada's Parliament decided they should be involved.

## Queen Victoria

Across Canada, there are cities, towns, mountains, lakes, rivers, bays, and buildings named for Queen Victoria (1819–1901). This is not surprising. Victoria sat upon the British throne for 64 years, longer than any other British monarch.

The British Empire grew so large during Queen Victoria's reign that places named for Victoria can be found all over the world. These include Victoria, British Columbia; Lake Victoria, in east Africa; and Victoria Harbour in Hong Kong, China. An asteroid that was discovered in 1850 in outer space is called 12 Victoria.

**Figure 6.3** This statue marks Queen Victoria's Diamond Jubilee. It sits in the English garden at Assiniboine Park in Winnipeg, Manitoba.

# The Boer War (1899–1902)

Wilfrid Laurier faced many challenges when he was prime minister. The hardest one took place almost half the world away, in a far-off colony on the southern tip of Africa.

In 1899, war broke out in South Africa. South Africa had been colonized by the Dutch in the 17th century. The Dutch settlers called themselves *Boers*. (This is a Dutch word meaning "farmers.") In 1797, the British took the colony from the Dutch. The Boers moved inland. There they founded new colonies called the Orange Free State and the South African Republic. For years, the Dutch republics and the neighbouring British Cape Colony did not get along with each other. In 1899, they went to war.

The Boers surprised the British. They were skilled marksmen and riders. On horseback,

they raided Britain's Cape Colony and pushed the British forces back. The cry for help went out to the Empire. Britain looked to Canada, Australia, and New Zealand for help. Thousands of Australians and New Zealanders responded.

Canada's response was much slower. Laurier found himself caught between the imperialists and the French-Canadian nationalists. The imperialists demanded that Canada do everything possible to help the British. The nationalists did not think that the war was Canada's business.

Laurier compromised. Canada, he said, would send 1000 volunteers to fight in South Africa. However, the war grew. More Canadians were needed. In all, more than 7000 young Canadians volunteered to fight in South Africa. It was the first time that a large force of Canadians fought in an overseas war.

**Figure 6.4** Soldiers from the thousand-strong Royal Canadian Regiment in South Africa. Another **regiment** was Lord Strathcona's Horse, a cavalry force made up of cowboys from the Canadian West. Their commander was the famous Mountie Sam Steele (see p. 35).

The Canadians fought in several tough battles. The Boers used hit-and-run tactics that frustrated the British and their allies. The British responded with a cruel tactic. They rounded up Boer people and forced them into prison camps.

By the time the Dutch republics gave up to the British, nearly 60 000 people had been killed. Thousands of Boer people died from disease in the British camps. More than 200 Canadians died as well. Many of them died from diseases they caught in Africa.

Back in Canada, the war drove another wedge between imperialists and French-Canadian nationalists. Both sides felt betrayed by Laurier. Although Britain won the war, the imperialists thought that Canada should have done more. On the other hand, nationalists thought that Canada should not have sent troops at all. They worried that Canada would now have to fight in every imperial war in the future. A young and talented Quebec politician named Henri Bourassa even left the Liberal Party in protest.

The list of disputes separating English Canadians from French-Canadians had been

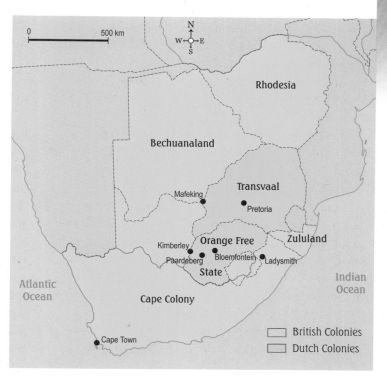

**Figure 6.5** *Boer War sites, South Africa*

growing. The Boer War was one more. These disputes would threaten Canadian unity in the decade to come.

## Henri Bourassa (1868–1952)

Henri Bourassa was the grandson of Louis-Joseph Papineau, who had led the Lower Canada Rebellions in 1837. Bourassa became mayor of the small town of Montebello, Quebec, when he was just 22 years old. As a member of the Liberal Party, Bourassa won a seat in Parliament six years later. He later left the Liberals, however. He did this to protest Laurier's decision to support Britain in the Boer War.

**Figure 6.6** Henri Bourassa

Bourassa became one of the leaders of the French-Canadian nationalists. He spent decades opposing the imperialists. Canada, he believed, should be an independent country within the British Empire. In later years, he was one of the few politicians to speak out against Canada taking part in the First World War.

He loved his home province of Quebec. However, he disagreed with those who wanted Quebec to separate from Canada. Instead, he wanted a greater voice for French people within Canada.

Bourassa spent much of his life in both provincial and federal politics. He also started one of Canada's great newspapers: Montreal's *Le Devoir*. He was its editor for 22 years. He died in 1952, having been a lifelong rebel, just like his famous grandfather.

## Wilfrid Laurier (1841–1919) PM

Wilfrid Laurier was prime minister of Canada for 15 years, from 1896 to 1911. For 45 years, Laurier struggled in Parliament for unity between French and English Canada. He once said that the "20th century will belong to Canada." Many years before he became Canada's first French-Canadian prime minister, however, Laurier had felt differently. As a young lawyer and newspaper editor in Canada East, Laurier opposed Confederation.

**Figure 6.7** Wilfrid Laurier

In time, Laurier changed his views. He was elected to Canada's Parliament as a Liberal in 1874. He disagreed with the execution of Louis Riel, and he supported Métis rights. In 1887, he became leader of the Liberal Party. In 1896, he led the Liberals to victory.

While Laurier was prime minister, Saskatchewan and Alberta became provinces. A second transcontinental railroad was started. There were also a number of disputes between French and English, Catholics and Protestants, and nationalists and imperialists. However, neither side was happy with Laurier's efforts at **compromise**. His government was defeated in the election of 1911.

Laurier spent the rest of his life as leader of the Opposition. He did his best to hold his party together during the hard years of the First World War. He lived long enough to see Canada's victory. Millions of Canadians were saddened by his death in 1919. Even his political opponents remembered him as a great Canadian. Today, he is thought to be one of Canada's greatest prime ministers.

**DID YOU KNOW?** In 1885, Ottawa became the first city in the world to have electric lights on all of its streets.

# Technology and Change in the Late 19th Century

Imagine a *habitant* from the year 1700 who has travelled through time to the year 1800. He might be disappointed by the future. He would be surprised to find himself under British rule. However, he would find most other things about day-to-day life much the same as he had known them. Most people still lived in drafty homes on farms. Horses plowed their fields. Sickness and disease were still a mysterious and dangerous part of life.

Now, imagine the same habitant has travelled to the year 1900. He would find himself in a world beyond his imagination. He would be in a world of steamboats and steam locomotives. It would be a world of telegraphs and telephones, where doctors talked about *germs* that caused disease. Even stranger, those doctors would tell him to bathe regularly. The habitant from 1700 almost never bathed. Getting wet was considered dangerous! In cities, he would find people pedalling around on a strange invention: the bicycle. Sometimes, people would even ride them after dark. After all, places such as Ottawa, Toronto, and Montreal were lit up at night by electric lights.

**Figure 6.8** This advertisement for a bicycle appeared in an 1899 magazine.

Now, imagine the habitant's surprise if he visited a farm. Although horses and oxen still did most of the work, he might see a huge steam-powered tractor in the field. At that point, the time-travelling habitant would probably want to return to the world of 1700!

Science and technology advanced very slowly for much of history. In the late 19th century and early 20th century, however, one new invention led quickly to another. The telegraph led to the telephone. The telephone led to the radio. The steam engine led to the gasoline engine and the automobile. The discovery of viruses led to new medicines. Yet decades passed before all Canadians could share in these new discoveries. At the end of the 19th century, for instance, very few homes had electricity. Most people did not own cars. Quick-spreading diseases still killed many people. Still, there is no doubt that Canada in 1900 was a very different place from Canada in 1800.

## Urbanization and Industrialization

By 1900, more than five million people were living in Canada. Since Confederation, the number of people living in towns and cities had increased three times. By contrast, the number of people living on farms or in small villages had grown only slightly.

The growth of towns and cities is called **urbanization** [ur-bin-eye-ZAY-shun]. By the start of the 20th century, Canada was quickly becoming an urban society. By the late 1920s, more than half of Canadians lived in cities.

As the country changed, so did the kinds of work people did. Farming, fishing, and forestry were still the country's main trades. However, more and more Canadians found work in industry. Thousands of Canadians worked in mining, pulp and paper, manufacturing, and construction. Thousands more worked on the railroads, which now crossed the entire country. In the Maritimes, shipbuilding became

### Alexander Graham Bell (1847–1922)

Most Canadians believe that Alexander Graham Bell invented the telephone. In fact, Bell was one of several brilliant inventors who worked on telephone designs at around the same time. It was Bell, however, who was best at promoting the telephone. He started the Bell Telephone Company in 1876 and became very rich.

Bell was born in Scotland. Later, he came to Canada. In Brantford, Ontario, his experiments led to the development of the telephone. He later moved to the United States, but he continued to spend summers in Canada.

Bell is best known for his work on the telephone. However, he had many other interests. He researched everything from airplanes to hydrofoils.

**Figure 6.9** Like many inventors, Alexander Graham Bell looked to the future. In a paper he wrote in 1917, he said that "a sort of **greenhouse effect**" would one day be the result of burning **fossil fuels**.

He even developed something like a cell phone. Bell called it the *photophone*. It carried sound over a beam of light. Although he could never get it to work right, Bell thought the photophone to be his most important invention.

important. Canadian shipyards were known for building very fine ships.

Industrial work, then as now, could be very dangerous. In 1905, more than 200 railway workers were killed on the job. Mining was even more dangerous. Poor and unsafe working conditions led many workers to join unions. If people were in a union, they could demand better treatment from their employers.

## Social reform movements

There were new problems as Canada changed and grew. People in cities faced overcrowding and poverty. There was unemployment, crime, and pollution. In the late 19th century, social reform movements were formed to fight these problems. One such movement was called the *Social Gospel*.

Social Gospel was the idea that **Christian values** could be used to solve social problems such as poverty and crime. Most social gospellers were educated, well-to-do people. They believed that they had a Christian duty to help others.

Many social gospellers supported **temperance**. One of them was Nellie McClung (see p. 109). Temperance reformers thought that the use of alcohol led to many of the world's problems. Crime and poverty were two of them. Temperance reformers wanted to **moderate** or even stop the drinking of alcohol. The social gospel and temperance movements would be very influential in Canada until the 1920s.

**The Home VERSUS The Saloon.**

Protect the home from the saloon, or the saloon will destroy the home.

The ballots of freemen must defend the homes of freemen.

I consider the temperance cause the foundation of all social and political reform—COBDEN.

Use your ballot as a weapon to defend your home, just as the liquor men use their ballots to defend the saloon.

Had the bullet in battle shot your noble boy, you would have honored his name, and decked his grave; but let the liquor traffic ruin him and sink his manhood, and earth has no compensation for the shame that would shadow his name.

The liquor traffic must be suppressed, or it will suppress the home.

To cast a saloon vote is to say to your son that he may legally become a drunkard.

Your ballot is the constitutional defence of wife, and children, and home. Dare you use it to offend them, and defend the saloon?

The saloon is in politics. Why not put home there? It has a better right to be there.

The liquor traffic is in the crisis of a death-struggle for supremacy over the Canadian home.

God is silently but surely sifting the Canadian people into two classes —home-defenders and saloon-defenders; these two forces now confront each other. The victory will be won when every freeman votes for the home as against the saloon.

Every wretched home is made out of a possible happy one; therefore,

**VOTE PROHIBITION.**

**Figure 6.10** This leaflet urged readers to vote for candidates in the next election who supported temperance.

# Canada's "Forgotten Four"

Canada's prime minister can serve for as long as Parliament supports him or her. For instance, John A. Macdonald was prime minister from 1878 to 1891. Wilfrid Laurier was prime minister from 1896 to 1911. In the five years between Macdonald and Laurier, however, Canada had four prime ministers. They were John Abbott, John Thompson, Mackenzie Bowell, and Charles Tupper.

John Abbott (1821–1893) became prime minister in the summer of 1891. Macdonald died in office, and Abbott replaced him. Abbott did many things during his life. He led a choir. He had been a bookkeeper, a lawyer, and a university professor. He was also president of a railway, a member of Parliament, mayor of Montreal, and a senator.

**Figure 6.11** Like many of Canada's prime ministers, Sir John Abbott was a lawyer. This photograph shows him when he was Dean of the Faculty of Law at McGill University in Montreal.

Abbott did not really want to be prime minister. "I hate politics," he once said. Perhaps he liked teaching better. Wilfrid Laurier was one of his students. Abbott quit as prime minister after less than a year and a half because of poor health.

John Thompson (1845–1894) was the next prime minister, from 1892 to 1894. Like many of Canada's prime ministers, Thompson was a lawyer. His law career took him all the way to the Supreme Court of Nova Scotia. Later, he played an important part in John A. Macdonald's government as minister of justice. Thompson was also an early supporter of women's right to vote.

In 1894, Thompson died of a heart attack. He had been visiting Queen Victoria in England.

**Figure 6.12** Sir John Thompson died in Windsor Castle in December 1894. This painting shows Queen Victoria at a mass that was held for Thompson in Windsor Castle.

He had been knighted only hours before. Saddened, the Queen ordered that her battleship *Blenheim* be painted black and return Thompson's body to Canada.

Mackenzie Bowell (1823–1917) became prime minister at age 71 after Thompson's death in 1894. Bowell owned and edited a newspaper in Belleville, Ontario. He was also in Belleville's **militia** company. He was elected to Parliament the year of Confederation. In 1892, he became a senator.

A Conservative, Bowell was not very popular in his own party. After only a year and four months as prime minister, he lost his party's support. He had to resign. However, he returned to the Senate and worked until he retired at age 83 in 1906.

At age 74, Charles Tupper (1821–1915) was the oldest person ever to become a Canadian prime minister. He is also the only medical doctor ever to be a prime minister. He was also a lawyer and

**Figure 6.13** Sir Mackenzie Bowell was in a rifle company in the Canadian militia in the 1860s. This photograph shows him in his militia uniform.

former premier of Nova Scotia. He led his province into Confederation. Then he was elected to Canada's new federal Parliament. He played many roles in John A. Macdonald's Conservative governments.

Finally, on May 1, 1896, Tupper became prime minister. Soon after, there was an election. The Liberals under Wilfrid Laurier defeated Tupper and the Conservatives. Tupper was prime minister of Canada for just 69 days. It is the shortest term of any prime minister.

From Confederation to 2008, Canada has had 22 prime ministers. The "forgotten four" are likely the least known of them. This is because they did not have the job for very long. However, each one led a remarkable life even before becoming prime minister. They should be remembered not for their short terms as prime minister, but for the years of service they gave to Canada.

**Figure 6.14** Although Sir Charles Tupper was Canada's prime minister for just 69 days in 1896, he served for more than 30 years in public office.

# Relations with the United States

Britain was not the only country that Canadians thought about in the early years of the 20th century. The United States had always had a great effect on Canada. There was the arrival of the United Empire Loyalists after the American Revolution. The British and Canadians fought against the Americans in the War of 1812. Then there was Canadian Confederation in 1867.

By 1900, the United States was one of the world's strongest countries. It was a huge place. It had many natural resources. There were 76 million people living there – twice Britain's population. It also had 18 times Canada's population.

When Wilfred Laurier was prime minister, Canada had two big issues with the United States. The first was the Alaska Boundary Dispute. The second was reciprocity [*ress-i-PROSS-it-ee*], which means trade without tariffs.

The United States bought Alaska from Russia in 1867. Alaska borders the Yukon and northern British Columbia. These areas were remote, and few people lived there. The Klondike Gold Rush changed that (see p. 40). Thousands of prospectors

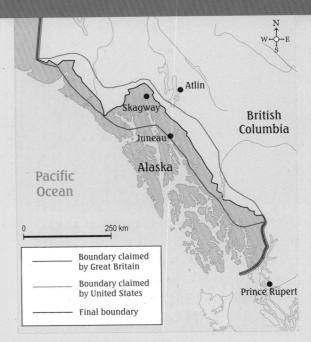

**Figure 6.16** *The Alaska Boundary Dispute*

arrived in the north looking for riches. Canada and the United States began to argue over the location of the border.

A group of men met to settle the dispute in 1903. In the group were two Canadians, three Americans, and one British member. Surprisingly, the British member sided with the Americans. When news reached the rest of Canada, even some Canadian imperialists were angry at the British government. Almost everyone was angry at the United States.

The boundary dispute helps to explain Canadians' feelings about reciprocity. For many years, Canada's leaders had argued about whether or not to sign a reciprocity agreement with the United States.

In 1911, Wilfrid Laurier said that his government wanted to make such a treaty. Once again, both imperialists and nationalists were unhappy. Imperialists wanted closer ties to Britain, not to the United States. Nationalists feared that reciprocity was a step toward Canada becoming a part of the United States. This opposition to reciprocity was one thing that led to the defeat of Laurier and the Liberals in the 1911 election.

**Figure 6.15** A surveyor marks the Canadian-Alaska border in August, 1916, after the Alaska boundary dispute was settled.

# Canada's Navy

On February 10, 1906, the British Royal Navy launched a new battleship. It was named the *HMS Dreadnought. Dreadnought* was the biggest and most powerful warship in the world. Huge guns and torpedo tubes lined its deck. Thirty centimetres of solid armour covered its hull.

Other countries hurried to build similar ships. They all came to be known as *dreadnoughts*. Soon, Britain and Germany were racing to build even bigger and more powerful ships. Many more dreadnoughts and super-dreadnoughts began to appear on the world's oceans.

These new warships were costly to build. Once again, Britain asked Canada to help defend the empire. The British wanted Canada's government to help pay for more dreadnoughts.

In Ottawa, Prime Minister Wilfrid Laurier again faced a crisis. Canadian imperialists wanted the federal government to give the British the money they needed to build up their navy. French-Canadian nationalists feared that Canada would become part of the dangerous rivalry between Britain and Germany.

Laurier tried to please both sides. Canada would not give the British money to build up their navy. Instead, Canada would build a navy of its own. In peacetime, this navy would patrol Canada's shores. If war broke out, the navy would fight under British command. Laurier's Naval Service Bill of 1910 created the Royal Canadian Navy. It also created a naval college to train its officers.

Canada did not have enough money for its own dreadnoughts. Instead, the navy bought two old British ships. They were called the *Rainbow* and the *Niobe*. The *Rainbow* sailed out of Esquimalt, British Columbia. It patrolled Canada's West Coast. Halifax was the home port of the *Niobe*. It patrolled the Maritimes.

Neither side liked Laurier's plan. Canadian imperialists felt that this tiny navy would not help Britain very much. On the other hand,

**Figure 6.17** *HMCS Niobe.* The *Rainbow* and the *Niobe* were the first ships in the Royal Canadian Navy. Both served in the First World War. However, neither ship fought in a battle.

French-Canadian nationalists, such as Henri Bourassa, did not think Canada's navy should be used to help Britain at all.

Bourassa called the Naval Service Bill a "backwards step" for Canada. Laurier was attacked from both sides. The Liberal Party lost support in both English and French Canada. It was another reason the Liberals lost the 1911 election.

# Conclusion

Canada's new prime minister was Robert Borden. He was leader of the Conservative Party. He promised to keep the Canadian navy. He also promised to help Britain build more dreadnoughts.

Liberals and French Canadians still disagreed with the government. However, that no longer mattered very much. In 1914, Borden would have to lead his divided country through the greatest crisis the world had ever known – the First World War.

# III Canada Grows Up

**1**

I n 1914, in faraway Europe, World War I broke out. Canada sent its soldiers to Europe's battlefields. With its victory at Vimy Ridge in 1917, Canada earned the world's respect. Yet by war's end in 1918 more than 60 000 young Canadians had been killed.

Canadians hoped the worst was behind them, but peace and prosperity were still out of reach. Flu killed thousands. Jobs disappeared as factories closed. The 1930s brought even greater ruin. In the Great Depression, almost one third of Canadians lost their jobs, and drought destroyed thousands of farms.

Again, the outbreak of war in Europe in 1939 changed everything. In 1945, at the end of the World War II, Canadians held their heads high. Not only could they move forward, but so could the world.

**4**

CAMP-FIRE
CHORUSES

THE SOLDIERS' SONG BOOK

Compiled by
S. EDMUND JONES, B.A.
TORONTO, CANADA

Price, 15c. a copy

HUMPHREY M
Oxford University Pr
TORONTO, CAN. and LONDON, ENG

LIBRARY / CWM
BIBLIOTHEQUE / MCG

GREETINGS
FROM SOMEWHERE IN FRANCE

**2**

**3**

MIDSUMMER TERM REPORT.

MIDSUMMER TERM REPORT.

Of Clifford Hanson Aged, 8.
BIG WOODY SCHOOL, MAN.

Days Attended. 95½  Days Absent. 16½

Arithmetic. V.G.
Reading & Recitation. V.G.
Spelling. 95.    MENTAL. 46.
Composition. 95.    WRITING. 92.
Grammar.
History.
Geography. V.G.
Drawing. G.
Handwork. V.G.
Health.
Grade July 1920. I  Grade July 1921. II

Signed. Kathleen Pocock. July 1921.

**5**

# In the Memory Box...

**1** These medals were awarded to Tommy Prince of Manitoba, one of Canada's most decorated Aboriginal war heroes.

**2** Soldiers in WWI sent home postcards such as these. They were not allowed to reveal where they were or what they were doing, in case the enemy read the cards, but they could let loved ones know that they were all right.

**3** The child who received this report card from 1920 was likely taught in a one-room schoolhouse.

**4** Soldiers kept their spirits up by singing. Many songs could be found in songbooks such as this one.

**5** During the Depression, store-bought toys were a luxury. Instead, children played with homemade toys, like this doll, sewn from a used sugar bag.

**6** A handbook shows how to send messages by carrier pigeons, which were used during the First World War.

**7** Members of the International Brotherhood of Electrical Workers would have carried a parade banner much like this as members of the Winnipeg General Strike in 1919.

**8** Women on the home front during war time were encouraged to preserve food at home so that soldiers overseas could be fed properly. They also recycled paper, which was in short supply.

**9** In 1942, the Canadian government sent many Japanese Canadians families to sugar beet farms in Manitoba, where they used knives such as this to harvest sugar beets.

**10** During the First World War, women assembled comfort bags, such as this one, for soldiers overseas. The bags were filled with things like soap, razors, toothpaste, hand-knitted socks, candy, and other small comforts.

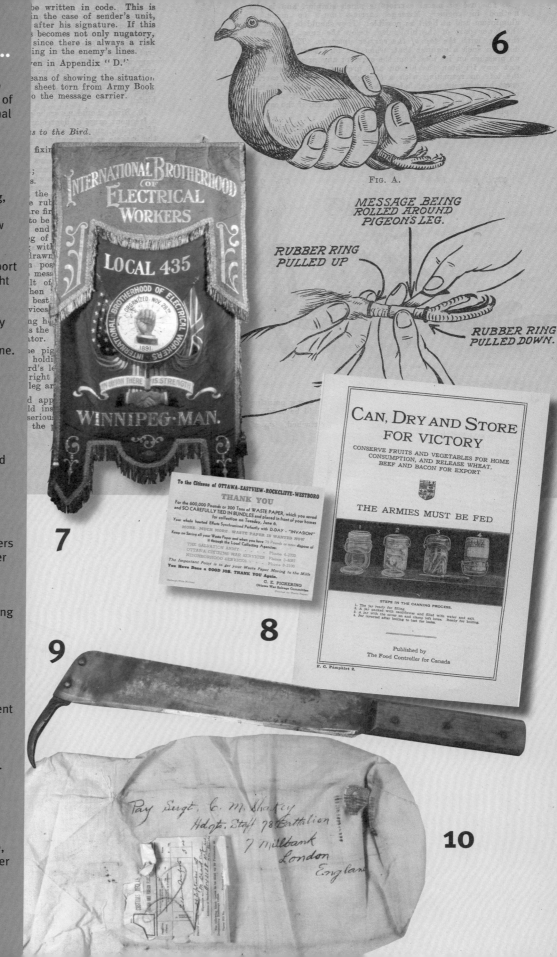

# 7 World War I
## 1914–1918

World War I began with the murder of one man. On June 28, 1914, the Austrian Archduke Franz Ferdinand was assassinated by Gavrilo Princip in the city of Sarajevo [*SA-rah-YEH-vo*]. Princip was a Serbian who wanted his people's independence from Austria-Hungary. Franz Ferdinand was heir to the throne of Austria-Hungary. With just one shot, Princip started a war in which 20 million people would die.

For a hundred years, the nations of Europe had been at peace. However, old rivalries were still there. By 1914, tensions were very high. All the nations of Europe were getting ready for war. Pre-war Europe was a *powder keg*. In other words, Europe was like a barrel containing gunpowder that needed only a tiny spark to set it off. Franz Ferdinand's assassination was that spark.

Within a month, Serbia and Austria-Hungary had declared war on each other. A system of alliances drew other nations into the war. Russia and France were on the side of Serbia. Germany was allied with Austria-Hungary. To attack France, Germany first had to invade through neighbouring Belgium. Belgium's ally was Great Britain. Suddenly, the entire British Empire was at war. This included Canada.

Across the Atlantic, Canadians found it hard to believe they were at war. Many had never heard of Serbia or Franz Ferdinand. Still, when the war was announced, huge crowds of people met in town squares and city centres to

**Figure 7.1** The government produced thousands of posters like this one to convince men to join the armed forces.

### AS YOU READ, THINK ABOUT

- what caused World War I
- why Canada joined the war
- what life was like on the battle front
- how Canadians contributed to victory
- the effect of the war on returning soldiers and people at home

celebrate the news. People cheered. They waved banners and sang patriotic songs. Tens of thousands of men rushed to join the army. They were afraid that the war would be over before they got the chance to fight. Fathers and sons enlisted together. Men who were too old to serve claimed that they were younger. Boys who were too young swore that they were older. Desperate for soldiers, the tiny Canadian army took them all.

Today, it is hard to imagine celebrating the outbreak of war. But in 1914, most English-speaking Canadians were very proud of Canada's ties to Britain. Many Canadians were from Britain. They believed that Britain's war was *their* war. Most French-Canadians did not share such feelings. However, they were angered by Germany's attack on Belgium and France.

Hardly anyone knew how terrible the war would be. People expected a short, glamorous war from which the soldiers would return as heroes. When a regiment of soldiers from the University of Toronto left for the war, their principal told them, "You will not regret this. When you return your romance will not vanish with your youth. You will have fought in the Great War, you will have joined in the liberation of the world." Yet the war turned out to be very different from what anyone had predicted.

**DID YOU KNOW?** In 1914, Canada was still a colony of Great Britain. That meant that when Britain declared war on Germany on August 4, 1914, Canada was also at war.

**Figure 7.2** *EUROPE, 1914.* In August 1914, the small war between Austria-Hungary and Serbia dragged in all of Europe because of the alliance system.

**Figure 7.3** Troops leave Union Station in Winnipeg, 1915. From ports in eastern Canada, they travelled to the battlefields of World War I. When this photo was taken, no one knew what the war would really be like.

# Trench Warfare

At seven-thirty on the morning of July 1, 1916, one of the worst battles in the history of the world began. One hundred thousand British soldiers left the protection of their **trenches** and dashed toward the German lines along the Somme River in eastern France. For a week before the attack, British **artillery** had bombarded the German defences. British soldiers hoped that any surviving Germans would surrender to them. The British were grim-faced and ready. Their rifles were loaded. They kept away from the muddy shell craters and found paths through the enemy barbed wire. Then something terrible happened.

Machine-gun fire roared from the German trenches. Hundreds of British soldiers fell, struck by bullets. Unknown to the British, the Germans had built **dugouts** strong enough and deep enough to protect themselves from the artillery bombardment. Too many shells had missed their target or failed to explode. When the British stopped firing, the Germans came out of their dugouts and manned their machine guns. As the British attacked, the Germans mowed them down with a wave of bullets.

Near a tiny village named Beaumont Hamel, a regiment of soldiers from Newfoundland, was almost totally destroyed that morning. Just 68 of its 800 men survived unharmed. In all, the British Army suffered 60 000 dead and wounded on July 1. But the Battle of the Somme was not over. The fighting went on for another five months. Through it all, the Germans held their position.

The Battle of the Somme was fought almost two years after the First World War began. It was just one of dozens of similar battles in the war. When the war began in August 1914, most Canadians believed it would be over by

## Living in the trenches

Life in a front-line trench was filthy, cold, and wet. Soldiers had to put up with horrible smells. At the front, no one could bathe. The bodies of fallen soldiers were often left in no-man's land, because no one could reach them. Soldiers grew used to the smells, but they never got used to the rats and lice that tormented them day and night. Frozen winters in the open trenches were worst of all. Still, the trenches kept soldiers safe from bullets and exploding shells. Trenches were also very difficult for the enemy to capture. In battle after battle, soldiers in the trenches defeated waves of attackers.

**Figure 7.4** Canadian soldiers in the trenches, 1916. Life in a trench was dirty and cold, but it kept soldiers safe from bullets.

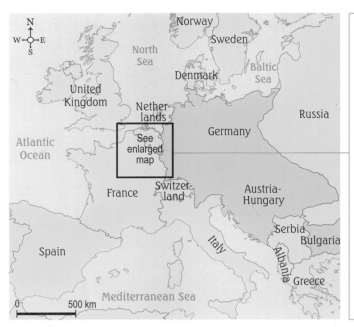
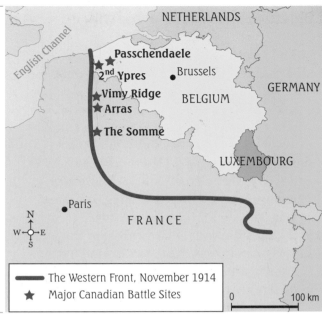

**Figure 7.5** *MAJOR BATTLES OF WORLD WAR I*

Christmas. They thought there would be few deaths. By 1917, they started to think that it would never end. No one had imagined that the war would so terrible. What made it like that?

The answer is technology. During the 20th century, technology had advanced greatly. For instance, a soldier in the War of 1812 travelled on foot or horseback. He was armed with a musket that he could fire only twice per minute. In the First World War, steamships and trains carried soldiers to the **front.** Airplanes soared overhead. An army's orders arrived by telegraph. Weapons were much more deadly. One machine gun could fire 600 shots per minute.

To protect their soldiers in the open fields, both sides dug trenches that spread out for hundreds of kilometres. The space separating the trenches of the two sides was called *no-man's land*, because neither side could control it. Over the four years of the war, millions of soldiers would live and fight and, sometimes, die in the trenches. Nearly half a million of them were Canadians.

**Figure 7.6** Artillery churned up the earth, and rain turned it to mud. In some places, the mud was so thick that men and horses drowned in it. Here are some Canadian soldiers in the mud at Passchendaele, Belgium, 1917.

World War I, 1914–1918    93

# Canada's Military Effort

The First World War ended in November 1918. British prime minister David Lloyd George wrote:

> The Canadians played a part of such distinction that … they were brought along to head the assault in one great battle after another. Whenever the Germans found the Canadian Corps coming into the line, they prepared for the worst.

Lloyd George's comment was very high praise. In 1914, no one could have thought that Canada, a country of just eight million people, would play such a big role in the war. When war broke out, Canada's armed forces were not ready. The army had just 3000 officers and men. Canada's militia had 60 000 poorly trained men. Many did not have rifles or even uniforms. Canada's navy had only two large ships. By comparison, Germany's army had nearly *three million* well-trained soldiers when the war began. Its navy had hundreds of warships.

**Figure 7.8** The Canadian government built one of the largest war memorials in the world at Vimy Ridge. It sits on land given to Canada in 1922 by the government of France as a gift of thanks. Thousands of people gathered for the dedication of the memorial in 1936, above.

## Sir Robert Borden (1854–1937) PM

Robert Borden was born in Grand Pré, Nova Scotia. Borden never attended university. However, he was an intelligent and well-read man who became a successful lawyer. Borden entered politics in 1896. Five years later, he became the leader of the Conservative Party.

**Figure 7.7** Sir Robert Borden

He led the Conservatives to victory over Wilfrid Laurier's Liberals in the federal election of 1911.

Borden was prime minister when World War I broke out in August 1914. Today, he is remembered as a man who led Canada through some of its most difficult years. He supported Britain. However, he also worked to give Canada a greater voice of its own in the world. He resigned as prime minister in 1920.

With the declaration of war came a flood of **recruits**. The Canadian Army grew very quickly. By December 1914, a force of 30 000 soldiers was ready to go overseas. During the war, 400 000 more followed them. They were known as the Canadian Expeditionary [*eks-puh-DISH-in-air-ee*] Force (CEF).

Canada's army was known for being tough, brave, and skilled. At the 2nd Battle of Ypres [*EE-pr*], in April 1915, the Canadians fought on while other Allied forces ran from a new German weapon: poison gas. In late 1916, the Canadians defeated the Germans near the French village of Courcelette [*KOOR-suh-let*]. But the Canadian Army's most famous victory came in April 1917 at the German stronghold of Vimy Ridge.

Vimy Ridge was a rocky hill in eastern France. The Germans had captured the ridge early in the war. The British and French armies had tried several times to take it back. However, they always failed. In April 1917, the Canadians seized Vimy Ridge after a fierce battle. At Vimy, all four **divisions** of the Canadian Expeditionary Force fought together for the first time.

Pierre Berton, a Canadian writer, once wrote, "Canada became a nation at Vimy Ridge." What Berton meant is that the Battle of Vimy Ridge was the first time that Canadians from across the country had accomplished a great task by working together. It was something in which all Canadians could take pride. Yet the cost of Vimy Ridge had been very high. Nearly 11 000 Canadian soldiers were killed or wounded.

## War at Sea and in the Air

Canada's navy was just three years old when the war broke out in 1914. It had only a few warships. These included the *Rainbow* and the *Niobe* and two submarines. The Royal Canadian Navy (RCN) remained very small during the war. However, Canadians played a big role in a new service the British had created: the Royal Flying Corps (RFC).[1]

Airplanes had been invented in 1903, only 11 years before the war began. At the time, airplanes were slow and dangerous to fly. Pilots sat in open cockpits and did not have parachutes. When the war began, airplanes were used mainly to spy on the enemy. Later, they were armed with machine guns. The fighter plane was born. Every country involved in the war had pilots known as *aces*. An ace was a pilot who shot down five or more enemy planes.

Since Canada did not yet have its own air force, Canadians who wanted to be pilots during the war had to join one of two British services. They could join the RFC or the Royal Naval Air Service (RNAS). Many of the most famous aces were Canadians, including Billy Bishop, Raymond Collishaw, and William Barker.

More than 650 000 Canadians served in the armed forces during the war. As well, hundreds of thousands of Canadian civilians served in other ways on the **home front**. Some Canadians, like the flying aces, are remembered in books and films. Many others have been forgotten.

1 It was renamed the Royal Air Force in April 1918.

### William "Billy" Barker, VC (1894–1930)

Billy Barker was born in 1894 in the town of Dauphin, Manitoba. When war began, Barker enlisted in the Canadian army. After a year in the trenches, he transferred to the RFC. Barker shot down 50 enemy aircraft and was one of the war's top aces. In 1918, he was awarded the Victoria Cross, Britain's highest medal for bravery, after downing four planes in a single battle.

**Figure 7.9  Billy Barker**

### Sir Arthur Currie (1875–1933)

In June 1917, Arthur Currie was given command of the CEF. He was the first Canadian general to lead the force. Currie was considered one of the best generals of the war. In one famous battle in September 1918, he sent his forces on a daring nighttime mission across a canal near Cambrai, France. In the morning, the Canadians surprised the Germans and won the battle. After the war, Currie became the president of McGill University in Montreal.

**Figure 7.10  Sir Arthur Currie**

**DID YOU KNOW?** Canada created its own air force, the Royal Canadian Air Force (RCAF), in 1924.

## The youngest hero

Alan Arnett MacLeod was only 15 when World War I began. As a boy in Stonewall, Manitoba, he dreamed of a job in the military. He tried to enlist many times. It was not until after his 18th birthday in April 1917 that he joined the Royal Flying Corps. Soon he began flying missions over France.

On March 27, 1918, MacLeod and gunner A.W. Hammond were attacked by eight German planes. An enemy bullet struck their plane's fuel tank. It set the plane on fire. MacLeod was wounded, but he climbed out on the wing of the plane to avoid the flames. From there, he continued to maneuver the plane so that Hammond could keep firing on the enemy. The pair shot down three enemy planes before crashing. Despite his injuries, MacLeod dragged Hammond to safety. MacLeod was shot again, then passed out from his injuries.

On September 4, 1918, at Buckingham Palace in London, MacLeod was awarded the Victoria Cross, the highest award for bravery in the British Commonwealth. He was the youngest of 70 Canadians fighting in World War I to receive the award. Soon after, MacLeod returned to Manitoba to recover from his wounds. He died from the Spanish flu just two months later. He was 19.

**Figure 7.11**  Alan Arnett MacLeod

# Forgotten Heroes

World War I was the first total war. Total war means that all of a country's strength is devoted to the war effort. Millions of Canadians dedicated themselves to winning the war. Some did so by joining the armed forces. Others worked on the home front. Not all Canadians who took part in the war are remembered as they deserve to be.

## Canada's nursing sisters

Women were not allowed to fight in the First World War. However, more than 3000 Canadian women served as nursing sisters. They saved the lives of many wounded soldiers. Many nurses served in emergency hospitals very close to the front lines. Working so close to the battles, the nurses were exposed to danger. In all, 46 nursing sisters died during the war.

## Women war workers on the home front

With hundreds of thousands of men in the armed forces, there were serious shortages of workers back in Canada. Factories and shipyards began to hire large numbers of women for the first time.

**Figure 7.12**  Soldiers nicknamed nursing sisters *bluebirds* because of their blue uniforms.

**Figure 7.13** This painting by Henrietta Mabel May shows women in a factory making artillery shells. Women were paid less than men even though they were just as good at their jobs.

By 1916, more than 30 000 women were working in factories, helping to build weapons and make supplies. Thousands of women took other jobs once thought to be for men only. Women drove streetcars in Ontario. They worked on farms on the Prairies. Across the country, they helped the war effort through volunteer work. Women knitted socks, sweaters, and scarves for the soldiers fighting overseas. They set up **rallies** to sell Victory Bonds (see p. 100). However, when a group of women tried to start a women's home guard to defend Canada from attack, the government stopped them. The idea of women handling rifles was too much for the men of the time!

## The No. 2 Construction Battalion

The Canadian Army needed all the soldiers it could get in 1914. However, recruiting officers still turned away African-Canadians who wanted to join the CEF. Eventually the army decided to create a unit of African Canadians. The members of this unit, the No. 2 Construction Battalion, were not allowed to fight. Instead, they went overseas to clear forests, dig trenches, and build railway lines. It was important work, and they did it well.

The battalion was based in Pictou, Nova Scotia. It accepted African-Canadian recruits from across the country. The battalion's officers were all European-Canadian. However, there was one exception: Captain William White, the battalion's chaplain. He was the only African-Canadian officer in the entire British Empire during the First World War.

**DID YOU KNOW?** Leo Clarke, Frederick William Hall, and Robert Shankland all lived on Pine Street in Winnipeg. They all fought in World War I, and received the Victoria Cross for acts of bravery. Only Shankland survived the war. The City of Winnipeg later changed the name of Pine Street to Valour Road in honour of the three brave soldiers who had lived there. The words *For Valour* are written on the Victoria Cross.

# Aboriginal Volunteers

As many as 7500 Aboriginal Canadians served in the Canadian Expeditionary Force. In some First Nations, all of the young men went overseas. Many came from far-off regions of the country where there was no pressure on them to join the struggle. Still, they joined.

Some Aboriginal Canadians went to war for adventure. Others went for the promise of steady jobs. Some went for the sake of tradition. First Nations had fought with the British in the Seven Years' War, the American Revolutionary War, and the War of 1812. Others hoped that by being in the war, the Canadian government would start to treat Aboriginal peoples more fairly. Whatever their reasons, they fought with bravery and skill. More than 300 Aboriginal soldiers never came back from the war.

First Nations women also served. In 1917, Edith Anderson was a nurse from the Six

## Aboriginal heroes

Tom Longboat (1887–1949) was a member of the Onondaga First Nation. He was born on the Six Nations Reserve near Brantford, Ontario. In 1907, he won the Boston Marathon with a record-breaking time. He became one of the most famous athletes in the world. During the First World War, Longboat served as a dispatch runner on the front lines of battles. Telephones and radios were not reliable, so armies used runners to carry important messages. It was dangerous work. Longboat was wounded twice. Once he was wounded so badly that he was declared dead by mistake.

Henry Louis Norwest (1884–1918) was a Métis from Fort Saskatchewan, Alberta. He became an inspiration to the entire CEF. Henry was a former rodeo performer and an excellent shot with a rifle. He earned some of Canada's highest military honours for bravery. A fellow soldier said of him, "Henry Norwest carried out his terrible duty superbly because he believed his special skill gave him no choice but to fulfill his indispensable mission." Sadly, this expert soldier was killed in action three months before the war ended.

**Figure 7.14** Tom Longboat, right, buys a newspaper in France, 1917.

ONE OF THE BUFFALO BOYS SPINNING A ROPE

BELL Photo

**Figure 7.15** Henry Louis Norwest

Nations Reserve in Ontario. She served with the American army in Vittel, France, treating wounded soldiers. "We would walk right over where there had been fighting. It was an awful sight – buildings in rubble, trees burnt, spent shells all over the place, whole towns blown up." After the war, Anderson went back to Six Nations. There she married and raised a family. She kept nursing until 1955.

Many Aboriginal soldiers were awarded for bravery. Francis Pegahmagabow, of Parry Island First Nation, was decorated three times for bravery in action. Brothers Alexander George Smith and Charles Smith, from the Haudenosaunee (Iroquois) Six Nations Reserve, each received the Military Cross. Many Aboriginal soldiers came home as heroes. However, they were still not allowed to vote in the country they fought for during the war.

## After the war

During the First World War, Aboriginal soldiers had been treated equally and fairly. However, when they came back to Canada after the war, they did not have the same benefits

**Figure 7.16** Frederick Loft, above, founded the League of Indians of Canada in 1919. It was the first Aboriginal political organization in the country.

that non-Aboriginal veterans had. In some cases, First Nations reserve lands were actually taken by the government and offered to non-Aboriginal veterans as land grants.

Aboriginal veterans questioned their unfair treatment. They had fought bravely for their country during the war. Frederick Loft, a Kanienkehaka [*gah-nah-geh-HA-gah*] (Mohawk) veteran from the Six Nations Reserve, argued that Aboriginal

**Figure 7.17** The Aboriginal War Veterans Monument in Ottawa is a tribute to Aboriginal soldiers who served in Canada's armed forces. The monument shows Aboriginal contributions to Canada's war and peacekeeping efforts. The statue includes spirit guides. The thunderbird at the top symbolizes the spirit of Aboriginal peoples.

peoples' sacrifices during the war entitled them to equal rights:

> As peaceable and law-abiding citizens in the past, and even in the late war, we have performed dutiful service to our King, Country and Empire, and we have the right to claim and demand more justice and fair play as a recompense.

# The Home Front

Getting a country ready for war is called *mobilization*. Canada had never mobilized for war before. There were many problems that no one expected.

## Industry

Britain wanted to buy weapons from Canada. However, when the war began, Canada had only a few factories able to make weapons. One Canadian factory, for instance, made only 75 artillery shells a day. In battle, soldiers might use as many as 100 000 shells in just a few hours.

It took time for the Canadian government to build more factories. However, by 1917 there were more than 600. When the war ended, Canadian factories had made nearly 25 million artillery shells. This was about one-third of all the shells used by British gunners during the war.

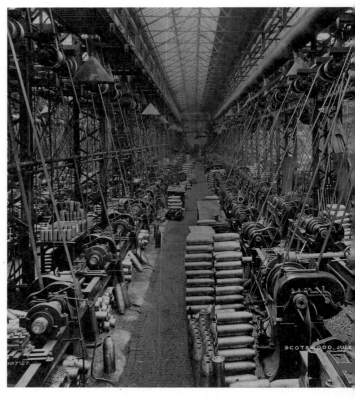

**Figure 7.19** Workers in this factory produced artillery shells. The war sped up the growth of industry in Canada.

## Victory Bonds

The Canadian government sold Victory Bonds to raise money to help pay for the cost of the war. People who bought the bonds could cash them in after the war. The government would give back the money paid for the bond. It would also pay an extra amount of money known as *interest*. Millions of dollars worth of Victory Bonds were sold.

**Figure 7.18** Poster promoting Victory Bonds

## The conscription crisis

Canada's army used volunteers at first. However, by 1915 and 1916, the army had lost many men. Prime Minister Borden believed in **conscription** to replace them. Conscription was an emotional issue. Many French-Canadians did not like the idea of being forced by law to fight for Britain. Many farmers worried that their crops would fail if more farm workers had to join the army.

Borden's government won the election of December 1917. Then it brought in conscription. In Quebec, people had once cheered the war. Now they protested in the streets. They shouted, "Down with Borden!" Some Quebeckers began to think about separation from Canada.

The war ended before many of the conscripted soldiers could be sent overseas. Only 25 000 actually served in the trenches. Despite this, the conscription crisis put national unity in danger. It was a lesson that future Canadian prime ministers would not forget.

## Fear and prejudice on the home front

After the war began, many Canadians did not trust other Canadians who had come from Germany or from countries that were Germany's allies. Many thought that German-Canadians might be spies. Canadians grew so fearful that they wanted nothing to do with German-related things. Schools stopped teaching the German language and German literature. Orchestras stopped playing music by German composers such as Beethoven and Mozart.

Another clue to the way many Canadians felt about Germany could be found in the city of Berlin, Ontario. Berlin was also the name of the capital of Germany. In 1916, people living in the Ontario city did not want to look like they were against their own country. They decided to change the city's name.

**Figure 7.21** During World War I, about 80 000 Europeans were named enemy aliens. They were mainly from Germany and the Austro-Hungarian and the Ottoman (Turkish) empires. About 8000 lived in internment camps. This is one of them – the Otter Internment Camp in Yoho National Park in British Columbia. Men worked as labourers in national parks or for government building projects.

## The Halifax Disaster

There were several disasters in Canada during the war. In February 1916, a fire destroyed most of the Parliament buildings in Ottawa. Seven people died. In September 1916, 11 people were killed when the Quebec Bridge suddenly collapsed into the St. Lawrence River.

The worst disaster of all, however, took place in Halifax, Nova Scotia. Halifax was the gateway to Europe during the war. Most Canadian troops and supplies left from its busy harbour. On December 6, 1917, at 9:00 am, a French ship, *Mont Blanc*, accidentally hit another ship, the *Imo,* in Halifax harbour. The *Mont Blanc* caught fire. A crowd gathered to watch the burning ship. No one knew that it was filled with explosives. Suddenly, a huge explosion sent a fireball more than a kilometre into the air. The *Mont Blanc* was gone.

The explosion shattered whole buildings. It uprooted trees. It blasted the ship's anchor two kilometres inland. Much of Halifax was destroyed, and more than 2000 people were killed.

Each of these tragedies was later shown to be an accident. However, at the time, many people thought that German spies were to blame.

**Figure 7.20** After the Halifax disaster

**Figure 7.22** Children on the home front help their families by carrying bags of fuel.

They considered the names of *Hydropolis* and *Industria*. Finally, they renamed the city *Kitchener*. (This was after Lord Kitchener, Britain's secretary of war.) It is still called Kitchener today.

In some cases, the Canadian government saw German-Canadians and other immigrants as *enemy aliens*. More than 8000 of these people were **interned** even though they had done nothing wrong. Most were either German or Ukrainians from Austria-Hungary. They were held in prison camps across the country, far from their families and homes. Many had to do heavy labour.

In 2005, Canada's prime minister, Paul Martin, called these events "a dark chapter" in Canadian history. He apologized for internment during the war.

**DID YOU KNOW?** Not only did Berlin, Ontario, changed its name to Kitchener in World War I. Did you know that Britain's Royal Family changed its name, too? In 1917, their German-sounding surname Saxe-Coburg was changed to the name still used today: Windsor.

# The End of the War

In April 1917, three years after Canada entered World War I, the United States declared war on Germany. In the spring of 1918, Germany made a desperate attempt to defeat the **Allies** before the Americans arrived. The Germans failed, and the Allies counterattacked. The Allies scored a series of hard-fought victories. Canadians took the lead in many of these attacks. Exhausted, the Germans and their allies asked for peace. World War I ended on the eleventh hour of the eleventh day of the eleventh month – 11:00 AM on November 11, 1918. Ever since, November 11 has been marked as a day to remember the war – Remembrance Day.

## After the war

The war brought many changes to Canada. It sped up industrialization. It changed the way that people thought about women's rights. It gave Canada a greater voice in world affairs. The price of the war had been very high. Thousands of men had gone cheerfully to war in 1914. Few returned unharmed. More than 60 000 Canadians died fighting the First World War. Most families lost a father or son. In some

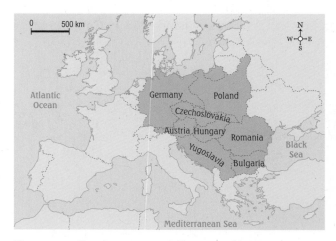

**Figure 7.23** *EUROPE AFTER THE TREATY OF VERSAILLES.* The war changed the map of Europe. In the peace treaty, signed in 1919 at Versailles [*Ver-SYE*], France, new countries were created and old ones broken up (see p. 91). Germany was blamed for the war and forced to pay for its cost. Some people believe that the peace treaty simply created more problems, leading to World War II.

**Figure 7.24** F.H. Varley's painting *For What?* portrays the destruction of war.

small towns, nearly all of the young men had been killed overseas.

Many soldiers returned to Canada badly wounded. Thousands lost their arms or legs. Others had been terribly burned or blinded. The government built veterans' hospitals for those soldiers who needed constant medical attention. In addition, many veterans suffered what people called *shell shock*. Shell shock was a form of mental breakdown caused by witnessing the horrors of war. Today, the condition is known as *post-traumatic stress syndrome*.

Because of all the death, some people grew very gloomy about life. Many Canadians believed that the war had been a terrible mistake. Others felt great pride in the role Canada had played in the war. They believed

## Remembrance Day

In Remembrance Day ceremonies, Canadians take time to remember those who died fighting for Canada. Remembering does not mean that war is a good thing. Rather, Remembrance Day services are held once a year to remember and honour soldiers who served in the wars. What will happen to Remembrance Day when so much time has passed that no one remembers those soldiers? It is up to all of us to keep the memory of the past alive. That way we can avoid the mistakes that led to the wars in the first place.

| | | | |
|---|---|---|---|
| PRIVATE | Carew, John Joseph (651) | | July 1, 1916 |
| | Royal Newfoundland Regiment | | |
| PRIVATE | Carew, John Joseph (1028) | | July 1, 1916 |
| | Royal Newfoundland Regiment | | |
| PRIVATE | Carew, Victor | | November 20,1917 |
| | Royal Newfoundland Regiment | | |
| PRIVATE | Carew, Vincent | | July 10, 1917 |
| | Royal Newfoundland Regiment | | |
| PRIVATE | Carrigan, Edward | | July 1 1916 |
| | Royal Newfoundland Regiment | | |
| CORPORAL | Carroll, Bernard, MM | | April 14, 1917 |
| | Royal Newfoundland Regiment | | |
| SERGEANT | Carroll, Thomas | | July 1, 1916 |
| | Royal Newfoundland Regiment | | |
| PRIVATE | Carsons, John | | July 1, 1916 |
| | Royal Newfoundland Regiment | | |
| PRIVATE | Carter, George Blake | | August 15, 1917 |
| | 26th Battalion, Canadian Expeditionary Force | | |
| SERGEANT | Carter, James Henry | | November 20,1917 |
| | Royal Newfoundland Regiment | | |
| LANCE-CORPORAL | Carter, Llewelyn James | | July 2, 1916 |
| | Royal Newfoundland Regiment | | |
| LANCE-CORPORAL | Carter, Thomas | | May 4, 1917 |
| | Royal Newfoundland Regiment | | |
| CORPORAL | Cave, Joseph | | July 10, 1917 |
| | Royal Newfoundland Regiment | | |
| SERGEANT | Chafe, Edward Bartlett | | November 0,1917 |
| | 73rd Battalion, Canadian Expeditionary Force | | |
| PRIVATE | Chafe, Ernest Leslie | | July 1, 1916 |
| | Royal Newfoundland Regiment | | |

**Figure 7.25** At the Peace Tower in Ottawa, the Books of Remembrance record the names of Canada's war dead. This page from the Newfoundland Book of Remembrance includes the names of six soldiers killed on July 1, 1916. It also includes the name of one soldier who died July 2, possibly from wounds received the day before at the Battle of the Somme.

In Newfoundland, July 1 is still called Memorial Day, in memory of the men of the Newfoundland Regiment who died at Beaumont Hamel.

that Canada had helped to defend freedom. They also felt that the war had made Canada a real nation, ready for full independence. But not everyone agreed that the war brought Canadians together. Many French-speaking Canadians felt betrayed by conscription.

## Conclusion

Some people called the First World War "the war to end all wars." They believed that the nations of the world would never fight again, now that they knew how terrible modern war really was. At the end of 1918, Canadians looked toward the future with hope.

# 8 Between the Wars
## Change and the Depression

In late 1918, a soldier named Arthur-Joseph Lapointe returned to his home in Gaspé, Quebec. Arthur had fought in some of the First World War's bloodiest battles. However, nothing prepared him for the shock he received when he returned home. Arthur's father met him at the train station and told him terrible news: three of Arthur's brothers and two of his sisters had just died from the flu.

It was the same across Canada. Everywhere people were sick. They shivered, coughed, and wheezed. Doctors called the sickness the *Spanish flu*. It was an **epidemic** that had spread around the world. Soldiers returning to Canada and the United States from the war accidentally brought the flu home with them.

The flu attacked both young and old. Governments made huge efforts to stop the disease from spreading. The sick were **quarantined** [*KWOR-un-teened*] indoors. Nearly everyone who went outside wore a doctor's mask. Towns and cities made it illegal for people

**Figure 8.1** During the Spanish flu epidemic in 1918 and 1919, some people wore masks outdoors to protect themselves from flu germs.

to shake hands. Schools and churches closed. Despite all this, one-quarter of Canadians got the flu. Doctors could do little to stop it. Hospitals overflowed with patients.

The epidemic lasted until late 1919. Fifty thousand Canadians died. The flu killed more people around the world than had died in the First World War. It was a bad beginning to this new era of peace.

---

**AS YOU READ, THINK ABOUT**

- why workers went on strike in Winnipeg in 1919
- what women did to gain new rights
- how new inventions changed the way people lived
- what life was like during the Great Depression
- how governments dealt with the hard times

---

**DID YOU KNOW?** The 1918–1919 flu epidemic was called the Spanish flu because it was first reported from Spain. However, it is now thought that the flu actually began in China. Chinese soldiers who served on the Western Front during World War I accidentally carried the disease to Europe with them.

## The Group of Seven

Canada's most famous group of painters called themselves the *Group of Seven*. The members of the group painted pictures of the wilderness of the Canadian Shield. They also painted scenes of the Rockies and the Prairies. Their colourful paintings of the windswept Canadian outdoors were different from any art Canadians had ever seen. Not everyone liked their paintings at first. Soon, however, the Group of Seven was famous across Canada.

Over time, new members joined the Group of Seven. The last painter to join was Winnipeg's L.L. Fitzgerald. Fitzgerald was called the "Painter of the Prairies."

**Figure 8.2** *A September Gale*, by Arthur Lismer, was painted at Georgian Bay, Ontario, in 1921.

The Group of Seven held its first show in 1920 and its last show in 1931. In a little over ten years, these painters changed the way that Canadians thought about art. Original paintings by members of the group hang in art galleries across Canada. Their art can also be seen in books, calendars, and even on postage stamps.

When the war ended, Canadians hoped to make Canada a country "fit for heroes." This meant that they wanted Canada to become a country worthy of their brave veterans. Instead, Canada faced many problems. The flu made millions of people sick. Jobs were needed for the returning soldiers. Hospitals had to be built for the wounded. Many Canadians were poor. Meanwhile, in Winnipeg, the biggest **strike** in Canadian history was about to occur.

> I HAD A LITTLE BIRD
> Its name was Enza
> I opened the window
> And in-flu-enza
> —*A popular children's skipping rhyme, 1918*

## The Statute of Westminster

Not many Canadians would think about celebrating on December 11. Perhaps they should – it is Canada's independence day. On December 11, 1931, the British Parliament passed an important law. The law was called the *Statute of Westminster*. It stated that British laws would never again apply to Canada unless Canadians wanted them to. In other words, the Statute of Westminster made Canada independent. The Statute of Westminster was also used in Australia, New Zealand, South Africa, Ireland, and Newfoundland.

# The Winnipeg General Strike

"This is not a strike," read the *Winnipeg Citizen* on May 19, 1919. "It is just plain, ugly revolution. … all true citizens must unite to defeat the Revolution."

The Winnipeg General Strike began on May 15, 1919. That day, more than 30 000 workers walked off their jobs. Metal and construction workers, factory workers, even department-store clerks marched into the streets of Winnipeg. They were joined by many jobless veterans. No one could have known how big the strike would become or that it would last for six weeks. Stores and factories closed. Newspapers stopped printing. Even mail delivery and telephone service ended. Businesses and services refused to operate without the permission of the strike's leaders (known as the *strike committee*). When the police decided to join the strike, the city fired them. The city then hired *special constables* to replace the police.

Why did some people think that the strike was the beginning of a **revolution**? For the answer to this question, it is important to know

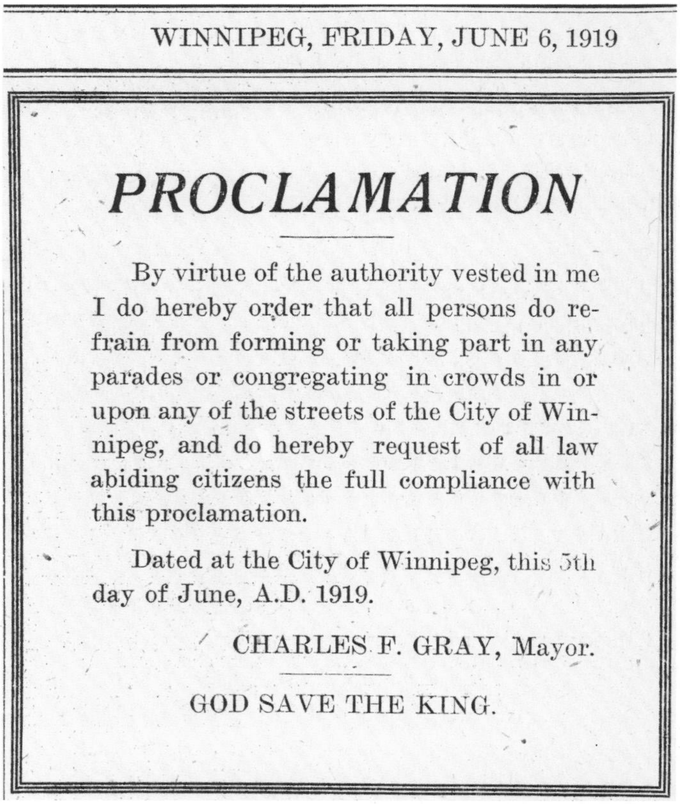

WINNIPEG, FRIDAY, JUNE 6, 1919

## PROCLAMATION

By virtue of the authority vested in me I do hereby order that all persons do refrain from forming or taking part in any parades or congregating in crowds in or upon any of the streets of the City of Winnipeg, and do hereby request of all law abiding citizens the full compliance with this proclamation.

Dated at the City of Winnipeg, this 5th day of June, A.D. 1919.

CHARLES F. GRAY, Mayor.

GOD SAVE THE KING.

**Figure 8.4** In a notice in the *Winnipeg Citizen* newspaper, the mayor of Winnipeg, Charles Gray, warns citizens not to strike.

**Figure 8.3** On what became known as *Bloody Saturday*, June 21, 1919, police charged down Main Street in Winnipeg to break up a crowd of strikers. Two people were killed and 30 were wounded.

what happened in Russia near the end of the First World War. In 1917, there was a revolution in Russia. A political party called the **Bolsheviks** [*BOLE-sheh-viks*] took power. The Bolsheviks killed Russia's monarch, the Czar, and his family. The Bolsheviks wanted *communism*. This is a political system where the government owns all property. The Bolsheviks created a dictatorship and called on workers in other countries to join them in a worldwide revolution.

Some people in Winnipeg feared that what happened in Russia was about to happen in Canada. Some believed that the Winnipeg strike was also led by Bolsheviks and "dangerous" immigrants. (Most of the strike leaders were, in fact, British born). A group of Winnipeg business owners who opposed the strikers formed the Citizen's Committee of 1000 to try to stop them.

In fact, very few of Winnipeg's strikers wanted a revolution. Most had gone on strike to protest their bad working conditions and poor pay. Workers believed their employers had made huge profits during the war and were unwilling to share them.

The Citizens' Committee of 1000 asked the government to end the strike, although the strikers were peaceful. The North-West Mounted Police were sent to Winnipeg to break up the strike. On June 21, mounted police charged down Main Street, swinging clubs and firing revolvers. People pushed and ran. Two strikers were killed and thirty others were wounded. The strike's leaders were arrested. Among them was J.S. Woodsworth (see p. 117). Charges against Woodsworth were dropped. Other members of the Strike Committee were sent to jail for as long as two years.

After the strike, people in the government tried to find out what caused it. They concluded that the strikers had not wanted a revolution. They also agreed with some of the strikers' demands. The citizens of Winnipeg, however, would continue to argue about whether or not the strikers had been right for many years to come.

## Sir Arthur Meighen (1874–1960) PM

Arthur Meighen was one of the greatest public speakers in Canada's Parliament. He dazzled other members of Parliament with his gift for language. Meighen was born in Ontario. However, he represented the Manitoba riding of Portage la Prairie for many years, beginning in 1908.

**Figure 8.5** Sir Arthur Meighen

Meighen was minister of justice under Prime Minister Borden. He played an important role in breaking up the Winnipeg General Strike in 1919. Meighen was Canada's prime minister from 1920 to 1921. For three months in 1926, he was again prime minister.

Meighen was not prime minister for very long. Yet he had an important political career. He served for many years as leader of the Conservative Party. He also served as a senator. Meighen retired from politics in 1942.

**Figure 8.6** Nearly 30 000 workers went on strike in Winnipeg on May 15, 1919, closing down factories, businesses, and transportation. Business leaders and their supporters protested the strike at this rally on June 4.

# The Struggle For Women's Rights

In the late 19th century, Canadian women could vote only in the municipal (town or city) elections. Even then, they were allowed to vote only if they owned property. Voting for a mayor or school-board trustee is an important right. However, women did not have the more important right to vote for members of the provincial legislatures or federal Parliament.

For decades, women formed groups to fight for the right to vote. One of the first was the Toronto Women's Suffrage Association, created in 1883. In the Canadian West, the struggle for **suffrage** was led by the Women's Christian Temperance Union (WCTU). This group thought that it could reach its temperance goals if women had the right to vote (see p. 84).

The women who led the fight for voting rights were suffragists. Many important Canadian suffragists were from the West. Among them were Manitoba's Nellie McClung and Alberta's Emily Murphy. They fought for women's rights for decades. They gave speeches, held rallies, and wrote letters to politicians.

Opposition to women's suffrage was strong. Many men thought that women were not suited for politics. A famous Canadian writer named Stephen Leacock said, "Women need not more freedom, but less." Some women agreed.

However, support for women's suffrage grew during the First World War. Thousands of women had joined the work force and proved themselves the equal of men. In January 1916, Manitoba became the first province in Canada to give women the right to vote. Other provinces followed. By April 1917, women could vote in Saskatchewan, Alberta, British Columbia, and Ontario. These rights only applied to provincial elections. Women still could not vote in federal elections.

That began to change in 1917. In September, the Wartime Elections Act gave some women the right to vote. These women had to be British subjects who were enlisted or had a close relative in the armed forces. In May 1918, the federal government extended the right to most women aged 21 or older, granting the same voting rights as men in federal elections. First Nations women (and men) with Indian status and Asian women (and men), however, were not yet allowed to vote.[1]

Some Canadian provinces, however, were slow to give women the right to vote in provincial elections. In Quebec, for instance, women could not vote until 1940.

**Figure 8.7** Emily Murphy was one of the Famous Five and the first woman appointed to be a magistrate anywhere in the British Empire.

## The Persons Case

Women won the right to run for election in the House of Commons in 1919. Two years later, in 1921, Ontario's Agnes MacPhail became the first woman elected to Canada's Parliament. However, women could still not be appointed to the Senate. According to the British North America Act, senators had to be "qualified persons." Yet women were not considered "persons" under the law.

In the late 1920s, five women from western Canada – Emily Murphy, Henrietta Muir Edwards, Irene Parlby, Louise McKinney, and Nellie McClung – fought to change that. However, Canada's Supreme Court would not change the law. The *Famous Five,* as these women became known, **appealed** the decision all the way to Great Britain. (In those days, Britain still had power over such laws.)

---

1  Chinese- and Indo-Canadians gained the vote in 1947; Japanese Canadians in 1948, and status First Nations people in 1960.

In October 1929, Britain's Privy Council (its highest court) struck down the Canadian law. According to the members of the Privy Council, this law was a "relic of days more barbarous than ours."

Many Canadians hoped that Prime Minister King would appoint one of the Famous Five to the Senate. In fact, none of the five ever served as a senator. Instead, King chose Cairine Wilson, a friend of the Liberal party, to be Canada's first woman senator in 1930. Wilson went on to be a great Canadian senator.

Earning the right to vote and to be a senator were important steps toward equality. The struggle for women's rights was not over, though. Many people still thought that women were not equal to men. Even today, women hold only 20 percent of the seats in Canada's Parliament. Real equality means changing the way people think. That struggle continues.

Figure 8.8 This statue on Canada's Parliament Hill honours the Famous Five and the Person's Case.

## Nellie McClung (1873–1951)

Nellie McClung spent much of her life fighting for women's rights. She was born in Ontario but raised in Manitoba. There, she taught school and joined the suffrage movement. McClung was also a writer. She wrote a best-selling novel. Her articles were featured across Canada in newspapers and magazines.

McClung was famous for her intelligence and quick wit. Indeed, many men were humiliated while trying to **debate** her. Stephen Leacock wrote that men had rights because of their superior strength. McClung replied, "No man has the right to citizenship because of his weight, height, or lifting power: he exercises this right because he is a human being, with hands to work, brain to think, and a life to live." She thought women should have the same rights, because they are human beings, too.

In 1915, McClung and her family moved to Alberta. There, she continued to fight for suffrage and other causes. Even after women won the right to vote and were, legally, seen as "persons," McClung kept doing important work. She served in the Alberta legislature. She worked for the Canadian Broadcasting Corporation (CBC). She also wrote more than a dozen books.

Figure 8.9 Nellie McClung

# A Rapidly Changing World

The First World War moved industry and technology forward. When peace came, new industries and new inventions changed Canada. Everything seemed to be moving faster. Automobiles and streetcars whisked people to work. Airlines, some of them started by veteran flying aces, carried people from city to city.

People talked about the *mod cons* – modern conveniences. These were things such as electric stoves, refrigerators, toasters, record players, radios, and automobiles. More and more, people shopped in big department stores. These stores included Eaton's, Simpson's, and the Hudson's Bay Company. The age of **consumerism** was born.

**Figure 8.10** Advertisements from the 1930s for modern appliances.

Not everyone could share in the new technologies. For instance, most farm homes in Canada did not have electric power. Many farms in Manitoba did not have electricity until the late 1940s. There was, however, an invention that farmers were more likely to own than city-dwellers – the automobile.

## The car comes to Canada

Imagine the excitement at the picnic on a hot June day in 1866 when Prince Edward Islanders saw a car for the first time. A parish priest named Father Antoine Belcourt was the proud owner of a strange new machine. It was a steam-powered carriage, which he had bought from an American inventor. He decided to show it off to his congregation. Belching steam and putting along at only two or three kilometres an hour, the steam carriage was still too much for Father Belcourt to control. It went off the road, crashed through a fence, and rolled. Luckily, no one was hurt. Father Belcourt is remembered for two reasons: he owned the first car in Canada, and he had the first car accident!

The automobile soon became very important to Canadians. During the 1920s, hundreds of thousands of Canadians bought cars. By the end of the decade, more than a million cars and trucks clogged Canada's roads.

In Ontario, American companies, such as General Motors and Ford, built factories. They produced hundreds of cars every day. Canada soon became the world's second-biggest producer of automobiles (after the United States). In 1926, more than 250 000 cars rolled off Canada's assembly lines.

Cars changed the way Canadians lived. In cities, people could now live farther away from where they worked. Families began to take vacations in other provinces. Houses were built with garages. Cities built more and wider roads, and governments built highways linking towns and cities.

**Figure 8.11** The first automobile ever built in Canada was this "horseless carriage," built in 1867 by Henry Seth Taylor in Stanstead, Quebec. Canada Post issued this stamp in 1993 to mark the event.

**DID YOU KNOW?** Father Belcourt, the owner of Canada's first car, led an interesting life. He lived among the Métis for 17 years and wrote the first Anishinabe (Ojibwa) dictionary. He also christened Louis Riel.

**Figure 8.12** These actors perform in a radio play from station CNRO in Ottawa, c. 1920s.

## The radio age

In the days before television, families often listened to the radio. The first radio program in North America was a concert broadcast in 1920 from station XWA in Montreal. Soon thousands of Canadians were buying radios for their homes.

At first, there were very few stations in Canada. Most Canadians listened to American radio programs. In the 1930s, the government of Canada created a nationwide network of radio stations. The network was named the Canadian Broadcasting Corporation (CBC).

One of the most popular programs in Canadian history got its start in November 1931. On Saturday nights, Canadians from coast to coast gathered around their radios to listen to

## Sir Frederick Banting (1891–1941)

After Frederick Banting failed his first year of studies at the University of Toronto, no one would have guessed that he would become one of the most famous men in the world. Returning to school, he studied medicine and then served as a doctor in the First World War. In 1921, Banting and his friend Dr. Charles Best discovered insulin. Insulin is used to control **diabetes**. Before the discovery of insulin, people with diabetes did not live for very long. For this discovery, Banting was knighted and awarded the Nobel Prize. Sadly, Banting was killed in an airplane crash in 1941.

**Figure 8.13** Sir Frederick Banting

*Hockey Night in Canada.* The show's announcer was Foster Hewitt. He became famous for his phrase, "He shoots, he scores!" By the end of the 1930s, three-quarters of Canadian homes had radios.

## The first trans-Atlantic radio message

Today, we use cell phones and computers that let us communicate in an instant with people around the world. We have sent spacecrafts millions of kilometres into space and marvel at pictures sent back to us from Mars. Until the early 20th century, such things were found only in science fiction. Then, an Italian inventor named Guglielmo [*goo-lee-EL-moe*] Marconi made history at Signal Hill in St. John's, Newfoundland.

On December 12, 1901, Marconi, the inventor of the radio, received the first radio signal sent across the Atlantic. Marconi's radio used an antenna nearly fifty

metres long. He used kites to carry the antenna high into the sky. Shortly after noon, he received a signal from his friend in Cornwall, England. It was the letter *S*, sent in Morse code.

Radio was called the *wireless* in the early days. (Radios, unlike telephones and telegraphs, did not need wires to carry a message.) From this simple signal over the wireless, the modern world of telecommunications began. In 1902, Marconi sent longer messages back and forth to England. Soon, radios were sending human voices over long distances.

# The Great Depression

Dear Sir: I am a girl thirteen years old, and I have to go to school every day. It's very cold now already and I haven't got a coat to put on. My parents can't afford to buy me anything for this winter. I have to walk to school four and a half miles [*7.2 km*] every morning and night and I'm awfully cold every day. Would you be so kind to send me enough money so that I could get one?

R.B. Bennett, Canada's prime minister, received this letter in October 1933 from a girl in Passman, Saskatchewan. He sent her five dollars. This was enough to buy a winter coat in those days. This was just one of the thousands of letters that the prime minister received during these years of poverty and hopelessness.

In the 1930s, the world went through an economic crisis called the *Great Depression*. The causes of the Great Depression were complex, and people still debate them. The First World War left the world's economy unstable. Even the economic boom of the 1920s did not solve many problems. Like Europe in 1914, the world economy in 1929 was a powder keg

**Figure 8.15** During the Depression, cities and towns ran soup kitchens, like this one in Montreal, where hungry people could get meals.

awaiting a spark. That spark was the New York stock-market crash in October 1929.

The effect of the stock-market crash in the United States spread rapidly to Canada. **Stocks** lost their value. Fortunes were wiped out. Banks went bankrupt. Families lost their savings. Without money to spend, people stopped buying things. Stores went out of business. This put people out of work.

Canada was hit harder by the Depression than any other country. In part, this was because so much of what Canada's farms and factories produced was exported (sold to other countries). Other countries stopped buying Canadian products during the Depression. Farmers could not sell crops. Factories could not sell products. By 1933, one third of Canadian workers did not have jobs. For millions of people, the 1930s was a decade of hardship. These years are known as the *Dirty Thirties*.

In Canada, there was no **welfare** system to help the needy. The federal and provincial governments argued for years about who should pay for a welfare plan. In the meantime, provincial governments did what they could to help people. Cities and towns set up soup kitchens and gave **relief** to those most in need.

**Figure 8.14** Jobless men left their homes and looked for work wherever they could find it. With no money, they would ride freight trains from place to place.

There were just too many people to help. In Saskatchewan, nearly two-thirds of farmers needed relief by 1933. One after another, the poorer provinces went bankrupt trying to provide help for people who needed it.

Across Canada, many young men *rode the rails*. They travelled illegally on freight trains from town to town, hoping to find work. Thousands of families sold their possessions to raise money. Some people worked only for food.

In 1935, Prime Minister Bennett promised Canadians welfare. His promise came too late. Canadians had already blamed him for the Depression. He lost the election in 1935 to Mackenzie King. King believed that relief was the responsibility of the provinces. He also believed that the Depression would not last much longer. But for millions of Canadians, every passing day brought greater sadness and hardship.

**Figure 8.16** Some Canadians were so poor during the Great Depression that they could not afford gasoline. Instead, they hitched their cars to horses. These cars were named *Bennett Buggies*, because people blamed the Depression on Prime Minister R.B. Bennett.

**DID YOU KNOW?** People on relief relied on food vouchers. These vouchers could be traded for food and other things that people needed. In Ontario, vouchers were worth $8 per week for a family. In Prince Edward Island, they were worth just $2. However, the government estimated that families needed $28 per week to survive.

## R.B. Bennett (1870–1947)    PM

R.B. Bennett came from a poor New Brunswick family. He became a schoolteacher at age 16. He saved every penny he earned to pay for law school. He practised law until 1911, when he was elected as a Conservative Party member of Parliament for Alberta, representing the riding of Calgary East.

In 1930, Bennett became prime minister of Canada. He had the misfortune of being prime minister during the worst years of the Depression. Bennett was a very kind man who did his best to help Canadians during the Depression. He often gave money from his own pocket to needy people. However, many Canadians blamed him for the country's troubles. He lost the election of 1935. Angry at Canada and Canadians, Bennett moved to England. He died there in 1947.

**Figure 8.17** R.B. Bennett and his sister, Mildred, campaigning in 1930.

# The Dust Bowl

It is hard to imagine anything making the Great Depression worse. However, between 1929 and 1937, one of the worst droughts in history hit North America. Year after year, the sun scorched the Prairie fields. Little rain fell. Crops failed and the soil turned to dust. Dry winds howled across the Prairies, kicking up dust clouds that buried fences and barns. People called the drought the *Dust Bowl*.

By the mid-1930s, the size of the harvest had dropped to just one-third of what it had been before the drought. On some farms, there was not even enough hay to feed the livestock. Nearly 14 000 prairie families boarded up their farms and left, hoping to find a better life. Those who stayed faced yet another problem: swarms of grasshoppers, attracted by the dry heat. While driving across Saskatchewan, a writer named James Gray came upon a cloud of grasshoppers. He later wrote:

> The swarm was on us so suddenly that our windshield was solidly encrusted with splattered insects in a matter of seconds … our car was a ghastly mess. The crashing grasshoppers had given it a sickly, stinking green coating. The windshield wipers only created a gooey smear. … In Weyburn (Saskatchewan) we made a deal with the son of a garage man to clean the grasshoppers off our car for a dollar. It took him almost two hours.

With the Depression in the cities and drought in the countryside, the 1930s were some of the worst years Canadians ever faced.

**Figure 8.18** Dry weather and high winds caused the Dust Bowl. The drought lasted from 1929 to 1937. Thousands of families lost their farms. Today, improved farming methods make it possible to work the land in dry years.

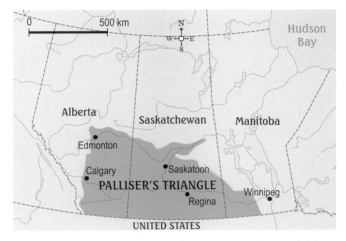

**Figure 8.19** *Palliser's Triangle*. This region of the prairies was the hardest hit by drought. It is known as *Palliser's Triangle* after the explorer Captain John Palliser. Palliser had told the British government in the 1850s that the region was too dry for farming, but he was ignored.

People looked to the government for relief. The bankrupt provinces could do little. In Ottawa, Mackenzie King returned to office in 1935. His government gave some money to the provinces to help unemployed workers and farmers, but it was not enough. Canadians were upset, and they began to look for new leaders with fresh ideas.

## Environment and agriculture

Farmers could not prevent the land from drying up – it was a result of the weather. However, they found they could make the effects of drought less severe.

In 1935, the federal government created an agency called the Prairie Farm Rehabilitation Administration. Its job was to help farmers find new ways to farm. For instance, farmers used dugouts to trap water. They planted rows of trees to prevent wind **erosion**. They also began to *strip farm*. In strip farming, long, narrow rows of crops were planted next to rows of fields that were left **fallow** (unused for the season). Farmers used modern machinery that was less likely to grind the soil into dust. These new methods made it possible to keep farming in areas where there was little rain.

## Relief camps and the On-to-Ottawa Trek

One of the federal government's few efforts to help the needy during the Depression was the creation of Unemployment Relief Camps. The camps provided food, shelter, and work for homeless, out-of-work men. Many of the camps were in British Columbia. There, workers cleared bush and planted trees. Living conditions in the camps were very poor, however.

In June 1935, there were strikes in several camps. A thousand men from the camps boarded trains bound for Ottawa. They wanted to protest to the prime minister. This event was called the *On-to-Ottawa Trek*. However, police in Regina stopped the trek. Although the trek's leaders finally met Prime Minister Bennett, there was a clash between the protesters and police in Regina. One officer died and several people were hurt. The On-to-Ottawa Trek was over. The following year, the Canadian government closed down the relief camps.

**Figure 8.20** Strikers from relief camps are stopped in Regina, June 1935.

**Figure 8.21** Jobless men found work in government relief projects, such as road-building in British Columbia. The men were fed, housed in tent cities, and paid a modest wage.

# New Political Parties

Three new political parties emerged in Canada during the Depression. The Co-operative Commonwealth Federation (CCF) was founded in Calgary in 1932. Its first leader was J.S. Woodsworth, a Methodist minister. The CCF was a **democratic socialist** party that believed in more government ownership of business and industry. The CCF was only three years old in 1935. However, in the election it won 10 percent of the popular vote.

Another political party, Social Credit, also began in Alberta. Its leader, William Aberhart, was a Christian preacher famous for his fiery radio sermons. He was known to his listeners as *Bible Bill*. Social Credit ideas included giving families money they could use to buy things that they needed. Under Aberhart, Social Credit swept to power in Alberta in 1935.

Another new party, the Union Nationale, arose in Quebec. Under its leader, Maurice Duplessis, the Union Nationale won the 1936 provincial election in Quebec. It promised relief programs and labour laws setting minimum wages, fewer hours of work, and better working conditions. It also supported publicly owned **utilities**. These promises were never fulfilled by Duplessis, however.

The three new parties could not end the Depression. However, they all had a great impact on Canadian politics. The Social Credit Party won nine elections in a row in Alberta. It stayed in power until 1971. The CCF won the provincial election in Saskatchewan in 1944. The CCF changed its name to the New Democratic Party (NDP) in 1961 (see p. 194). Except for four years during World War II, the Union Nationale remained in power in Quebec until 1960.

> **DID YOU KNOW?** Mackenzie King was not only Canada's longest-serving prime minister. He remains the longest-serving prime minister anywhere in the entire British Commonwealth.

## William Lyon Mackenzie King (1874–1950) PM

William Lyon Mackenzie King was the grandson of William Lyon Mackenzie, who led the Upper Canada Rebellions in 1837. It may seem strange that a rebel's grandson became prime minister. However, King not only became prime minister, he held the position longer than anyone else in Canadian history. King was Canada's prime minister during most of the 1920s and again from 1935 to 1948 – a total of almost 22 years. He was Canada's best-educated prime minister, with five university degrees.

Even though he kept winning elections, King was never very popular. People thought he was dull. He never married and had few friends. After his death, historians read King's diaries. They discovered that secretly he had been a **spiritualist**. He believed he had spoken to the spirits of dead prime ministers and historical figures such as Joan of Arc. Today King is remembered as Canada's leader through some of its most difficult times, including the Great Depression and World War II.

**Figure 8.22** Prime Minister Mackenzie King with his dog Pat in 1940

## J.S. Woodsworth (1874–1942)

Today, J.S. Woodsworth is remembered as one of the founders of the Co-operative Commonwealth Federation (CCF) in 1932. However, he had a long and important career before then.

**Figure 8.23**
J.S. Woodsworth

James Shaver Woodsworth was born in Ontario, and grew up in Brandon, Manitoba. At the age of twenty-two, he became a Methodist minister. Woodsworth's life was shaped by two important ideas. One was the Social Gospel (see p. 84). The second was *pacifism*. Pacifism is the belief that all problems should be solved without violence. Woodsworth worked hard his whole life to help the poor and needy. In 1921, be became a member of Parliament for the riding of Winnipeg North Centre. He would hold that seat until his death in 1942. Woodsworth believed so strongly in pacifism that he was one of the only members of Parliament to oppose Canada's declaration of war on Germany in 1939.

# Conclusion

Canada changed a great deal in the decade after the First World War. Women won the right to vote. Cities grew rapidly. New technologies such as automobiles, stoves, refrigerators, and radios changed the way that people lived. Many Canadians were poor, however, and many people still worked under dreadful conditions. At the same time, people saw evidence of change everywhere they looked. Things seemed to be getting better.

Then the Depression hit. Hundreds of thousands of Canadians lost their jobs. Drought gripped the Prairies. Thousands of farms were left to the dust. Many Canadians began to lose hope in the future.

The drought ended naturally in 1937, but the Depression dragged on. Every effort to solve economic problems failed. No one – Bennett's Conservatives, Mackenzie King's Liberals, the CCF, Social Credit, or the Union Nationale – could end the Depression. That was because the Depression was a worldwide problem, not just a Canadian one. Ending it would require a global change. That change came in September 1939 when the Second World War broke out. The war created jobs in the armed forces and in industry. It put people back to work and gave them money to live on.

Many Canadians who lived through the hard years of the Depression developed habits that they would keep for the rest of their lives. They learned to be careful with money. They became good recyclers. They took good care of the things they owned to make sure that they would last a long time. They planted vegetable gardens in their yards so they would always have food to eat. They also demanded that the government take steps to prevent anything like the Depression from ever happening again.

In late 1939, Canadians were relieved that the Depression was finally over. However, there was another great task awaiting them before they could celebrate. They had to fight Germany once more. This time Germany was led by a **dictator** named Adolf Hitler.

# 9 World War II
## 1939–1945

In 1933, Adolf Hitler, a veteran of the First World War, seized power in Germany. Hitler and his followers called themselves National Socialists, or *Nazis*.

Few jobs were to be found in Germany after World War I. The country had many other problems, as well. Much of its land was given to surrounding countries. Its army, navy, and air force were cut in size. Germany was forced to accept total blame for the war and to pay all of the costs.

Many Germans, including Hitler, blamed the signing of the Treaty of Versailles for the state Germany was in. Hitler also blamed Jews and communists for Germany's problems. He promised to restore Germany's greatness.

The Nazis set up a ruthless dictatorship soon after taking power. They stripped all Jews of their rights. They killed or imprisoned anyone who opposed the government. Then they began to plan a war of **conquest.** That war began in September 1939, when Hitler ordered German forces to invade Poland. Britain and France declared war to stop the German invasion. A week later, on September 10, 1939, Canada declared war on Germany as well.

Canadians followed Britain into the war because they thought that Hitler and the

**Figure 9.1** In both the First World War and Second World War, the Canadian armed forces hired painters called *war artists*. It was their job to record the war in art. Some artists visited the front lines to sketch. Returning to their studios, they would then turn their sketches into paintings. Many famous Canadian artists of the 20th century began as war artists. Alex Colville made this painting, *Infantry, near Nijmegen* [NYE-may-gen] *Holland*, just after the end of the Second World War.

Nazis had to be stopped from invading other countries. This time, however, there were no celebrations or patriotic marches. The agony of trench warfare was still fresh in their minds. They also remembered the conscription crisis and how it had nearly torn the country apart.

In Ottawa, Prime Minister Mackenzie King shared their fears. He wanted to avoid the mistakes of the First World War. King did not want to send Canada's army into battle. He promised Canadians that there would be no conscription.

Once again, Canada's armed forces were caught unprepared. Once again, the war would

**AS YOU READ, THINK ABOUT**
- what caused World War II
- why Canada joined the war
- how the war affected people at home
- how Canadians contributed to victory

be different from what anyone expected. New weapons had been invented since the First World War. These included fast-moving tanks and dive-bombing airplanes. Germany used tactics that made good use of the new weapons. People called this new kind of warfare *blitzkrieg* [*BLITZ-kreeg*]. This is a German word that means *lightning war*.

Hitler's armies moved rapidly from one victory to the next. Poland fell in 1939. In 1940, Germany took over almost all of Western Europe, including France. Suddenly Great Britain was alone. Canada was its most important ally. Now the British needed everything from Canada: tanks, planes, ships, food, and soldiers.

World War II grew even bigger in 1941. Hitler invaded the Soviet Union (USSR) in June. In December, Japan attacked the United States, bringing both countries into the war. Obsessed with power, Hitler declared war on the United States, too. It was his biggest mistake. Germany and its main allies, Italy and Japan, called the **Axis**, were not strong enough to fight the USSR, the United States, and Great Britain and the British Commonwealth at the same time.

However, it took nearly four more years for the **Allies** to defeat Germany, Italy, and Japan and to free all the countries that the Axis had conquered. During those years, Canada mounted a huge war effort. Canada's navy chased down German submarines in the North Atlantic. Canadian bomber crews flew dangerous missions over Germany. Canada's army fought deadly battles in Hong Kong, Sicily, Italy, France, and the Netherlands. By the end of the war, 1.1 million Canadians had served in uniform. This was nearly twice as many as had served in World War I.

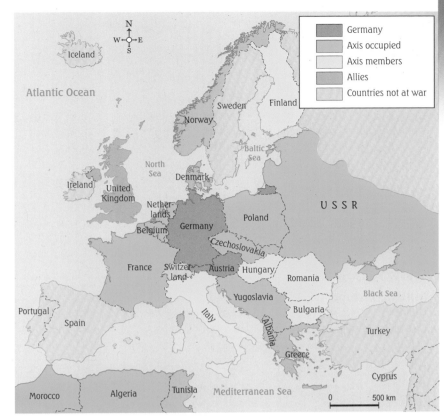

Figure 9.2 *Europe, November 1942*

## Dieppe

On August 19, 1942, Canadian troops raided the seaside town of Dieppe in **occupied** France. The raid was meant to surprise the Germans and get information that could be used for a future invasion. But the raid was a disaster. The Canadians had to advance into carefully placed German defences. Machine-gun and artillery fire hit them hard. Nearly 3000 of the 5000 Canadian soldiers who attacked were killed, wounded, or taken prisoner. After the Dieppe raid, a survivor from Verdun, Quebec, wrote to his family:

*I suppose you heard over the air* [radio] *that we were in France on the morning of the 19th. It is a morning I will never forget. I saw my buddies killed one after the other on all sides of me. We did what we went to do and that is main thing ... there were quite a few boys from Verdun like myself, and I am proud that some Verdun boys were in it.*

Although the raid went very badly, the Allies learned important lessons from it. These lessons saved many lives on **D-Day** (see p. 128).

## Bomber Command

In the summer of 1940, Hitler ordered his air force, the Luftwaffe, to bomb Britain. Over the next seven months, British cities, including London, Liverpool, and Coventry, were bombed almost every day. Nearly 40 000 British civilians were killed by these air attacks. Newspapers called the bombings the *Blitz*.

That same year, the British started bombing the Germans. The British bomber forces were part of a unit called *Bomber Command*. Waves of British bombers struck Germany every night. The bombers flew at night to hide from enemy fighters and anti-aircraft guns. At first, the targets were German factories, airfields, and railways. However, the British soon found that bombing small targets accurately was very difficult. Bombers at that time did not have good radar and targetting devices. Therefore, the British decided to try a new tactic called *area bombing*. With area bombing, **squadrons** of British planes attacked whole cities, hoping to destroy everything beneath them. By 1942, the British were sending more than a thousand bombers at a time to blast German cities. In January 1943, a Canadian force, the Number Six Bomber Group, joined Bomber Command's fleet. Over the next two years, Germany's cities were bombed into rubble. Nearly half a million German people were killed.

Flying in Bomber Command was one of the most dangerous missions of the war. Every night, bombers were shot down or crashed. In all, nearly 10 000 Canadians were killed flying for Bomber Command.

Figure 9.3 The Royal Canadian Navy had a vital mission during the war – to protect Allied supply ships crossing the Atlantic. This ship is HMCS *Halifax*. Canada's navy was the third largest in the world by 1945.

# Waging War From Home

World War II was a total war. Every part of life was aimed at the war effort. More than ever, the home front and fighting front worked together for victory.

## Canadian war production

Canada grew into an industrial powerhouse during World War II. Tanks, planes, ships, artillery, machine guns, rifles, and ammunition rolled off the assembly lines by the thousands. Canadians built them all.

Figure 9.4 Canadian factories built more than 850 000 vehicles in World War II, including more than 400 000 CMP trucks. This photograph shows CMP trucks being unloaded on a beach in Italy.

Canada's biggest aid to Allied war production was the simple, modest truck. In World War I, armies had still used horses to haul their supplies. Now armies needed motor vehicles.

In Canada, rival companies Ford and General Motors joined to make a vehicle called the *Canadian Military Pattern* truck (CMP). CMPs were a clever design, and the vehicle was used in many ways. They carried troops and supplies. They were used as mobile hospitals and radio stations. They were even used as anti-aircraft gun carriers.

## Women's labour

Once again, Canadian businesses needed women to fill the jobs left by men who had joined the armed forces. This time, however, the need was even greater. In World War II, women took ten times as many jobs in **munitions** plants as they did in World War I. In all, 600 000 women joined the work force in World War II. They did everything from building airplanes to driving buses to working on farms. By 1944, there were 1.2 million Canadian women in the work force. This is more than twice as many as there had been before the war.

Women also did other important jobs, just as they had in the First World War. They knitted clothing for soldiers overseas, collected scrap metal for recycling, and sold Victory Bonds. One woman remembered how she and her friends took war jobs *and* did volunteer work at the same time:

> The Red Cross supplied us with the wool and the whole lot of us set to work with [knitting] needles making socks for men of the services. Throughout the war, we made literally thousands and thousands of socks. Anytime there was a spare moment in the office the knitting needles would be out. We'd knit before work, during work, during our lunch hours, after work and at home.

Unfortunately, women in the work force had to fight prejudice. Many people felt that women should not be in the workplace, even though they were vital to the war effort. Women were often paid less than men for doing the same job. When the war ended, thousands of women lost their jobs.

## Victory Bond sales

The cost of war was not cheap. In 1939, the government spent $126 million on the military. In 1943, it spent over $4 billion, more than 30 times as much. Where did the money come from? Some came from new taxes that Canadians had to pay. Some came from the sale of Victory Bonds (see p. 100). Canadians bought billions of dollars worth of Victory Bonds, far more than in World War I.

**Figure 9.5** Factory workers in Montreal build a *Ram* tank. The Ram was designed in Canada for use by Canada's armoured forces.

**Figure 9.6** The government used posters like this one to advertise Victory Bonds. Buying bonds was one way that Canadians at home could help the war effort.

## British Commonwealth Air Training Plan

The British Commonwealth Air Training Plan (BCATP) trained pilots and aircrews at bases in Canada. In Canada, pilots learned to fly without fear of an enemy attack. Recruits came from around the world. While most were from Canada, Britain, Australia, or New Zealand, others had escaped from countries that Hitler had conquered, such as Poland, Czechoslovakia, and France. Over 130 000 pilots and crew members were trained in Canada.

**Figure 9.7** Pilots from the Royal Canadian Air Force were among those trained at BCATP bases throughout Canada.

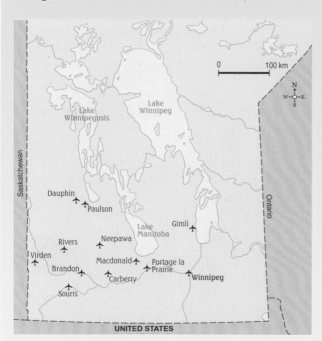

**Figure 9.8** *BCATP BASES, MANITOBA.* Many of the bases for the British Commonwealth Air Training Plan were in western Canada. This map shows the locations of the BCATP bases in Manitoba.

# Problems on the Home Front

## Rationing and shortages

Imagine going shopping only to find empty shelves in most stores. Or imagine not having enough gas for the family car. Life could be like that on the home front. Everything was needed for the war effort.

When factories started to build tanks, planes, and guns, they had to stop building cars, radios, refrigerators, stoves, and toasters. Gas was badly needed by the armed forces. Some people stopped driving their cars because so little gas was left over. Instead, they walked, rode bicycles or took buses or streetcars. With so many uniforms being made, there was not enough cloth for clothes. People had to make their old clothes last longer. Even some foods were hard to find. In wartime, ocean travel

**Figure 9.9** Because of shortages during the war, the government adopted rationing to make sure Canadian families received enough goods to meet their needs.

was so dangerous that there were fewer shipments of goods. Things like coffee and tea, for instance, which came from overseas, could be scarce.

In 1942, the Canadian government began to **ration** some goods. Coffee, tea, butter, sugar, meat, and gasoline were among them. Rationing meant that each person could buy only small amounts of these goods. Canadian families were given ration coupons. Once coupons were used up for the week, people could not buy any more rationed goods until the next week. Rationing in Canada ended when the war did. In Britain, shortages kept the government rationing for years after the end of the war.

## Internment of Japanese-Canadians

In December 1941, the Japanese bombed an American naval base at Pearl Harbor in Hawaii. The event brought the United States and Japan into the Second World War. The Allies were caught by surprise. They suffered many losses

**Figure 9.10** Japanese-Canadians board trucks to be relocated in 1942. The towns they were sent to often did not have electricity or running water.

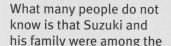
### David Suzuki (1936–)

David Suzuki is a Canadian environmentalist known around the world. He is the host of the CBC television program *The Nature of Things*. When the CBC asked Canadians to vote for the *Greatest Canadian* in 2004, David Suzuki came in fifth.

**Figure 9.11** David Suzuki

What many people do not know is that Suzuki and his family were among the Japanese-Canadians removed from their homes during the Second World War. Suzuki was born in Vancouver in 1936. In 1942, the government closed his parents' dry-cleaning business. Suzuki, his mother, and his sisters were sent to an internment camp. His father was sent to a different camp where he was forced to work as a labourer.

After the war, the family lived in London, Ontario. Suzuki studied science in university. Eventually he earned a PhD. Other Japanese-Canadians interned during World War II who later became famous include the writer Joy Kogawa and the painter Kazuo Nakamura.

on land and sea as the Japanese moved across the Pacific. Canadians feared a Japanese attack in British Columbia. As well, they did not trust Japanese-Canadians who were living in Canada. Canadians pressured the government to move the Japanese-Canadians somewhere else.

In February 1942, the government agreed. More than 21 000 Japanese-Canadians were uprooted and interned until the end of the war. Their schools and businesses were closed. Their possessions were taken from them. Some were sent to work camps. Others were sent to old mining towns in British Columbia for the rest of the war.

After the war, few Japanese-Canadians were allowed to return to their homes. Many settled elsewhere in Canada. Some returned to Japan, a country ruined by the war. Most Japanese-Canadians had done nothing wrong – just as Ukrainian-Canadians had done nothing wrong in the First World War. In fact, three-quarters of Japanese-Canadians had been born in Canada. Some of them had even fought for Canada in the First World War.

Why did the government relocate and intern the Japanese-Canadians? Some people think it was because most Canadians were prejudiced against the Japanese to begin with. Others argue that people in British Columbia honestly believed that some Japanese-Canadians might be spies. However, no Japanese-Canadian ever betrayed Canada. In 1988, the government of Canada finally apologized to the Japanese-Canadians who suffered during World War II. It paid each survivor $21 000.

### The conscription crisis of 1944

Conscription, which was so unpopular in Quebec, had nearly torn Canada apart in the First World War. In 1939, Prime Minister Mackenzie King wanted to make sure that there would not be another crisis like it. He told Canadians that only those who volunteered would be sent overseas. **Conscripts**, he said, would be used for home defence only.

Unfortunately, the Canadian Army lost a lot of men in the battles that came after D-Day (see p. 128). The army was unable to find enough soldiers to replace those it had lost. By late 1944, the situation was very bad. King had to break his promise. He decided that 16 000 conscripts would be sent overseas to fight. By the time most of them arrived, however, the war had already ended.

Fortunately, the conscription crisis in 1944 was not as bad as the crisis of 1917 had been. Many French-Canadians were angry. However, most realized that King had done his best to keep his promise. In the federal election of 1945, King and the Liberals won most of Quebec's seats.

# A Child's Eye View of the War

For Canadian children, the war was both an exciting and frightening time. Everywhere they looked, they saw men and women in uniform, army trucks rolling along city streets, and military aircraft crisscrossing the sky. Everything seemed to be moving at a faster pace. War could also mean that their fathers or older brothers were fighting overseas. Sometimes, letters arrived carrying the dreadful news that someone they knew was missing or had been killed in the fighting.

**Figure 9.12** Canadian comic books such as these, featuring Canadian war heroes and superhero Johnny Canuck, were very popular during the war. Sometimes, comics had to be printed in black and white, because there was not enough coloured ink.

Ordinary life went on, however. Children in wartime still went to school. They did their homework and chores. They played sports and listened to the radio. On Saturdays, boys and girls raced to the movies to see the latest blockbusters, such as the science-fiction adventure *Flash Gordon Conquers the Universe* or the mystery *The Maltese Falcon.* Afterward, they might ride their bicycles to the drugstore to buy a soda pop and a chocolate bar.

As the war went on, however, these things changed too. In school, teachers spoke of battles in faraway places, with names such as El-Alamein, Stalingrad, and Ortona. On Friday mornings, the CBC brought the war into classrooms with its national school radio broadcasts. After school, there was more work to do around the house, as more and more women were working outside the home. The radio played more news and less music. Short films about the war, called **newsreels**, were shown before the movies.

The drugstore had less soda pop and chocolate bars to sell. When children outgrew their bicycles or roller skates, they could not buy new ones because the metal used to build them was needed to build tanks and planes.

**Figure 9.14** *Be an Airman* was a board game where players pretended to join the British Commonwealth Air Training Plan.

**Figure 9.15** Children were encouraged to purchase War Savings stamps with money they earned from part-time jobs. Like Victory Bonds, War Savings stamps could be cashed in after the war.

**Figure 9.13** Wooden toys became popular, because metal was needed for the war effort.

# Forgotten Heroes

## Women in the armed forces

During the Second World War, the government made an important decision that changed Canada's armed forces forever. The government let women serve in uniform. Women were still not allowed to fight, however. Instead, they did important jobs behind the lines. The armed forces needed cooks, clerks, drivers, mechanics, messengers, and telephone operators. By

**Figure 9.16** A recruiting poster for the Canadian Women's Army Corps. This poster compares CWACs to Joan of Arc, the woman warrior of 15th-century France.

performing duties such as these, women freed men to serve at the front.

More than 45 000 Canadian women joined the armed forces in World War II. Special branches of the three services (army, navy, and air force) were created for them. Of the three services for women, the largest was the Canadian Women's Army Corps (CWAC). Over the course of the war, more than 22 000 women joined this service. They called themselves CWACs [*CEE-wacks*].

Women joined the armed forces for many reasons. Some enlisted because they believed it was their duty as Canadians. Many others just wanted a break from their daily lives. One CWAC from Quebec remembered:

> You enrolled for adventure. At seventeen … I lied about my age and told them my birth certificate was lost … I was working in Montreal and every day I'd pass a recruiting office. Take part in the war? Be a patriot? Replace a man? Perhaps … but for me it was really more for the fun of it and to see new places.

## The pilots of Ferry Command

How did airplanes built in Canada get overseas? We might think that that they flew — after all, today, hundreds of aircraft cross the Atlantic Ocean every day. In World War II, however, the idea of flying across the ocean was new. Most airplanes could not fly that far. At first, airplanes were carried overseas on slow-moving cargo ships. In 1941, the Allies created Ferry Command. It had a bold new mission. Its pilots flew the largest airplanes built in Canada on a dangerous trip over the North Atlantic. Some flew directly from Gander, Newfoundland, to Britain. Most took a slower but safer route — from Goose Bay, Labrador, to Greenland, and then to Britain. During the war, Ferry Command pilots delivered 9000 aircraft to Britain. It was a dangerous mission. Many pilots died when their planes crashed into the sea. Frederick Banting, the famous Canadian doctor (see p. 111), was killed when he was a passenger on a Ferry Command flight to Britain.

**Figure 9.17** These bombers await transport to Britain by Ferry Command pilots. Only the largest planes could fly directly across the Atlantic. Animals were also used in the war effort. This cat kept mice and rats away from airplanes.

**DID YOU KNOW?** The names of the other two women's branches of the armed forces were the Royal Canadian Air Force Women's Division (WD) and the Women's Royal Canadian Naval Services. Seventeen thousand women joined the RCAF and 7 000 joined the navy.

After the war, the government decided that women were no longer needed in the armed forces. However, the women who served proved that they could do important jobs in the military. In time, the government once again opened the military to women. Today, women also serve in combat roles.

## Aboriginal Canadians and the war

As they did in World War I, Canada's Aboriginal peoples served bravely in World War II. Many Aboriginal veterans of the First World War, such as Tom Longboat, volunteered in 1939. Since they were now too old for overseas service, Aboriginal veterans were sent to units such as the Veteran's Home Guard. The Home Guard helped to protect Canada from attack. It also performed duties such as guarding prisoners of war who had been sent to Canada.

Charles Henry Byce and Oliver Milton Martin were two of the thousands of Aboriginal Canadians who fought in World War II. In 1945, Byce, a Nehiyaw (Cree) soldier from Moose Factory, Ontario, took command of his company. He led its attack after all of its officers were killed or wounded by German tanks. For this heroic act, he was awarded the Distinguished Conduct Medal. Brigadier-General Martin, a Kanienkenaka (Mohawk) from the Six Nations Grand River Reserve, was the Aboriginal Canadian with the highest rank in the Second World War. More than 3000 Aboriginal Canadians served in the armed forces in the Second World War.

## Tommy Prince (1915–1977)

One of the best known of all Canadian soldiers was Tommy Prince. He was an Anishinabe (Ojibwa) soldier from Brokenhead First Nation in Manitoba. Prince was among the first to join the new parachute infantry. These soldiers jumped from airplanes onto enemy positions. Later, he became a member of the 1st Special Service Force. It was known as the *Devils Brigade*. Members of the Devils Brigade came from both Canada and the United States. Its soldiers were specially trained for the most dangerous missions.

In London, King George VI awarded Prince the Military Medal for his bravery during a mission in Italy. Prince had cleverly disguised himself as a harmless farmer. He then directed an artillery attack against unsuspecting Germans. He also won an American Silver Star for bravery, one of only 59 Canadians to receive the award.

Prince came back from the war to a country that would not let him collect veterans' benefits or vote. His once-successful business had failed while he was overseas. He decided to re-enlist in the armed forces. He served with distinction in the Korean War in the early 1950s. Prince was honourably discharged from the military in 1953. He then worked to provide Aboriginal Canadians with better jobs and education.

**Figure 9.18** Tommy Prince, right, with his brother Morris, at medal ceremony at Buckingham Palace, 1945.

# The Allies Sense Victory

## D-Day

June 6, 1944 is known as D-Day. That is when the Allies began the **liberation** of France. An Allied force of 8000 ships and 13 000 planes landed a huge army on the coast of Normandy, a province of France. British, American, and Canadian forces stormed up the beaches, overcoming strong German resistance. Canadians from the 3rd Infantry Division plunged farthest inland of all the Allied forces that day. Over the coming weeks, they would fight a series of bloody battles against some of Hitler's best troops. The Battle of Normandy ended in August with a victory for the Allies.

## Victory

On May 8, 1945, Canadians poured into the streets to celebrate. Hitler was dead, and Germany's armies had been defeated. The war in Europe was over, and the Allies had won. Ever since, May 8 has been remembered as V.E. Day (Victory in Europe Day).

In the Pacific, the war went on, however. Canadian troops were preparing to help the United States invade Japan. Then news arrived that the fighting had ended. The United States had used a terrifying new weapon – the atomic bomb. Two Japanese cities, Hiroshima [*HEER-oh-SHEE-muh*] and Nagasaki [*NAH-guh-SAH-kee*], had been totally destroyed. The Japanese surrendered.

American, British, and Canadian scientists had developed the atomic bomb in secret. The A-bomb, as it was known, exploded with the force of thousands of ordinary bombs. After the war, some people believed that A-bombs should not have been used, because so many innocent Japanese people had been killed. Others argued that the bombs saved many more lives by ending the war. In any case, Canadians celebrated again when the Japanese signed the surrender agreement on September 2, 1945. The Second World War was over. It had lasted almost six years.

# Conclusion

The Allies suffered many disasters on the road to victory. Once again, Canadians had played a major part in the Allied victory. Canadian soldiers fought all over the world – from the icy waters of the North Atlantic, to the jungles of Burma,

**Figure 9.19** No celebrations marked the start of World War II. Across Canada, however, people celebrated its end. Here, a crowd celebrates on the corner of Portage and Main in Winnipeg.

## The Holocaust

As the Allied powers advanced on Germany near the end of the war, they discovered that Hitler and the Nazis had committed a horrible crime. This crime is called the **Holocaust**. The *Holocaust* is the name we give to the murder of more than six million Jews, as well as more than five million people from other minority groups. These included the Roma, disabled, homosexuals, and political prisoners, among others. Some were shot. Others were enslaved and starved or worked to death. Millions were murdered in specially built *death camps*. The largest of the death camps was Auschwitz [*OWSH-vitz*]. Trains carried thousands of innocent people to Auschwitz every day. They were marched at gunpoint into chambers, where they were killed with poison gas. Historians estimate that 1.5 million Jews and other people that Hitler thought of as his enemies were murdered at Auschwitz alone. If Hitler had won the war, many more would have been killed.

Why did the Holocaust happen? Once Adolf Hitler was in power, he wanted to create a pure race of Germans. Hitler decided to get rid of certain groups of people by murdering them. Hitler told the citizens of Germany that the Jews and others were less than human. He claimed that they were the cause of Germany's problems. Many Germans agreed with Hitler's ideas.

**Figure 9.20** A Jewish family arrives at Auschwitz. Just moments later, these people were sent to the gas chambers and murdered by their captors.

Although the Allies knew about the camps early in the war, the full horror of what had happened was not discovered until the end of the war. The world was shocked. Governments and their leaders vowed to create a world where such mass murder could never happen again.

The Holocaust was such a terrible crime, that a new word was invented to describe it. That word is *genocide*. From the Greek words *genus* (race) and *cide* (killing), it means the murder of an entire group of people.

to the beaches of Normandy. On the home front, factories worked around the clock to make weapons of war. Canadians at home gave up all they could to help achieve victory. For Canada, the price of victory had been very high. Nearly 45 000 Canadians were killed in World War II.

The Second World War had a big impact on Canada. New industries, such as aircraft manufacturing, were created. Hundreds of thousands of women joined the work force. Cities grew. The government took the first steps toward creating a social safety net. Most importantly, Canada was ready to play a leading role in rebuilding the war-torn world. Many challenges lay ahead, but Canadians knew they could face them.

**Figure 9.21** Every May, Ottawa holds its famous Tulip Festival. In 1945, Princess Julianna of the Netherlands gave the Canadian people a gift of 100 000 tulip bulbs because Canada's army had freed her country from Germany. Today, the festival boasts more than three million tulips.

# IV Shaping Contemporary Canada

Canada was changing in the middle of a changing world. When World War II ended, the Cold War began. The USSR and the United States of America threatened each other by building bombs that could destroy the earth. Canada took its place on the world stage, promoting peace and cooperation.

Canada itself changed dramatically. New technology and industry pulled Canadians out of the poverty of the Depression. Immigrants from every corner of the earth came to make Canada their home. Yet many people in Quebec talked about separating from Canada. First Nations people joined together to speak out for their rights. The people who ran the country had to find a way for everyone to live together and get along.

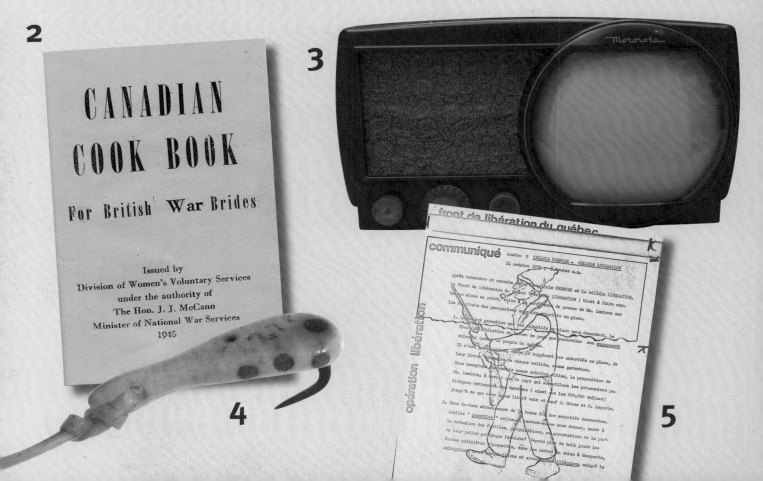

# In the Memory Box...

**1** A 1961 ad for Oldsmobile cars reflected growing incomes and growing families.

**2** The Canadian government issued cookbooks like this one to war brides, calling them "a practical form of welcome to the Canadian way of life." The war brides were new immigrants from Europe who had married Canadian soldiers from the Second World War.

**3** An early television, made in 1948.

**4** An ivory fish hook with baleen fishing line is an Inuit invention, one of many great Canadian innovations.

**5** In October 1970, the Front de Libération du Quebec kidnapped James Cross and Pierre Laporte. The group submitted this list of demands, telling the government what it would have to do to have the men released.

**6** This matchbox from 1962 advertises four Saskatchewan towns along the newly built Trans-Canada Highway.

**7** When Newfoundland joined Canada in 1949, this cartoon appeared in the Montreal *Gazette* with the caption "Welcome Aboard."

**8** Sweater pattern from the Mary Maxim Company, founded in Sifton, Manitoba after World War II. It sold knitting patterns, which often had Canadian designs, such as moose, beavers, deer, and maple leaves.

**9** Light blue berets like this one are worn by United Nations peacekeepers throughout the world.

**10** This article from a February 1968 Maclean's magazine shows how popular music influenced the fashions of the time.

# 10 Canada on the World Stage

On September 3, 1945, Canadians woke up to a new world. Japan had surrendered. The Second World War, which had begun exactly six years earlier, was over. There would be peace at last. Canadians emerged from the war with a new sense of pride. They had helped win the war. Now they would help keep the peace.

In 1945, the war-weary countries of the world started a new organization, the United Nations (UN). The UN was a place where different governments from around the world could settle their disagreements peacefully instead of through fighting. The UN's **charter** stated that all members would agree to "social progress and better standards of life" and "to practise tolerance and live together in peace."

These were fine ideas, and Canadians supported them. However, not all went as planned. Within a few years, the wartime alliance of the United States and the Union of Soviet Socialist Republics (USSR), also called the Soviet Union, fell apart. Each country feared and mistrusted the other.

Canadians also became suspicious of the USSR. Soon after the war, the Royal Canadian Mounted Police (RCMP) learned that the USSR was spying on Canada. Also, the USSR built an atomic bomb of its own in 1949. In Canada and the United States, people began to fear that a nuclear war could occur. Some Canadians even built **bomb shelters** in their backyards and basements.

## The North Atlantic Treaty Organization (NATO)

That same year, the United States, Great Britain, Canada, France, and eight other European countries joined together to form the North Atlantic Treaty Organization (NATO). NATO's job was to defend Western Europe and North America in case the USSR and its allies attacked them. Perhaps because of NATO, there was

**Figure 10.1** Flags of NATO member nations are flown at a meeting of the organization in the Netherlands in 2007.

**AS YOU READ, THINK ABOUT**

- the role of Canadians in the United Nations and its programs
- how Canada's involvement in other international organizations has grown since World War II
- Canada's role in world conflicts and peacekeeping since 1945
- how world events have shaped Canada's relationships with other countries

never an attack. Mistrust between NATO and the USSR lasted until the early 1990s. Historians call this period of tension the **Cold War.**

# The United Nations

In 1945, Canada and 50 other countries created the United Nations (UN). Today, more than 190 countries belong to the UN. The United Nations is a very large and complex organization with many important jobs to do. It includes agencies such as the following:

**The Security Council**. Members of the Security Council are the United States, Russia, Great Britain, France, and China. The Security Council keeps peace by acting as a global police

## The Korean War

In 1950, war broke out in Asia when North Korea invaded South Korea. For the first time, the United Nations acted to restore order. The UN sent a force of soldiers from many countries to defend South Korea. The Korean War was much smaller than either of the World Wars. When the war ended with a **truce** in 1953, more than 500 Canadians had been killed in the fighting. North Korea and South Korea remain divided to this day.

**Figure 10.2** Canadian soldiers during the Korean War comfort a child who has been injured.

## Louis St. Laurent (1882–1973) PM

Louis St. Laurent was born in Quebec. He became a lawyer in 1905. Later, he was a professor at Université Laval in Quebec City. He entered politics in 1942, and became prime minister six years later, in 1948. During St. Laurent's years in office, Parliament extended old-age pensions and created hospital insurance plans. St. Laurent helped bring Newfoundland into Confederation in 1949. The Trans-Canada Highway was built during his term. In 1957, his government lost to John Diefenbaker's Conservatives. A year later, St. Laurent retired from politics.

**Figure 10.3** Louis St. Laurent

force. The Security Council also runs all UN peacekeeping missions (see p. 134).

**The World Health Organization (WHO)**. The mission of the World Health Organization is to fight disease. WHO helps develop vaccines and medicines. It watches for the outbreak of diseases like SARS and AIDS.[1] Over the years, WHO has won major victories in the battle against disease. For instance, in 1979, WHO announced that smallpox had been wiped from the face of Earth. People had suffered from this terrible disease for thousands of years.

**United Nations International Children's Emergency Fund (UNICEF)**. UNICEF helps children in some of the world's poorest countries. The agency provides children with food, clothing, shelter, and education.

---

1  SARS, for Severe Acute Respiratory Syndrome, is a serious form of pneumonia caused by a virus. AIDS, for Acquired Immune Deficiency Syndrome, is a disease of the human immune system caused by the HIV retrovirus.

# Canada and Peacekeeping

The United Nations has many important duties. One of them is peacekeeping. Soldiers and civilians, known as peacekeepers, are often sent to places after the United Nations has worked out a truce between countries at war. It is their job to make sure that fighting does not break out again. The peacekeepers wear blue hats to identify themselves. They act like police officers. They use force only if they have no other choice.

Countries who are members of the UN send their own soldiers to run its peacekeeping missions. Since the UN was formed, more than one million soldiers from around the world have acted as peacekeepers. Of these, more than 80 000 have been Canadians. Canada has played a central role in more than 40 peacekeeping missions. Canada was there when UN peacekeeping missions began. It was during a crisis in one of the oldest countries in the world – Egypt.

## The Suez Canal crisis

The Suez Canal is an important waterway in Egypt. It links the Mediterranean Sea with the Red Sea. Before the canal was built, ships sailing from the Mediterranean to the Indian Ocean had to travel on a long voyage around the southern tip of Africa.

The Suez Canal was built in the 1860s. For almost a hundred years, the canal was open to the world. In 1956, the Egyptian government took control of the canal and decided who could use it. In November of that year, British, French, and Israeli forces invaded Egypt. Their goal was to seize the canal. They wanted to make sure that they could keep using it. All over the world, people feared that the invasion might start the Third World War.

When the Suez Canal crisis began, Lester B. Pearson was Canada's minister for external affairs. With the help of other UN members, he convinced both sides of the conflict to accept a truce.

Then, Pearson had a clever idea. He suggested that a large force of peacekeepers be placed between the two sides. This force would be made up of soldiers from many countries. It would make sure that the fighting did not start again. The first peacekeeping force included 1000 Canadians. It was named the *United Nations Emergency Force* (UNEF). It remained in Egypt for nearly 10 years.

> **DID YOU KNOW?** Canada's longest peacekeeping mission has been in the Mediterranean island of Cyprus. Canadian peacekeepers have been stationed in Cyprus since 1964.

**Figure 10.4** A Canadian peacekeeper in Haiti

**Figure 10.5** One of the newest monuments to Canadian soldiers is the peacekeeping monument in Ottawa. It is called *Reconciliation*. It shows soldiers standing in the rubble of a ruined town. Peacekeeping can be dangerous work. More than 100 Canadians have been killed on peacekeeping missions.

For his role in solving the crisis, Lester Pearson was awarded the Nobel Peace Prize in 1957. He became a hero to Canadians. Later, he became prime minister of Canada (see p. 139).

## Peacekeeping today

Canada still takes part in peacekeeping missions around the world. Since 1995, Canadian soldiers have been sent to places such as Haiti, Rwanda, and Bosnia-Herzegovina [*HERTZ-eh-go-VEE-nuh*]. However, the missions cost a lot of money. In recent years, the Canadian government has cut back on its help to UN peacekeeping efforts. Perhaps in the future, Canada will again take a leading role.

**DID YOU KNOW?** The Nobel Peace Prize has been awarded most years since 1901. It is presented in Oslo, Norway, to a person or group of people who have worked for peace. The prize was founded by a Swedish inventor named Alfred Nobel. Nobel invented the powerful explosive dynamite. He felt so guilty about his invention that he created the award, hoping it would promote peace in the world.

## John Humphrey and the Universal Declaration of Human Rights

On December 10, 1948, the members of the United Nations set out some of its most important ideas in a document called the *Universal Declaration of Human Rights*. The Declaration states that every person is born equal and has certain rights. For instance, everyone has a right to freedom of speech. Everyone is also free to choose his or her own religion.

All members of the UN are supposed to follow the Declaration. Many do not. However, the Declaration is an important step toward a more just and equal world.

John Peters Humphrey (1905–1995), a Canadian, wrote most of the UN Universal Declaration of Human Rights. Humphrey was a law professor at McGill University in Montreal. In 1946, he became the first director of the UN's human rights division. Humphrey worked hard for human rights until he retired in 1966.

**Figure 10.6** John Humphrey

# Canada and Other International Organizations

Canada is a large and rich country, but its population is small. In 2007, Canada had fewer than 32 million people. The United States has a population of more than 300 million people. China and India have more than one billion people each.

In a world with so many people, Canada's voice might be ignored. This is why the Canadian government has joined so many international organizations. In organizations like the UN, Canada is given the right to be heard by everyone. Canada's leaders know it is important to promote cooperation and understanding between countries. They see it as a way to prevent future wars from occurring. Cooperation gives Canada a greater influence than it would have working alone.

Besides the United Nations and NATO, Canada is also a member of several other international organizations.

## The Commonwealth of Nations

The British Commonwealth, as Britain and its colonies were known, saw great changes after the Second World War. This was because many nations that had been colonies of Great Britain gained their independence. India, Ceylon (Sri Lanka), and Burma (Myanmar) became independent in 1947 and 1948. Many other countries followed them in the 1950s and 1960s.

Today, there are 53 countries in the British Commonwealth. Each country is independent, or self-governed. Most recognize Queen Elizabeth II as head of the Commonwealth, however. Like the UN, the Commonwealth stands for understanding and cooperation between its members. Nations of the Commonwealth also share some culture and history. Every four years, athletes from the Commonwealth nations compete in the Commonwealth Games. Canada is one of the Commonwealth's richest members. It provides help to less developed members.

## The North American Aerospace Defense Command (NORAD)

During the Cold War, Canada and the United States started NORAD to protect North America from enemy attack. The organization is a good example of cooperation between Canada and the United States. NORAD's commander is always American. The second-in-command is always Canadian. The commanders report to both the president of the United States and the prime minister of Canada. NORAD's defence system includes a network of radar bases in Canada's far north. These bases were called the *Distant Early Warning Line* (DEW line) and are now called the North Warning System. They were built to provide early warning of an attack from the USSR.

**Figure 10.7** Fireworks display at the closing ceremonies of the Francophonie Games in Hull, Quebec, July 2001. The games are open to athletes from all the Francophonie countries.

## Decade of the World's Indigenous Peoples (1995–2004)

Every year, the United Nations declares special years for studying important topics that affect the world community. In 1975, the focus was on women. In 1990, it was literacy. In 1993, the world's **indigenous peoples** were the focus.

In December 1994, the UN's World Conference of Human Rights extended the Year of Indigenous People to the Decade of the World's Indigenous People. That meant the problems facing indigenous people of the world would be the focus for 10 years. Some of the issues studied were poverty, illness, and loss of culture and language. Ecosystems and indigenous knowledge were also studied. Many countries and indigenous communities joined together to focus on these issues. Canadian Aboriginal peoples were among them. Canada is one country that has started to write its own action plan based on the goals of the decade.

**Figure 10.8** Indigenous leader Rigoberta Menchu of Guatemala prays as Bolivian shamans light a fire to celebrate the approval of the UN Declaration on the Rights of Indigenous Peoples in 2007.

An important result of the ten years has been the Declaration on the Rights of Indigenous Peoples. In 2007 it was adopted by the General Assembly of the United Nations. Canada was one of four countries to vote against it.

## The Organization of American States (OAS)

Like many world organizations, the OAS was created after the Second World War. Countries from North America, South America, and the Caribbean belong to the OAS. It began in 1948 with 21 members. Canada did not join until 1990. This was because, until recently, many of the governments in South America and the Caribbean were dictatorships that Canada did not support. Canada now gives more support to the OAS than any country except the United States. Canada takes part in many OAS projects. The projects include efforts to make democracy stronger and to police the illegal drug trade.

## La Francophonie

La Francophonie is a French organization. Its members are former colonies of France. La Francophonie began in 1970 and meets every two years. Canada has three members. One represents the Canadian government. Two represent the two provinces with the most French-Canadians, Quebec and New Brunswick. As a member of La Francophonie, Canada hopes to promote closer relationships among the French-speaking nations of the world.

# Conclusion

"We will always be there," Prime Minister Jean Chrétien said in a speech in 1999. It is a fine idea, but it is not always true. The UN, NATO, the Commonwealth, NORAD, La Francophonie, the OAS – all of these organizations ask Canada to "be there." In addition, Canadians have problems of their own that federal and provincial governments must solve. Sometimes, Canada has so many things to do, it is impossible to do them all.

The world today has many problems. Poverty, disease, pollution, and war still exist. There are no easy answers to these problems. It can be hard for Canada's leaders to know how to deal with them. Sometimes, the answer to one problem can create another problem. For instance, industry and technology can lessen poverty. However, they can also cause pollution.

Sometimes a solution that works in one case might not work in another. For example, Canada has always looked for peaceful ways to end conflicts, such as in the Suez Canal Crisis. However, Canadian soldiers have fought in Afghanistan since 2002.

Still, many of the world's problems have been solved. Diseases like smallpox have been wiped out. Polio may soon be gone. No world war has been fought for more than 60 years. The Cold War ended peacefully. There are far fewer nuclear weapons in the world today than twenty years ago. Led by Canada, countries have taken great steps toward getting rid of land mines. There are far more democracies in the world today than ever before.

In addition, people today are more aware of problems in far-off regions of the world. This is due, in part, to television and the

**Figure 10.9** In August 2005, Hurricane Katrina devastated the city of New Orleans in the United States. Here, a Canadian worker walks down rows of hospital and emergency relief supplies that are ready to be sent to Katrina victims.

Figure 10.10 *Long Day at Doha* by war artist Edward Fenwick Zuber shows Canadian soldiers in the Persian Gulf. Canadian forces served in the region in 1991, as one of many countries that joined together to force the invading army of Iraq out of neighbouring Kuwait.

Internet. Before World War II, many Canadians would never have heard about a disaster such as a famine, earthquake, or tidal wave on the other side of the world. Now, within days of a disaster, Canadians send aid to help victims.

Canadians know that their own well-being depends on the well-being of other people around the world. This is why Canada must keep playing an active role in the world.

## Canada and the United States

Canada and the United States became close friends and allies during the First and Second World Wars. Today, Canadians and Americans enjoy a peaceful relationship. The two countries have not fought each other for nearly 200 years. Canadians watch American television programs and movies. Americans enjoy Canadian musicians. Every day, thousands of Canadians and Americans cross the border to shop or vacation.

However, the leaders of Canada and the United States do not always agree about **foreign policy**. In the 1960s and early 1970s, the United States fought a war in Vietnam. Canada stayed out of the war.

On the other hand, Canada fought alongside the U.S. in the Gulf War in 1991. This short war was fought after the dictator of Iraq, Saddam Hussein, ordered his armies to conquer the tiny country of Kuwait. In 2002, the Canadian government decided to help the United States fight in Afghanistan. However, Canadians chose not to fight in the Iraq War in 2003. Even though Canadians and Americans sometimes disagree, the relationship is an example of how two nations can get along.

## Lester B. Pearson (1897–1972) PM

Lester B. Pearson was born near Toronto in 1897. Pearson did well at almost everything he tried in life. He studied at the University of Toronto, where he was an excellent student and a great athlete. When he later became professor of history at Toronto, he coached the university's hockey and football teams.

During the First World War, Pearson was a fighter pilot in the Royal Flying Corps (RFC). Later, Pearson decided to become a diplomat. He played a key role in the birth of the United Nations. Soon after, when he was Canada's minister of foreign affairs, he won the Nobel Peace Prize for helping to end the Suez Canal Crisis (see p. 134). Pearson became the leader of the Liberal Party when Louis St. Laurent retired in 1958. He became prime minister in 1963. During his time as prime minister, Parliament passed

Figure 10.11 This photograph shows Lester Pearson (on the right) with three men he chose to be cabinet ministers in his government. They are Pierre Trudeau, John Turner, and Jean Chrétien. All three later became prime ministers.

many important laws. These include laws related to universal health care and old age pensions. He retired as prime minister in December 1967.

# 11 A Modern Industrial Nation

**F**rom 1930 until the end of World War II in 1945, Canadians faced hard times. The Depression had left many people without jobs and money. During wartime, there were more jobs, but Canadians had to ration food and fuel. By the time the war ended, Canadians were ready for change.

Canada's economy grew quickly after World War II. So did its population. Many people from Europe left behind their war-torn countries. They came to Canada for a chance at a new life. Canada welcomed these immigrants, as it needed workers for its new factories.

World War II also ushered in a period known as the *Baby Boom*. Between 1948 and 1957 almost five million babies were born. Why did families have so many children during these years? Here are some reasons:

- After years of being apart because of the war, husbands and wives were together again. They wanted to start families.
- The federal government gave families money to help with the costs of raising children. This money was called *family allowance*.

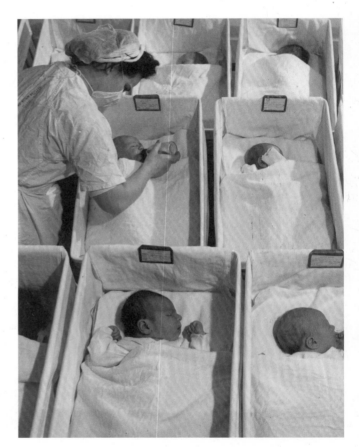

**Figure 11.1** In the 1950s, hospital maternity wards became busy places because of the Baby Boom.

- By 1948, businesses were doing well. People were earning more money. Parents could afford to take care of more children. Life for many Canadians became more comfortable.

Canadians first started buying television sets in the late 1940s. At first, there were very few channels. Programs were aired for only a few hours each day. However, Canadians were excited

**AS YOU READ, THINK ABOUT**

- how industry and technology affected the country
- how the Baby Boom affected Canadian society
- what Canadian inventors have contributed to the world
- what fads and fashions can tell you about how young people lived after World War II

Figure 11.2 Prosperity finally came after years of Depression and war.

on the floor for hours in a stuffy, overheated living room cannot be good for any child," they warned. "What effect will it have on their posture and eyesight?" Still, family life soon centred around the TV.

by the new invention. Families would even stare at the flickering black-and-white test pattern for hours before the shows started.

With TV came other inventions. Families set up fold-out TV tables in their living rooms. Then they could watch television during the dinner hour. A teachers' group in Toronto worried what television might do to children. "Surely crouching in a chair or stretching out

Figure 11.3 TV dinners, invented in the 1950s, were complete meals meant to be eaten while watching television.

## Toronto and Montreal: Wonder cities of tomorrow!

Toronto and Montreal had planned to build subway systems for a long time. However two world wars and the Depression made other concerns more important.

Finally, in 1950, Toronto broke ground for a subway system. Workers soon discovered a huge rock bed underneath Toronto's streets. They had to blast through it with dynamite twice daily. The noise was so terrible (and terrifying) that a radio jingle was written to cheer people up. It went:

Yes we're gonna have a subway
    in Toronto
We gotta get the working man
    home pronto
So bear the noise with a smile
And in a little while
We'll be ridin' in the new subway!

Toronto's subway opened for business in 1954. In Montreal, Mayor Jean Drapeau opened that city's subway system – the Métro – in 1966. The Métro had its own jingle called "Il fait beau dans le Métro."

Figure 11.4 The new Toronto subway at rush hour, 1954

There were fewer downtown traffic jams in Toronto and Montreal because of the new subways. New office and apartment buildings sprang up near the subway stations.

# The Industrial Boom

After World War II, many things in Canada became bigger, including cars, families, and cities. Even the country became bigger when Newfoundland joined Canada in 1949. For the first time in years, average Canadians had more money to spend. More people could afford new cars, clothes, and vacations. They could also afford new items, such as television sets and appliances.

Much of Canada's money came from its natural resources, such as oil, precious minerals, and powerful rivers. Profitable businesses, based on these resources, created many new jobs.

Oil is the source of gasoline, and as more and more people bought cars, the demand for gasoline grew. By 1950, the oil industry in Alberta was booming.

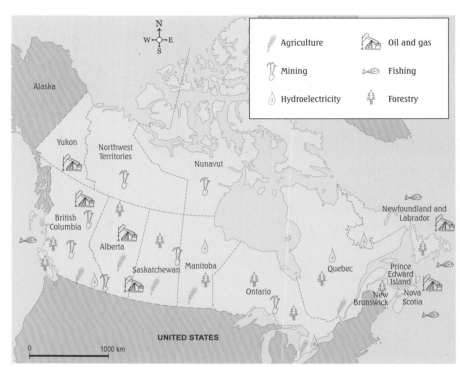

**Figure 11.5** *NATURAL RESOURCES IN CANADA*

Canadians also needed electricity to run their new electric appliances. Companies such as Hydro-Quebec and Manitoba Hydro built giant hydro dams on northern rivers. The hydro companies harnessed the power of crashing

## Anishinabe of the Grassy Narrows Reserve

The English-Wabigoon River flows into Grassy Narrows First Nation in northwestern Ontario. For years, the Anishinabe (Ojibwa) people who lived there ran profitable fishing businesses. In the 1950s and 1960s, many people worked as fishing guides for tourists. But upstream, 160 kilometres away in Dryden, Ontario, a paper mill regularly dumped mercury waste into the river. The deadly pollution flowed downstream toward the Grassy Narrows reserve, poisoning the fish. By 1970, the English-Wabigoon River was so polluted that people could no longer eat the fish they caught there. Tourists no longer went on fishing trips. The guides were out of work. Worse, the people of Grassy Narrows became sick from having eaten the poisoned fish for so many years.

**Figure 11.6** The English-Wabigoon River at Grassy Narrows

The story of the English-Wabigoon River shows how an industry can destroy the environment, a people's way of life, and even the people themselves.

river rapids to supply all the electrical energy people needed. Forestry became another important industry, as Canadians needed wood to build new homes.

The war gave Canada a head start in manufacturing. Factories that had been making tanks, uniforms, and machine guns were soon making cars, nylon stockings, and washing machines. Mining became important, providing metals for the many new things Canadians wanted.

These new industries were good for some Canadians, but not for everyone. Many of Canada's Aboriginal peoples found their way of life ruined by mines, pulp mills, and hydroelectric projects. Hydro companies flooded Aboriginal lands to create dams. The flooding

## Alberta strikes oil

During the Depression, Alberta, like other provinces, was very poor. In February 1947, a man named Vernon Hunter drilled for oil in Leduc, Alberta. Hunter found so much oil that Alberta went from rags to riches almost overnight. **Oil barons** moved into Western Canada and found even more oil. Billions of dollars soon poured into Alberta. That made it one of the richest provinces in Canada.

**Figure 11.8** Page from the *Western Examiner*, February 22, 1947

**Figure 11.7** This sign warns swimmers about polluted water, c. 1950.

destroyed **sacred** burial grounds, wild-rice areas, and longstanding villages. Forests were cleared by pulp and paper companies. This caused game animals to move elsewhere. Mining companies and paper companies polluted waters and surrounding lands.

In 1962, American biologist Rachel Carson wrote a book called *Silent Spring*. In her book, Carson showed how pollution from factories was poisoning air, rivers, and wildlife in the United States and Canada. Industry might be good for making money, but it could cause great harm to the natural world.

Another effect of more industry was the move to large cities. In 1951, 38 percent of all Canadians lived in rural areas. About half of all Canadians did not have refrigerators in their homes. Many people still used wood-burning stoves to cook their meals. Many did not have flush toilets or running water.

That would soon change. In the 1950s, more than four million people moved from farms and small towns to Canada's biggest cities. These people thought cities offered more jobs. They thought that life there would be easier.

# Canadian Inventions

Canadians have invented many things. Some of the inventions are known the world over because they have helped to improve people's lives. Other Canadian inventions are a little unusual. Yet all of them show how creative the minds of Canadians can be.

The canoe, kayak, snow goggles, snowshoes, and the game of lacrosse were all invented by Aboriginal peoples. Armand Bombardier, from Quebec, invented the snowmobile. The world can also thank Canadian inventors for Pablum baby food, the paint roller, ginger ale, and table hockey.

In the early 1950s, Harry Wasylyk of Winnipeg created the first plastic garbage bags. The Winnipeg General Hospital was always concerned with cleanliness. It had many garbage cans, which had to be washed over and over. Wasylyk's disposable garbage bags solved the problem. Later, an American company bought Wasylyk's idea. It started making garbage bags for household use in the late 1960s.

Another Canadian innovation saves lives around the world – the heart pacemaker. The

## Bill Konyk's perogie maker

Some Canadian inventions reflect the **ethnic** background of the inventor. Bill Konyk was a Ukrainian-Canadian restaurant owner from Winnipeg's North End. He saw how long it took to make perogies by hand. For each perogie, Konyk had to cut the dough, place the filling inside, fold the dough around it, and seal the edges. So Konyk invented a handy gadget to speed things up. His perogie maker could make 18 perogies in seconds.

**Figure 11.11** Perogies, made popular by Eastern European immigrants, are enjoyed by many Canadians

invention is used to regulate uneven heartbeats. It was invented in 1950 by a Manitoba electrical engineer named Jack Hopps. Many years later, Dr. Hopps himself used his invention when his own heart needed a pacemaker.

Canada has also contributed to space exploration. Satellites orbiting Earth often needed repairs. However, there was no way to catch satellites once they were in space. In 1979, Canadian scientists invented a robotic arm called the *Canadarm*. It grasped broken satellites and pulled them into the **space shuttle** for repairs.

**Figure 11.9** Snowshoes allowed people to walk on top of the snow by distributing their weight over a large area. This traditional Innu snowshoe is made from a wood frame woven with rawhide.

**Figure 11.10** Winnipeg's Harry Wasylyk, inventor of the green garbage bag.

**DID YOU KNOW?** Canada became the third country in the world to send a satellite into space. Following the Soviet Union and the United States, Canada sent the *Alouette I* into orbit in 1962 to study the atmosphere.

**Figure 11.12** The Canadarm

## Bearproof suit

Troy Hurtubise is a scrap-metal dealer from North Bay, Ontario. In 1986, he survived a grizzly-bear attack in the wilds of British Columbia. He soon found that scientists did not know very much about grizzlies. That was because it was too dangerous to study them up close.

Hurtubise wanted to know more about grizzlies. He decided to invent a suit that would protect him against a grizzly attack. That way he could safely watch the bears.

Hurtubise built the suit from scrap metal, titanium, chain mail, rubber, and plastic. He tested the suit before trying it out with a real bear: Hurtubise was hit by a 136-kilogram log and run over by a truck. He was even struck by arrows and baseball bats. "I never got a bruise!" said Hurtubise.

In 2001, Hurtubise finally went face to face with a 586-kilogram Kodiak bear. The gigantic bear was terrified of the strange-looking suit. It would not attack! Since then, Hurtubise has been redesigning the suit.

**Figure 11.13** A man tries to power saw through the Ursus Mark VII bear suit.

# Fads of the 1950s and 1960s

People can learn a great deal about a time period by looking at everyday fads and fashions. By looking at what was popular (and not so popular) in the 1950s and 1960s, we can find out

- how Canadians spent their money
- how young people expressed themselves
- how young people challenged their parents' generation
- how American and British culture influenced Canadian culture

Most popular fads and fashions in the 1950s and early 1960s came from the United States. Canadians loved American products, such as the Hula-Hoop, Elvis Presley music, and poodle skirts. They enjoyed television shows such as *I Love Lucy* and the *Ed Sullivan Show*.

At the same time, Canadians created some fads and fashions of their own. In the 1950s, *La Famille Plouffe* was broadcast on both French and English television. It reached audiences across the country. In the early 1960s, Canadian children all wanted *Ookpiks*. Ookpiks were stuffed sealskin owls made by the Inuit of Kuujjuak, Quebec.

**Figure 11.14** The Ookpik

## Hair

In the 1950s, many teenage boys copied the hairstyle of popular singer Elvis Presley. Teenage girls' hair went from ponytails to bobs to beehives. Hair got bigger – and longer!

By the mid-1960s, British music became popular. The British Invasion brought new fads and styles to Canada. Boys grew their hair into shaggy *mop tops* to look like the Beatles, the most popular musical group.

By the late 1960s, many teenagers did not agree with the ways of the older generation. They grew their hair longer and longer. One reason they grew it long was to show how unhappy they were with the war in Vietnam that was all over the news. Long hair was the complete opposite of the short, military buzz cuts of soldiers.

*The crew cut*

*The duck tail*

*The mop top*

*The hippie*

*The bob*

*The beehive*

*The flower child*

*The Afro*

**Figure 11.15** Hairstyles of the 1950s and 1960s

## Marilyn Bell: Canada's youngest sports hero

One September night in 1954, Marilyn Bell, a 16-year-old high-school student from Toronto, dove into Lake Ontario at Youngstown, New York and began swimming. Almost 21 hours later, she climbed out of the water at Toronto, on the other side of the lake. She became the first person to swim across Lake Ontario. Instantly, she became a Canadian sports legend. In 1955, Bell swam across the English Channel between Britain and France. In 1956, she swam across the Strait of Juan de Fuca in British Columbia.

**Figure 11.16** Marilyn Bell

## Canada's first pop star

In 1957, Paul Anka, a teenager from Ottawa, became an international pop star. When he was only 15 years old, he wrote a song called "Diana" about his Ottawa babysitter, Diana Ayoub. "Diana" became a big hit. Many more hit songs followed, and teenage fans mobbed Anka wherever he went. In Japan, they nicknamed him King Paul. Thousands of fans even waited for autographs outside his hotel in Japan in the middle of a typhoon!

**Figure 11.17** Paul Anka

**Figure 11.18** The hula hoop was a popular fad in the late 1950s.

**DID YOU KNOW?** In 1964, the first Tim Hortons doughnut shop opened in Hamilton, Ontario. Tim Horton, Canada's "Father of the Timbit," was a hockey player for the Toronto Maple Leafs when he went into the doughnut business.

## Don Messer's Jubilee

One of the most popular TV shows in Canadian history was *Don Messer's Jubilee*. It was a CBC music show from Halifax, Nova Scotia. It ran from 1959 to 1969. More than three million Canadians, mostly older viewers, tuned in every week to watch Don Messer play his Maritime jigs and reels on the fiddle.

In 1969, when the CBC cancelled the show, Don Messer's fans were very upset. Some of them came from across Canada to protest at the Parliament Buildings in Ottawa. One of the protesters even told a journalist, "We in Canada must fight for the Don Messer Show. The young generation and the CBC want to kill it!"

**Figure 11.19** Don Messer was a favourite of Canadian television viewers in the 1960s.

## Social Welfare

Between 1921 and 1941, two-thirds of Canadians lived in poverty. By 1951, only one-third of Canadians were poor. Things were better because there were more jobs.

The government, however, could not ignore those Canadians who were still poor. Many were elderly and lived in rural areas. Far too many

were Aboriginal or French-Canadian. New wealth, however, meant that the government of Canada could take care of its needy citizens as well. It introduced programs to provide help to those who needed it. These included

- family allowances
- **medicare** (see sidebar, right)
- old-age pensions, introduced in 1951 under Prime Minister St. Laurent

## Conclusion

In the 1950s and 1960s, many Canadians enjoyed a good life. However, as Canada approached its 100th birthday in 1967, Canadians wanted to do away with inequalities in their country. At the same time, they wanted to build a new society to reflect modern times. In the process, Canada would see some of the most dramatic events in its history.

**Figure 11.20** After World War II, families became larger. They had more money. The government received more tax money so it could afford to look after its growing population.

## Tommy Douglas's bad knee

In 1911, when Tommy Douglas was a boy in Winnipeg, he fell on a stone and hurt his knee. The injury did not heal properly.

Tommy's family did not have enough money to send the boy to the hospital. They were new to Canada. They lived in a poor neighbourhood in Winnipeg's North End. Tommy's father worked in an iron factory, where he was not paid very much. Without medical help, Tommy's knee got worse and worse. Soon he had to walk with crutches.

Winter came. Tommy's knee was so bad he could not climb over the ice and snow to get to school. A neighbour boy pulled Tommy to school every day on a sled. Soon the infection in Tommy's knee became very bad. His family faced a terrible choice: pay for an expensive operation or have the leg cut off.

There really *was* no choice. The family did not have enough money for the operation. Tommy was about to lose his right leg. At the last minute, however, Dr. Robert H. Smith offered to operate on the young boy's leg for free.

Dr. Smith fixed the knee. If Dr. Smith had not been so generous, the boy would have lost his leg. Tommy knew that he had been luckier than most people. Many people stayed sick, lost legs, or even died because they could not afford to pay their medical bills.

Tommy Douglas did not forget this experience. When he grew up and became premier of Saskatchewan, he worked hard to create a government program called *medicare*. It began on July 1, 1962. The program provided all of the people in the province with free medical care. Everybody in Saskatchewan – rich or poor – could see a doctor if they were sick.

Tommy Douglas went to Ottawa in 1962 as leader of the New Democratic Party. There he encouraged the federal government to create a nationwide medicare program. In 1966, Prime Minister Pearson set up medicare for every Canadian, based on Saskatchewan's example.

Figure 11.21  Tommy Douglas, 1944

Figure 11.22  This child at the Estevan Health Centre in 1963 was among the first Saskatchewan residents to have a medical checkup under the province's medicare program. In 1966, the federal government brought medicare to all Canadians.

# 12 A Changing and Diverse Society

In the 50 years following World War II, Canada went through many changes. Aboriginal people pressed for the right to take care of their own affairs. French-Canadians wanted respect for their language and culture. Some Quebeckers believed Quebec should separate from Canada and become its own country. Canada also became a homeland for people from every part of the globe. These new Canadians also wanted to be heard.

## First Peoples

In the decades after World War II, First Nations peoples of Canada began to organize themselves politically. The National Indian Brotherhood (see p. 152) represented many First Nations. It faced its first major political fight in 1969.

That year, Prime Minister Pierre Trudeau and Minister of Indian Affairs Jean Chrétien presented a **white paper.** It was a new plan for First Nations peoples. Trudeau believed First

(see p. 152)

**AS YOU READ, THINK ABOUT**

- how Aboriginal peoples made changes in their communities
- the people and events that caused change in Quebec
- how post-war immigration added to Canada's diversity
- how bilingualism and multiculturalism affected Canada
- what you are learning and how it connects to your life

**Figure 12.1** In the years after WWII, Aboriginal peoples worried about their place in the modern world, and with losing their traditional cultures. How does this painting, *Buffalo Dreams* by Jane Ash Poitras, show that concern?

Nations people were not fully part of Canadian life because they had different rights. He thought having different rights kept them from fully taking part. If Canadians were to be equal, Trudeau argued, they must all have the same rights. He suggested the treaties be cancelled. He said that Indian status should be taken away.

The National Indian Brotherhood (NIB) strongly protested the white paper. Alberta Nehiyaw (Cree) leader Harold Cardinal wrote a response which came to be known as the *Red Paper*. The National Indian Brotherhood said that the government plan would mean assimilation of First Nations. In the end, the government backed down. Treaties and Indian status stayed as they were. Trudeau admitted his white paper was a mistake.

For a long time, Aboriginal peoples have been frustrated by the way the government looks after their affairs. For example, in 1988, the Aboriginal Justice Inquiry in Manitoba found that Aboriginal people were treated unfairly by police and the courts. In 1998, the federal government apologized to First Nations people for the racism, abuse, and violence that their children often faced in Canada's residential schools. Yet, residential schools operated in

Canada for more than 100 years before they were closed for good.

Many Aboriginal people believe that they should run their own affairs. They say First Nations and the Canadian government are equal partners. This idea is known as Aboriginal **self-government.**

**Figure 12.2** In 1970, Harold Cardinal, as president of the Indian Association of Alberta, responded to the federal government's white paper with his Red Paper. It criticized the government's policies and promoted Aboriginal self-government. In later years, Cardinal, a Nehiyaw (Cree) lawyer and chief, became a legal expert on treaty rights and land claims, and advised the government about such issues. Cardinal was an important voice for Aboriginal peoples until his death in 2005.

## John Diefenbaker (1895–1979) **PM**

When John Diefenbaker was growing up in Saskatchewan, he told his mother that he would be prime minister one day. In 1957, the Progressive Conservative Party won a big **majority** in the federal government. Diefenbaker, as its leader, became prime minister. The promise Diefenbaker had made to his mother came true. He became one of the most popular politicians in Canadian history.

Diefenbaker knew what it was like to be a Canadian who was not English or French. His parents were German and Scottish. Many things Diefenbaker did as prime minister showed his concern for Canadian diversity and equality.

Diefenbaker created the Canadian Bill of Rights to help fight discrimination (see page 178). In 1960, his government granted status Indians the right to vote in Canadian elections. He opened Canadian immigration to all ethnic groups. At the Commonwealth Conference in 1961, Diefenbaker spoke out against **apartheid** in South Africa. Under apartheid, black South Africans did not have the same rights as other South Africans. Black citizens, who were the majority, could not even vote in elections. In 1961, Diefenbaker said South Africa should be removed from the Commonwealth until apartheid was stopped.

John Diefenbaker did not speak French very well, but he supported **bilingualism.** He set up a translation system in the House of Commons. When French-Canadian members of Parliament spoke in French, English speakers could understand what was being said. In 1959, Diefenbaker appointed Georges Vanier Canada's first French-Canadian governor general. Diefenbaker represented the people of Prince Albert, Saskatchewan, until his death in 1979.

**Figure 12.3** John Diefenbaker

After long talks, the Canadian government and the Inuit people of the Northwest Territories reached an agreement. Nunavut was created on April 1, 1999. Nunavut is an example of how Aboriginal self-government can work.

The word *Nunavut* means "our land" in the Inuktitut language. Not everyone who lives in Nunavut is Inuit. Yet life in Nunavut is shaped by traditional Inuit knowledge called Qaujimajatuqangit [*cow yee ma ya too kang eet*]. For example, the Nunavut government does not have political parties. Rather, the Nunavut legislature follows the Inuit tradition of consensus.[1] In other words, the government does not make a decision until all elected officials agree with it. The official languages of Nunavut are Inuktitut [*ee-NOOK-ti-toot*] and Inuinaqtun [*EE-noo-ee-NOK-ton*] as well as English and French.

**Figure 12.4** Nunavut's first premier, Paul Okalik, helped settle Inuit land claims. He is one of the founders of Nunavut.

1 Consensus government is also used in the Northwest Territories

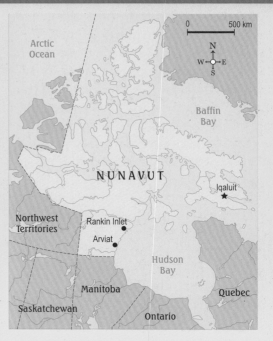

**Figure 12.5** *NUNAVUT.* Nunavut covers 2.2 million square kilometres of land.

**Figure 12.6** The Nunavut flag features the *inuksuk*, a landmark that guides people and marks sacred places.

## Aboriginal organizations

First Nations, Inuit, and Métis are distinct cultural groups. Therefore, they have different people to speak for them.

The National Indian Brotherhood (NIB) was formed in 1968. In 1982, it became the Assembly of First Nations (AFN). The AFN now brings the concerns of 630 First Nations peoples to governments. These concerns include land claims (restoring land that First Nations believe they are entitled to), **self-government**, health, and social development.

The Inuit are concerned about many of the same issues that First Nations people are. Issues include control over their land and resources

**Figure 12.7** Phil Fontaine, national chief of the Assembly of First Nations, is from the Sagkeeng First Nation, Manitoba.

**Figure 12.8** Clem Chartier, president of the Métis National Council (left) and David Chartrand president of the Manitoba Métis Federation, at the gravesite of Louis Riel in Winnipeg in 2005. A ceremony was held to commemorate the 120th anniversary of the Métis leader's death.

and the loss of their language and culture. In 1971, Inuit from five regions of the north formed the Inuit Tapirisat of Canada (now known as *Inuit Tapiriiat Kanatami*).

The Tapiriiat was the organization that reached an agreement with the Canadian government over the creation of Nunavut. It negotiated land rights and the new territory's role in Canada. The organization is now concerned with the effects of global warming on the environment and on traditional ways of life.

The Métis National Council (MNC) was formed in 1982. It is concerned with Métis rights. Its members include groups from Ontario, Manitoba, Saskatchewan, Alberta, and British Columbia. (The Manitoba Métis Federation represents Métis in Manitoba.) Prior to 2005, the federal government did not treat the Métis as a distinct people. The council worked to change that. In 2005, the council signed an agreement

with Canada that accepts the Métis as a people with its own language, culture, and traditions. The agreement also says the Métis nation has rights to territory and self-government.

## The Oka crisis

In Quebec, where the St. Lawrence and Ottawa rivers meet, is a place called *Kanesatake* [*kuh-neh-suh-TAH-kay*]. For over 300 years, the Kanienkehaka (Mohawk) people have claimed Kanesatake as their homeland. They have always fought to keep their land. In the 1970s, they asked the federal government to give reserve status to Kanesatake. The government did not agree to their request.

For more than 300 years, European-Canadians used the lands in this area. They built missions, sawmills, and established the town of Oka. In the 1950s, Oka built a golf course without asking the Kanienkehaka people for permission. Forty years later, in 1990, the mayor of Oka decided to build a bigger golf course. He planned to use part of an ancestral graveyard belonging to the Kanienkehaka.

This was not acceptable to the Kanienkehaka. They built a barricade on the road to the building site to stop builders from moving onto their land. For months they stayed put, guarding the barricade.

After almost six months, the mayor called in the Quebec Provincial Police. He asked the police to remove the protestors. The police arrived with tear gas, assault weapons, and grenades. Things got violent. One police officer was killed. Other police ran away. Soon after, Quebec Premier Robert Bourassa called in the Canadian army. The standoff ended a month later without any more bloodshed.

The events at Oka showed First Nations' determination to protect their land. As a result, Prime Minister Brian Mulroney set up a **Royal Commission** on Aboriginal peoples. The Commission reviewed what had happened at Oka. It also recommended what could be done to avoid future conflict.

# The New Quebec

After World War II, francophone Quebeckers asked themselves: What is the best way for us to live in the modern world without losing our language and culture? As they tried to answer this question, several changes were taking place in Quebec and French Canada.

# The Great Darkness

Maurice Duplessis was the premier of Quebec from 1944 to 1959. He was leader of the Union Nationale Party (see p. 116). Duplessis wanted Quebeckers to live their lives as they had in the past, based around family, rural life, and the Catholic Church.

At the same time, most Quebec industries and resources, such as hydroelectricity, were run by a few English-speaking businesspeople. Francophones often faced discrimination in the business world. In general, they were much poorer than English Quebeckers.

In the 1950s, francophone Quebeckers were not able to get the same education that anglophones did. Even though most Quebeckers were French-speaking, there were only two francophone universities. Anglophones, who were much fewer in number, had four.

Some Quebeckers refer to this time as the *Great Darkness*. Quebeckers felt they were held back from their dreams.

# The Quiet Revolution

By the late 1950s, Quebeckers were ready for change. They knew they could have a better life. They thought a new government could make that happen. In 1960, they elected the Liberals, led by Jean Lesage, to replace the Union Nationale.

Lesage's message was "Maîtres chez nous." That means "Masters in our own house." René Lévesque was minister of natural resources in Lesage's government. Lévesque bought Hydro-Quebec from the small group of anglophones who owned it. It became a public industry. As it was Quebec's biggest industry, everybody was able to share the wealth, not just English businesspeople.

Things began to change in Quebec. Francophone Quebeckers began to take their place in government, business, and culture. The new era was called the *Quiet Revolution*.

## Quebec sovereignty

In the 1960s, more and more Quebeckers started to think that the province should leave Canada. They wanted Quebec to become its own nation. That way, Quebec could be part of North America without losing its language and culture. This idea is called **Quebec sovereignty**.

## René Lévesque (1922–1987)

René Lévesque was one of Quebec's most popular leaders. He was born in Gaspé and educated in Quebec City. Lévesque first had a career as a journalist. When he entered politics, he was a **federalist**. By 1967, however, he believed sovereignty was the best choice for Quebec.

Not all Quebeckers agreed with Lévesque's ideas. However, most liked him as a man and as a leader – Lévesque was bold, charming, and had a good sense of humour. Quebeckers voted against sovereignty in 1980, but they still wanted Lévesque as their premier. They re-elected him in 1981.

**Figure 12.9** René Lévesque

In 1968, René Lévesque founded a new **sovereignist** political party called the Parti Québécois. In 1976, the Parti Québécois won the provincial election. Lévesque became Quebec's first sovereignist premier. The Parti Québécois was peaceful, moderate, and democratic, in keeping with the spirit of the Quiet Revolution.

However, there were other sovereignist groups that were not moderate. The *Rassemblement pour l'indépendence national* (RIN) held angry street protests against the British queen and federalism. The group *Front de Libération du Quebec* (FLQ) believed the only way for Quebec to be on its own was through violence. The FLQ used dynamite to blow up banks, mailboxes, a statue of General Wolfe, and other symbols of English control.

## A Canadian Crisis

In 1963, Prime Minister Lester B. Pearson wanted to know how anglophones and francophones were getting along. He sent a team of people to travel across Canada. They talked to Canadians and found that anglophones and francophones did not understand each other very well.

Pearson's team reported that there was still hope for a united Canada. They advised that French and English should become the official languages of Canada. That way, French-Canadians would feel like equals. They said that Quebec needed special powers to keep its language and culture. This idea was called *special status*.

### Trudeau and the bilingual experiment

In 1965, a Montreal **intellectual** joined Lester B. Pearson's Liberal government. His name was Pierre Elliott Trudeau. Three years later, he would become prime minister of Canada. He was a federalist who did not believe in sovereignty or special status.

When Trudeau arrived in Ottawa in the 1960s, the government was run almost entirely

### Francophones in Canada

The number of francophones in Canada has grown over the years, from just over a million people in 1871, to 4.1 million in 1951, to 6.8 million in 2001. For many years, the francophone population held at around 30 percent of the population. This started to change after 1951 partly because of an increase in immigration. Another reason was francophones had fewer children than the rest of the Canadian population.

#### *Percentage of Canadians with French as their mother tongue*

|  | In Canada | In Quebec | In Provinces Outside Quebec |
|---|---|---|---|
| 1951 | 29 | 82.5 | 7.3 |
| 2001 | 23 | 81.4 | 4.4 |

in English. Trudeau believed bilingualism was the way to keep Canada together.

When he became prime minister, Trudeau decided that federal government would now do business in both English and French. In 1969, he passed the Official Languages Act, which made both languages equal.

As a result, Canadians started seeing French on their cereal boxes. They started hearing more French in airports, on the radio, and in the prime minister's speeches. French immersion schools were set up across Canada in the 1970s. So were student exchange programs where young people could learn both official languages.

Not everyone liked Trudeau's bilingual dream. Many Canadians thought it was too expensive. Others said bilingualism would never work. However, Trudeau wanted to show French-Canadians that they could speak their language anywhere in the country, not just in Quebec. He thought bilingualism would keep Quebec from leaving Canada. Trudeau also believed anglophones should have equal rights in places where English was a **minority**, such as in Quebec. In this way, the English and French would not be separate. Canada would be a united, bilingual country.

# The October Crisis

On the morning of October 5, 1970, four gunmen broke into the Montreal home of British diplomat James Cross. "We are the FLQ," one of them said. They forced Cross into their getaway car and sped away. Five days later, the FLQ kidnapped Pierre Laporte, minister of labour in the Quebec government. In a **ransom** note, the FLQ demanded money. They also wanted certain FLQ members to be released from prison. They asked for safe transportation to Cuba. Finally, they demanded that their **manifesto** be read on national television. If they did not get these things, the hostages would be killed. Quebec Premier Robert Bourassa asked Prime Minister Trudeau to invoke the **War Measures Act.** On October 15, he did.

On October 17, the body of Pierre Laporte was found in the trunk of an abandoned car. He had been strangled. Canadians were horrified by the senseless murder. René Lévesque said that the FLQ were "inhuman." James Cross was rescued a few days later.

The government uses War Measures Act in times of extreme emergency. It may be used during war or when a country's security is threatened. Under the act, police have the right to arrest anybody. During the October Crisis, the police could put someone in jail just for knowing someone in the FLQ – even without proof. More than 450 people were jailed. Trudeau also made it illegal to be a member of the FLQ. He sent the Canadian army to guard the streets of Montreal.

Many people were upset with Trudeau for using the War Measures Act. They believed it took away peoples' **civil liberties**. As it turned out, the FLQ was only a tiny gang, not a big organized group. Most people who got arrested had nothing to do with the FLQ and were against violence.

Trudeau did not apologize, however. He said that the government had to be tough. Otherwise, the FLQ's violence would not end.

## Pierre Elliott Trudeau (1919–2000) PM

In 1968, Trudeaumania broke out all across the country. Canadians went wild for Pierre Elliott Trudeau's style and charm. They elected him as their 15th prime minister.

Trudeau was born into a wealthy Montreal family in 1919. His father was French-Canadian and his mother came from a Scottish background. Trudeau was a brilliant student. He studied at l'Université de Montreal, Harvard University, and the Sorbonne in Paris.

Trudeau was adventurous and curious about the world. He learned to speak Spanish. He backpacked through the Middle East and Asia. He paddled to Cuba in a canoe. He was prime minister of Canada from 1968 to 1979 and again from 1980 to 1984.

**Figure 12.10** Pierre Elliott Trudeau, April 1968, after winning the leadership of the Liberal party.

## Oui ou Non?

In 1980, the Parti Québecois government held a **referendum** in Quebec. Quebeckers were asked if they wanted to separate from Canada, *oui ou non* (yes or no). Quebec premier Lévesque wanted Quebeckers to vote *oui*. Trudeau wanted

**Figure 12.11** Residents of this duplex in Vanier, Quebec, take sides in the 1980 referendum on Quebec sovereignty.

them to vote *non*. He promised to make things better for Quebec if they stayed in Canada.

In the end, a majority of Quebeckers – almost 60 percent – voted to stay in Canada. (In another referendum in 1995, Quebeckers again voted to stay – by a narrow majority of 50.58 percent!

# French Canada Outside Quebec

In the 1960s and 1970s, Quebeckers were not the only francophones in Canada who wanted change. About a million francophones lived outside of Quebec, mainly in Ontario, New Brunswick, and Manitoba.

## The Acadians

About one third of the population of New Brunswick are French-speaking Acadians. Like many Quebeckers and Aboriginal people, some Acadians think of themselves as a nation within Canada. In 1977, a political party called the *Parti Acadien* wanted to create a new province of Acadia.

In the 1960s, Acadians in New Brunswick went through their own Quiet Revolution. It began when Louis Robichaud became the province's first Acadian premier. Robichaud set up a francophone university in Moncton in 1963. In 1968, he turned New Brunswick into Canada's first (and only) bilingual province.

## Georges Forest and francophone rights in Manitoba

One winter morning in 1975, Georges Forest of Winnipeg found a parking ticket on the windshield of his car. He had received a five-dollar fine for illegal overnight parking, payable to the City of Winnipeg. The ticket was written in English, but Forest, a francophone, knew his rights. He decided to challenge the ticket in court.

**Figure 12.12** Georges Forest

When Manitoba joined Confederation in 1870, one condition was that French and English would be equal languages in the province. That meant, for example, that both English and French had to appear on government documents. This condition was made into law with the Manitoba Act (see p. 29). However, the government ignored that part of the law for more than 100 years.

Georges Forest took his parking ticket all the way to the Supreme Court of Canada. He argued that Manitoba was a bilingual province. The different levels of government in Manitoba, he said, had to serve people in both English and French. Every Supreme Court judge agreed with Forest. The language rights Louis Riel had won for Manitoba in 1870 were finally granted to francophones. And Forest never had to pay that parking ticket!

**Figure 12.13** The Acadian flag was created on Prince Edward Island in 1884 by Marcel-François Richard.

# Changes in Canada's Population

One reason Canada's population grew after the Second World War was the Baby Boom. It also grew because of a flood of new immigrants. Between 1945 and 1957, 1.5 million people came to Canada. Most came from different parts of Europe. Some were war brides who had married Canadian servicemen during and after the war. Many others moved to Canada because they had lost their homes during the war. Some were survivors of concentration camps or political refugees. Canada offered new beginnings for all.

In 1967, the Canadian government started a new immigration system. It was called the *points system*. It gave immigrants points for their level of education, their age, and their

ability to speak English or French. Under this policy, many new immigrants from Asia, the Caribbean, the African Commonwealth states, and the Middle East settled in Canada. New Canadians spoke many different languages and practised different religions.

**Figure 12.14** Ellen Fairclough, above, was the first woman in Canadian history to be a minister in the federal government. She worked as minister of citizenship and immigration between 1957 and 1962. Fairclough helped change the immigration policy. Since 1962, Canada has chosen its immigrants based on what they can contribute to Canada as individuals, and not on the colour of their skin or their ethnic background.

## Refugees

In 1949, Hungary lost its independence to the Soviet Union. In 1956, thousands of Hungarians fought back, but Soviet tanks moved in and crushed the uprising. More than 200 000 Hungarians fled their homeland. Canada set up immigration offices in Hungary. It even rented a ship and an airplane to bring some of the refugees to Canada for free. Close to 40 000 Hungarians moved to Canada at the time.

The Canadian government had not always been so helpful. Canada had strict immigration laws before World War II. For example, in the 1930s, Canada closed its doors to Jewish refugees who were fleeing the Nazis in Germany. The Canadian government did not want Jews in the country.

**Figure 12.15** Hungarian refugees, 1956

With the war over, many people wanted immigration laws to be loosened. They argued that Canada should welcome homeless European refugees out of simple humanity. Others said immigrants would be good for Canadian business. Canada was doing well, and new industries needed more workers. Prime Minister Mackenzie King's government let in many immigrants. However, the new immigration policy still followed the old rules. It would still accept or reject new immigrants based on their race. As a result, it was easier to immigrate to Canada if you came from the United Kingdom, the United States, or France.

**Ten leading source countries of immigrants to Canada**

| 1951 | 2005 |
|---|---|
| United Kingdom | China |
| Germany | India |
| Italy | Philippines |
| Netherlands | Pakistan |
| Poland | United States |
| France | Colombia |
| United States | United Kingdom |
| Belgium | Republic of Korea |
| Yugoslavia | Iran |
| Denmark | France |

**Figure 12.17** In 1939, close to 1000 Jews from Germany boarded the ship *S.S. St. Louis* to escape the Nazis. Canada, Cuba, and the United States would not accept them, so the ship returned to Europe. Many passengers found refuge in countries in Western Europe. However, when Germany conquered those countries during World War II, most of those refugees were murdered in the Holocaust.

**DID YOU KNOW?** The United States, Australia, and Canada have the highest rates of immigration in the world. Canada was the first of these countries to stop accepting or rejecting immigrants based on their race or nationality.

**Figure 12.16** Starting in April 1975, hundreds of thousands of people escaped from the war-torn countries of Vietnam, Laos, and Cambodia. They travelled in unsafe boats across the South China Sea. Many starved or drowned. By 1980, approximately 60 000 *boat people*, as they were called, had found safe homes in Canada.

**Figure 12.18** At the end of the Second World War, women known as war brides married Canadian servicemen and moved to Canada. The children of the war brides became part of Canada's Baby Boom.

# Cultural Diversity

As immigrants changed the face of the country, many people in Canada were neither French, English, nor Aboriginal. They spoke other languages and came from many different cultures. Between 1945 and 1971, more than three million immigrants made Canada their home. Many ethnic groups, such as Ukrainians, Mennonites, and Icelanders, had been in Canada for generations. Now there were many others. How could so many different people share the same country?

Some Canadians say that immigrants to Canada should leave their old ways behind and join the mainstream of Canadian life. To them, diversity weakens Canada. They believe that if everyone shares the same habits and values, a strong Canadian identity will be formed. This idea is called a *melting pot*. In a melting pot, all differences are melted down and mixed into one culture. The United States, where Americans of all ethnic groups have created a national identity, is considered a melting pot. Prime Minister Diefenbaker thought this would be a good idea for Canada.

Other Canadians describe their country as a **mosaic**. In a cultural mosaic, many different cultures live together.

# Multiculturalism

On October 8, 1971, Prime Minister Trudeau announced in the House of Commons that Canada would have a mosaic policy of **multiculturalism** in a bilingual society. French and English would remain the official languages of Canada. Different ethnic groups would keep their cultural traditions and contribute them to Canadian life.

## Speaking Out for Multiculturalism

When Prime Minister Pearson sent his team across Canada in 1963, a Ukrainian-Canadian man told them, "The other day, I heard a French-Canadian from Quebec on television. He was saying that the new Canadians … could not expect to obtain the same privileges as French-Canadians, who developed a large part of the country. Well, we were pioneers too, in other parts of the country which we settled before anyone else arrived!"

In the 1960s, Ukrainian-Canadians spoke out for all cultural communities that felt they had been left out of Canadian **biculturalism**. They asked Prime Minister Trudeau to support multiculturalism. The day after Trudeau announced multiculturalism in the House of

**Figure 12.19** Brazilian drummers (left) and a Japanese dancer (right) perform at Folklorama, a long-running multicultural festival in Winnipeg, Manitoba.

Commons, he flew straight to Winnipeg to announce it in person at the Congress of Ukrainian Canadians.

Many people wonder how Canada can be bilingual and multicultural at the same time. If Canada is truly multicultural, why are Ukrainian or Japanese not official languages along with French and English?

Trudeau answered that Canada's two official languages had nothing to do with the length of time that the English and the French had lived in the country. If that were the reason, then Canadians would also have to speak Cree, Inuktitut, Salish, and many other Aboriginal languages.

Trudeau said bilingualism was just realistic. French was an official language because more than 25 percent of Canada's population spoke French every day. If that many people spoke Ukrainian, Trudeau said, it too would be an official language.

## Official Multiculturalism

The Multiculturalism Act (1988) means that both federal and provincial governments must protect Canadian diversity. Governments help ethnic communities keep their cultural traditions. Governments also support schools that teach other languages, such as Japanese, Ukrainian, and Hebrew.

Canada was the first country in the world to adopt an official policy of multiculturalism. Other countries, such as Australia, the United Kingdom, and the Netherlands, have followed Canada's example.

Multiculturalism encourages Canadians to respect one another's differences. Cultural diversity is valued and respected instead of feared and rejected, as it had been in the past. Think about the head tax on Chinese immigrants, Japanese internment camps during World War II, or residential schools for Aboriginal peoples. These groups were not treated as

**Figure 12.20** Certain communities across Canada are traditional neighbourhoods for new immigrants. The different ethnic groups living in Toronto's Kensington market, above, give the neighbourhood its unique character.

equals by their own government. A policy of multiculturalism requires that such prejudices be eliminated. Since the Multiculturalism Act was put in place, the Canadian government has apologized to Aboriginal peoples, Japanese-Canadians, and Chinese-Canadians for the racism they faced in the past.

## Conclusion

As Canada celebrated its 100th birthday in 1967, Canadians faced many new challenges. It was clear that Canada was more than just a simple arrangement between English, French, and Aboriginal peoples. It was, more than ever, an immigrant society. The idea of a sovereign Quebec emerged. Aboriginal peoples worked to bring about a new relationship with Canada.

Multiculturalism, bilingualism, sovereignty, and federalism show how Canada has grown. Since World War II, it has become a unique nation, made up of diverse cultures.

# V Canada Today

**1**

By the time of its 100th birthday, Canadian culture was still influenced by the United States and Britain. Canada's birthday celebration, Expo 67, brought about a great change, as the country showed the world what it could do. Soon, the work of Canadian writers, artists, performers, and filmmakers reflected what it meant to be Canadian. At the same time, Canada's government sought to refine its laws to be fair for all people and regions of the country.

Today, a new constitution and the Charter of Rights and Freedoms aims to provide justice for all Canadian citizens. Today, Canadians can be part of the democratic process through their elected representatives, who are responsible to the Canadian people.

**2**

**3**

**4**

# In the Memory Box...

**1** The song "Canada," written by Bobby Gimby for Canada's centennial in 1967, was a huge hit in both English and French. A video of the song featured schoolchildren from across Canada singing, as they followed Gimby and his trumpet.

**2** In the 1968 election campaign, this poster for Conservative leader Robert Stanfield asked voters to "Turn on with the Tories."

**3** Canadian folksingers often sang about Canadian subjects: Ian and Sylvia sang about Alberta ranch life, Buffy Ste. Marie about her Aboriginal heritage. Rock musicians like Winnipeg's Guess Who were proud of their prairie roots. These early pioneers of Canada's music industry became famous around the world.

**4** The mace is a symbol of the Crown. It empowers the House of Commons to make the country's laws and must be present at all official government sessions. The use of the mace in Parliament dates back to 1792.

**5** Postcard from Expo '67 showing the Canada pavillion.

**6** In modern times, the Canadian magazine *Maclean's* has reported on important Canadian issues.

**7** This souvenir tray shows Expo '67 pavilions from Russia, France, Germany, Great Britain, the United States, and Canada.

**8** Painting on birchbark by Nehiyaw artist Jackson Beardy. Beardy (1944–1984) depicted traditional legends in his modern paintings.

# 13 What Makes Us Canadian?

**B**y the 1950s, Canada had fought in two world wars. It had signed the Statute of Westminster. It had been in a Confederation for almost 90 years. Canadians began to think of Canada as a nation in its own right, instead of a part of faraway Britain. However, Canada still flew the British flag above the House of Commons in Ottawa. Canadian children still sang "God Save the Queen" in school. All of Canada's governor generals had been born in Britain. The government still had to ask for Britain's permission to change its constitution.

American movies, music, television shows, and fast-food restaurants had moved into Canada. At the same time, talented and well-educated Canadians were moving to the United States looking for success. Was American culture threatening Canadian identity? Was it important to be different from the United States

### Emily Carr (1871–1945)

Artist Emily Carr was a painter In British Columbia in the 1920s and 1930s. She was one of the first artists to paint uniquely Canadian subjects. Carr was inspired by the natural landscape of the West Coast and by the art of Aboriginal peoples, especially the Haida. This painting, *Chill Day in June*, was done in 1939. It was a hard time for a single woman to make a living as an artist. Carr had to support herself by running a boarding house.

**Figure 13.1** *Chill Day in June*

### AS YOU READ, THINK ABOUT

- the qualities that define Canada as a country
- how the natural environment affects the way Canadians live
- how our government preserves and protects Canadian identity
- how national, regional, group, and personal identities define Canadians
- Aboriginal peoples' unique perspective on Canadian identity
- what you are learning and how it connects to your life

and Britain? If so, how *was* Canada different? These were the questions Canadians asked themselves after the Second World War.

In 1949, Prime Minister St. Laurent asked Vincent Massey, a former diplomat, to lead a Royal Commission. The Massey Commission,[1] as it became known, looked at Canadian culture, including movies, music, books, theatre, dance, and visual arts. The commission found that many Canadians did not support their own culture.

**Figure 13.2** Beethoven at centre ice

The commission also found that Canadian artists had a hard time making a living or showing their work. Canadian symphony orchestras did not get to play in concert halls, as they did in America and Europe. Instead, orchestras often played in hockey rinks. There was a gallery of Canadian art in Ottawa, but it was hidden behind the dinosaurs at the National Museum.

The Massey Commission suggested ways to develop culture in Canada. One idea was to create an organization that would give Canadian artists money. Then they could create books, plays, music, dance, and visual art. In 1957, the government set up the Canada Council of the Arts to do just that.

1 The full name was the Royal Commission on National Development in the Arts, Letters, and Science.

**Figure 13.3** Canada came out of the Second World War with a strong sense of nationhood. However, Canadians were still defined as British subjects. The Canadian Citizenship Act, which came into force January 1, 1947, made Canada's people Canadian citizens. Above, the first official Canadian citizenship ceremony was held at the Supreme Court building in Ottawa, January 3, 1947. These new citizens, from Poland, Switzerland, Russia, Rumania, and Scotland, among other places, would have the same rights and responsibilities as people born in Canada. Second from the right in the top row is Yousuf Karsh, an Armenian from Turkey, who was a renowned Canadian portrait photographer (see page 72).

# Canadians and Nature

Some people say Canada's true identity is found in nature. They say the landscape and climate make Canadians who they are. Canadians think of themselves as a northern, nature-loving people. Prime Minister Mackenzie King once said Canadians have more geography than history. After all, Canada is the second biggest country in the world. It has vast areas of land, yet few people.

## Living on the land

The natural environment has always influenced the ways Canadians live.

Aboriginal peoples have lived on the land for thousands of years. Their cultures have been shaped by the environment they lived in. Water provided transportation and **sustained** people and animals. Plants provided food and materials for such things as boats and shelter. Animals – like the salmon of British Columbia, the moose of the eastern Canada, and the seals of the north – also provided food, shelter, and clothing.

The land also influenced where new settlers chose to live. Some settled near rivers, which provided transportation and irrigation. Woodlands supplied materials for shelter. The Prairies held rich farmland.

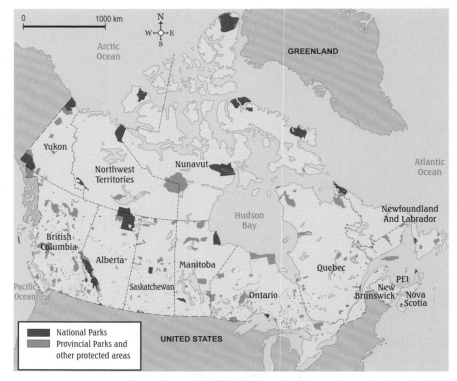

**Figure 13.5** *CANADA'S NATIONAL AND PROVINCIAL PARKS*. This map shows Canada's main national and provincial parks. By 1965, the Trans-Canada Highway was complete, and Canadians could explore new national and provincial parks throughout the country. There, they could camp, go bird watching, call moose, swim, and canoe.

Legend:
- National Parks
- Provincial Parks and other protected areas

**Figure 13.4** The importance of the environment can be seen in this sculpture, *Man with Spear*. Not only is it carved from local stone, it shows the Inuit way of living on the land.

Some places, like Halifax harbour, gave shelter from ocean storms.

The environment also influences how many Canadians support themselves. Farmers, hunters, fishermen, and miners all need the land to make a living.

## Brrrr!

Canadians take pride in being a tough, northern people who can survive in a cold climate. As the popular Québécois folk singer Gilles Vigneault sang:

*Mon pays*
*Ce n' est pas un pays*
*C' est l' hiver!*

Which means:

*My country*
*Is not a country*
*It's winter!*

**Figure 13.6** Bus Griffiths was a logger in British Columbia his entire life. When he was not logging, he created drawings and paintings showing the work he did. This painting, *High Rigger*, shows a lumberjack chopping the lower limbs off a tree before cutting it down.

## Protecting nature

Many new industries created wealth for Canada. Yet they also polluted the environment and threatened wildlife. When that started to happen, some Canadians wanted to protect nature for the future.

In 1971, a group of **conservationists** in Vancouver started an organization known as *Greenpeace*. Its members thought big businesses were more interested in making money than protecting the environment. They held protests to try to get industries and governments to stop killing whales, dumping poison in the oceans, and hunting seals. Some people criticized Greenpeace for their protests, while others supported them.

Today, Greenpeace works in 41 countries around the world. A famous Greenpeace slogan goes, "When the last tree is cut, when the last river is poisoned, and the last fish dead, we will discover that we can't eat money."

## The canoe

The canoe is a First Nations invention that has become a symbol of Canadian identity. For many Canadians, a canoe ride is a way to enjoy nature. When canoeing, people can imagine what life was like for First Nations, fur traders, and explorers.

The Kanienkehaka (Mohawk) poet Pauline Johnson became famous for her poem about canoeing called "The Song My Paddle Sings." In Quebec, a popular folktale tells about the ghosts of voyageurs returning home in a flying canoe. In the 1980s, a Canadian comedy troupe called *The Frantics* created a character called Mr. Canoehead. Mr. Canoehead had a large canoe where his head should be. He was always knocking things over.

**Figure 13.7** Mr. Canoehead.

## How Canadians See Themselves

Canadians have many myths about their identity. Like all myths, they are partly true and partly made-up. Canadians think of themselves as polite and friendly. Lester B. Pearson, Anne Murray, and Mr. Dress-up are examples of friendly and polite Canadians. Some Canadians are not always so polite. Don Cherry, the blustery former hockey coach and host of CBC's *Coach's Corner,* is an example. In 2004, Cherry said European and French-Canadian hockey players were not "tough guys" because they wore visors on their helmets. Many people were insulted by Cherry's remark.

Canadians also claim they are different from Americans. That is partly true. Canada has two official languages instead of one. Canada has a prime minister instead of a president. Canadians say "zed" instead of "zee." However, many Canadians love watching American television. They like to listen to American music and shop at American stores.

**Figure 13.8** Postcards from Expo '67

Canadians may find it hard to explain what makes them different. However, there have been some special moments in the 20th century that helped Canadian identity become stronger.

### Expo!

In 1967, Canadians celebrated their country's 100th birthday, or **centennial.** They celebrated in many ways. A centennial train travelled from sea to sea. The Order of Canada was founded. It is an award for people who make an outstanding contribution to the nation. The centennial project for Bowsman, Manitoba, was a new sewer system. That town celebrated Canada's 100th birthday by burning all its outhouses!

The most important celebration was Expo '67, a world's fair in Montreal. Expo '67 was a showcase of culture and technology from nations around the world. Expo was a high point for Canadian pride. For a long time, Canadians believed that Canadian culture did not measure up to countries like Britain, France, and the United States. Expo '67 gave Canada a chance to prove itself to the world. Some 50 million visitors from around the world came to Montreal. They saw what Canada had to offer.

## Paul Henderson's winning goal

To many Canadians, the 1972 world hockey series between Team Canada and the Soviet Union was one of the greatest sporting events of the 20th century. After seven games, each team had won three games and tied one. The last game, in Moscow on September 28, would decide the winner. Three thousand Canadians travelled thousands of kilometres to the Luzhniki Arena in the Soviet Union to cheer on their team. "*Da! Da!* Canada! *Nyet! Nyet!* Soviet!" they shouted. Back home, 12 million Canadians, more than half of Canada's population, watched the game on television in the middle of a Wednesday afternoon. The game was tied until the final seconds of the game. Suddenly, Paul Henderson scored a goal. Canada won the game – and the series.

Team Canada's goalie in 1972 was Ken Dryden. He said that the 1972 series was not just a game. It was meant to prove that Canadians were the world's best hockey players.

The 1972 series had a dark side, as well. Some people said the Canadian players wanted to win at any cost. It was said that in one game, a Canadian player deliberately broke the ankle of Valery Kharlamov, the star player of the Russian team. "This series was not

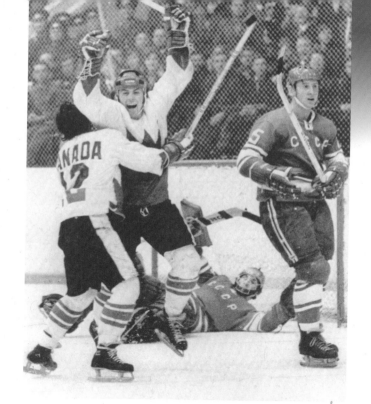

**Figure 13.9** Paul Henderson scores the winning goal in the Canada-Russia hockey series, September 28, 1972.

conceived in the spirit of brotherhood and understanding," said Dryden.

Nevertheless, the 1972 Canada-Russia hockey series was a high point for Canadian pride. It proved that hockey was, first and foremost, "Canada's game."

## Does anyone here speak Canadian?

Words and language can tell a lot about the people who use them. Here are a few examples of Canadian English. (They can be found in the *Canadian Oxford English Dictionary*.) Canadians are the only people in the world who use these words. What do they show about Canadian culture?

**Dépanneur** (from French. Also shortened to *dep*.) A convenience store

**Gitch** (Canadian slang. Also called *gonch* and *gotch*.) Underwear

**Jambuster** (Manitoba & Northwestern Ontario only) A jelly doughnut

**Kielbasa** (from Ukrainian) A garlic sausage

**Toque** (from French) A winter hat

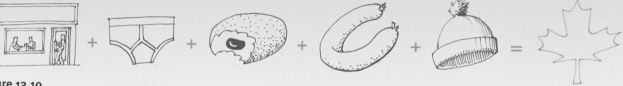

Figure 13.10

# Canada in the Media

In 1969, Prime Minister Pierre Trudeau visited Washington, D.C., in the United States. He was guest of honour at a National Press Club dinner. Trudeau described how Canadians felt being a neighbour to the powerful United States. "Living next to you is like sleeping with an elephant," Trudeau said. "No matter how friendly and even-tempered the beast … one is affected by every twitch and grunt."

Trudeau had found a funny way to make a serious point. American culture has a strong effect on Canada. Americans express their culture through media (movies, music, magazines, radio, and television). Since English is the main language in the United States, English Canada is a good market for American culture.

Canadian governments have tried to protect Canadian culture from being squashed by the American elephant. They encourage the creation of Canadian media. One all-Canadian agency is the Canadian Broadcasting Corporation (CBC). It has broadcast radio since 1933 and television since 1953.

In 1950, the Canadian government formed the National Film Board of Canada (NFB). Its job is to

**Figure 13.11** Canadian filmmakers Deepa Mehta (1996); Claude Jutra (1977), and Donald Brittain (on location in Sicily, 1962).

## Children's television in Canada

Did you know that Canada has been one of the largest creators of children's television in the world?

The CBC has created many classic children's shows. *The Friendly Giant* (1958–1985), starred Bob Homme as a giant named Friendly. He played songs on the recorder alongside a giraffe and a rooster (see right). *Mr. Dressup* (1967–1996) would find costumes in his tickle trunk. He was friends with a boy named Casey and a dog named Finnegan.

Many early television shows spread Canadian culture. In the 1960s, for example, Hélène Baillargeon and a mouse named Suzie taught anglophone children how to speak French. Her show was called *Chez Hélène* (1959–1973).

**Figure 13.12** The Friendly Giant

create films that "interpret Canada to Canadians and other nations." The NFB produces unique films that reflect different Canadian viewpoints. These come from filmmakers such as Montreal animator Norman McLaren, Abenaki documentary maker Alanis Obomsawin, Ontario's Donald Brittain, and Western Canada's Roman Kroitor. (He invented the IMAX film format). In Quebec, the NFB became important in the 1960s and 1970s for expressing Quebec culture. Today, Quebec has one of the richest film cultures in the world. Nearly all of the movies in English-Canadian movie theatres, however, come from the United States.

The Canadian government also has laws that limit the amount of American media Canadians hear or see. It makes sure to reserve space for Canadian media. Canadian radio was full of mostly American music until 1971. That year, the Canadian Radio and Television Commission (CRTC) brought in Canadian content requirements (CanCon). Since then, 30 percent of the music that radio stations play between 6:00 AM and midnight has to be Canadian.

Some people do not believe the government should control the media. Other people think CanCon is a good idea. They say it gives Canadian performers a chance to be heard by Canadian audiences. That way, they can compete with American media.

When Canadians began hearing their own musicians on the radio, it set off a homegrown music industry. Canadians became fans. Canadian recording studios sprang up. Canadian musicians no longer had to move to the United States to record their music. In 1964, the Juno Awards for Canadian recorded music were founded. By the mid-1990s, the Canadian music industry was doing very well. It had close to 200 music labels and many well-known Canadian musicians.

## I feel good! Pour moi ça va!

In the mid-1960s, francophones did not have laws to protect their language as they do today. They had to find ways to overcome American cultural influence.

The Quebec rock band Les Beethovens loved American-style rhythm and blues. In 1966, they became famous in Quebec for their French translation of James Brown's hit song, "I Got You" (see below). Lead singer Pierre Perpall sang and danced, imitating Brown.

**I Got You!**

*Whoa! I feel good!*
*I knew that I would now.*
*I feel good! I knew that I would now!*
*So good! So good! I got you!*
*HEY!*

**Pour Moi Ça Va**

*Pour moi ça va. Depuis que tu es là.*
*Pour moi ça va. Depuis que tu es là.*
*Ça va! Ça va! Je suis amoureux!*
*HÉ!*

**Figure 13.13** Pierre Perpall (right) with James Brown (left), 1968.

# Many Different Identities

In Canada, some people think that their ethnic or cultural identity is more important than their Canadian identity. They call themselves French-Canadians, Hungarian-Canadians, or Japanese-Canadians. Other people think Canadian identity should come first.

Prime Minister John Diefenbaker thought this way. He did not like people calling him a German-Canadian. He wanted everyone to be simply Canadians. He thought people should be unconnected to the countries of their ancestors.

Diefenbaker wanted a *civic identity* for Canada. That means identity is not based on the languages people speak or where their families come from, but on the citizenship everyone shares – Canadian. Diefenbaker believed Canadians should concentrate on what they shared rather than on what made them different. For Diefenbaker, that was good enough.

However, Canada is also made up of many different groups. Group identities are important to people. Many Quebeckers, for example, think of themselves as Quebeckers first and Canadians second. Some Newfoundlanders, Albertans, and First Nations people feel the same way. Diefenbaker would say that this kind of thinking divides people. Others say that strong group identities make it easier for people to live together.

## Understanding Quebec nationalism

Maka Kotto was born in Cameroon, Africa. When he was a young man, he moved to France. As an actor in Paris, Kotto used theatre to speak out against racism and discrimination. In the 1980s, he visited Quebec. He liked the province so much that he decided to stay. In

**Figure 13.14** Nationalist Quebec politician Maka Kotto.

## Joe Clark (1939–) PM

Joe Clark was Canada's 16th prime minister. He led the Progressive Conservative Party from 1976 to 1983. He served a short term as prime minister from 1979 to 1980. Clark, from High River, Alberta, was popular among Western Canadians. He also learned French so he could talk to Quebeckers in their own language.

**Figure 13.15** Joe Clark

Joe Clark's political rival, Liberal leader Pierre Trudeau, believed Canada needed one national identity if it was going to stay together. Clark disagreed. He believed Canada's different regional identities made Canada stronger, not weaker.

"In an immense country," Clark argued, "you live on a local scale." To Clark, Quebeckers, Albertans, Aboriginal peoples, and Maritimers were all Canadians in their own different ways. He said Canada was a "community of communities."

2004, Maka Kotto became a Quebec politician. He believes that Quebec should separate from Canada and become its own country.

Many Quebeckers believe that Quebec is not just a province like the others, but its own nation. Not all Quebeckers believe, like Maka Kotto, that Quebec should be separate from Canada. It is, however, the only place in Canada where most people speak French. Quebeckers are proud of that. They believe that Quebec's culture makes it a unique nation. That belief is called **Quebec nationalism.**

Many Canadian prime ministers, including John A. Macdonald, Lester B. Pearson, and Brian Mulroney, thought of Quebec as a nation. In 2006, Stephen Harper became the first prime minister in Canadian history to officially state that Quebec is a nation within Canada.

Some people do not like the idea of Quebec nationalism. They say only French-Canadians are welcome in Quebec, and other citizens are left out.

Racism *does* exist in Quebec, just as it does elsewhere in Canada. However, most Quebec nationalists would say that Quebec welcomes all cultures. In Quebec today, there are francophone Quebeckers whose parents are Vietnamese, Moroccan, Jewish, Greek, and British. Someone like Maka Kotto shows us that not all Quebec nationalists are French-Canadian.

## "The West wants in!"

Like Quebec, Western Canada has its own regional identity. Western Canada includes the three Prairie provinces (Manitoba, Saskatchewan, and Alberta) and British Columbia. Feelings of Western-Canadian identity are very strong in Alberta. A few politicians there have said Alberta should separate from Canada. Mainly, however, the West wants a stronger voice within Canada, not a separate country.

In 1986, an Albertan named Preston Manning founded a political party for Western Canadians called the *Reform Party*. Manning entered politics to stop **Western alienation**. He thought that some politicians spent too much time on Quebec and Ontario. They did not pay enough attention to the needs of Western Canadians. The Reform Party wanted to end bilingualism and high taxes.

**Figure 13.16** Preston Manning, former leader of the western-based Reform Party.

It said the federal government had too much power. It also said the provinces should run more of their own business. The Reform Party's first slogan was "The West wants in!"

## Canada's new flag, 1965

For its first 98 years, Canada had no flag of its own. It was the British flag that flew above Canada's schoolyards, hockey rinks, and Parliament buildings.

When Lester B. Pearson became prime minister in 1963, he wanted a new, all-Canadian flag. French-Canadians, new Canadians, and young anglophones agreed. Many older people who had fought under the British flag in the world wars disagreed with Pearson.

The government asked people to send in their flag designs. More than 2000 designs were received. Yet no one could agree on the best one. In the end, Pearson himself chose the maple leaf flag Canada has today. It flew for the first time above the House of Commons in 1965.

**Figure 13.17** The Red Ensign, used officially from 1945–1965.

**Figure 13.18** Flag design by A.Y. Jackson, a member of the Group of Seven.

**Figure 13.19** Pearson's first design for the flag, which John Diefenbaker mocked as the "Pearson Pennant."

**Figure 13.20** Canada's flag, adopted in February 1965.

# Aboriginal Perspectives

Many Aboriginal people are famous in Canada and the world. The Anishinabe (Ojibwa) war hero Tommy Prince, the Inuit filmmaker Zacharias Kunuk, the Métis architect Douglas Cardinal, the Nehiyaw (Cree) playwright Tomson Highway, as well as Nehiyaw actor and politician Tina Keeper are all among Canada's cultural leaders. Aboriginal people know that doing well in mainstream North American society is not the only thing that is important. They also have important responsibilities to their cultures and identities.

## First Nations: What does it mean?

In 1975, the Dene people of the Northwest Territories made a statement to Canada and the world. The Dene people were a nation. In their Dene Declaration they wrote: "Our struggle is for the recognition of the Dene Nation by the Government of Canada and the peoples and governments of the world."

Canada has often been described as a partnership between two founding nations: the French and the English. Aboriginal peoples are also founding nations in Canada. When we talk of First Nations, we are saying they are the original inhabitants of Canada.

The term *First Nations* reflects the way Aboriginal people see themselves in Canadian history. The ancestors of First Nations, Métis, and Inuit people were here thousands of years before Canada became a nation. First Nations peoples think of themselves as partners in Confederation. By signing treaties, they agreed to share their land and their

**Figure 13.21** The Canadian Embassy in Washington, D.C., is home to *The Spirit of Haida Gwaii*, a massive bronze sculpture by Haida artist Bill Reid. The 13 mythical characters in the boat show the world of living things.

culture with European newcomers. They did not agree to hand it over or give it up.

## Aboriginal identity

The Indian Act (see p. 60) gave certain rights to people registered as status Indians. Under the act, the government is responsible only to people who have Indian status.

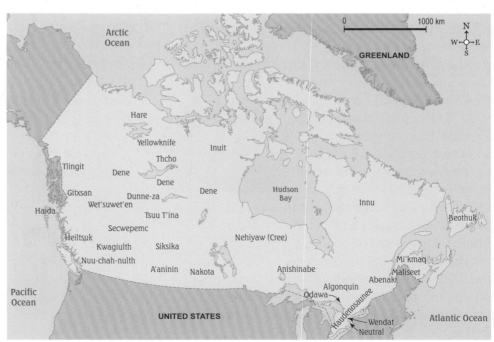

**Figure 13.22** *TRADITIONAL TERRITORIES OF ABORIGINAL PEOPLES AROUND 1600.* This map shows how Canada looked from a First Nations' point of view before contact with Europeans.

## Aboriginal people and the environment

*In every deliberation, we must consider the impact on the seventh generation.*
– From the Great Law of the Iroquois

Many Aboriginal people are concerned about how nature has been changed by industry and modern life in the past 150 years. The law of the seventh generation, from the Great Law of the Iroquois, expressed their commitment to a healthy earth. That law says that, when making decisions about the natural world, people must think about how those actions will affect people seven generations from now (or in about 175 years).

For thousands of years, Aboriginal peoples have lived by certain beliefs and values. Many believe that

- everything in the natural world is sacred

- nature will provide all that a person needs

- a person must live in harmony with nature, not control it

- people must never take more than they need

- all living things are connected

Many Aboriginal people have worked to make sure that the earth's resources are not used up. Billy Day, an Inuk elder from Inuvialuit, Northwest Territories, works to protect northern wildlife. He has studied how pollution affects sea animals that supply the Inuit with food. He has also worked on land claims to ensure that Inuit people control how their land is used.

Mary Thomas, a Secwepemc [*suh-WEP-muh*] elder, has worked for decades protecting the salmon rivers near her central British Columbia community. She educates young people in the importance of looking after the environment according to First Nations traditions.

People with Indian status can live on reserves. They can claim ancestral land. They have treaty benefits such as hunting and fishing rights. Status is based on a person's First Nations ancestry.

First Nations identity is also determined by culture. Sometimes, First Nations have adopted people from other ethnic groups into their communities. For example, Henry Mills, an African-American man, married a woman from the Kainai (Blood) Nation of southern Alberta in the 1800s. Mills could not get status, but he adopted Kainai culture. He and his children were accepted as members of the Kainai nation.

The Royal Commission on Aboriginal Peoples (1996) said that First Nations are not racial groups. Rather, they are cultural groups that often include people of different ethnic backgrounds.

Many Aboriginal people do not agree with laws that try to tell them who they are. "Why is the government concerned about defining who is an Indian and who is not?" asked author Thomas King. "There's not an Italian Act that defines who is and who is not Italian. Or a Russian Act. Or a Greek Act." King, of Cherokee, Greek, and German background, says that Aboriginal people, not the federal government, should decide who they are.

## Conclusion

Over the years, Canadians have looked at Canadian identity in different ways. Some believe that everyone should share a common identity. Others believe Canada is richer for having many different cultures.

To explain what makes us Canadian is not easy. However Canadians have come up with many ways of doing so. The government introduced bilingualism and multiculturalism. It promotes Canadian content in the media. Canadians express their identity through art, music, literature, film – and hockey.

# 14 Toward a Fair and Just Society

What is a *right*? A right is something that a person is allowed to do or have. People are born with certain rights. Other rights are given by the law.

Here are some rights that people in Canada have:

- **Human rights** are the rights that all people have because they are human beings. These rights belong to every person in the world. They include freedom of speech, the right to practise the religion of one's choice, the right to be treated equally before the law, and even the right to go to school.
- **Civil rights** are the rights given to people because they are citizens of a country, such as the right to hold public office. Someone who is not a citizen of Canada, for example, does not have the right to run in an election. Some civil rights are granted by age, such as the right to vote in elections at age 18. Civil rights are often written into a country's constitution.
- **Collective rights** are sometimes called *group rights*. Human and civil rights in Canada

**Figure 14.1** Even though women held the same jobs as men, they were often paid less. In the 1960s, these women marched for equal pay.

protect individuals. Group rights protect whole groups of people. The right of Franco-Manitobans to send their children to French-language schools is a collective right.

Rights come with responsibilities. For example, freedom of speech is a right. That means people can say what they think in public – within limits. With the right to speak freely should come the responsibility to be fair and not to hurt other people with what is said.

---

**AS YOU READ, THINK ABOUT**

- why people in the world became concerned with rights after World War II
- the different rights that people are entitled to as human beings, as members of distinct cultures, and as citizens
- how the Charter of Rights and Freedoms protects Canadians
- how Canadians have had to fight for equality in the past and present

# The Concern for Rights

After World War II, the world's nations became more concerned about human rights than ever. The war and the Holocaust forced people everywhere to face the cruel and unfair ways in which humans often treated each other. People thought there should be laws made to protect each human being. These laws would help to make sure everyone was treated fairly.

Around the world, people began demanding their rights. In the 1950s and 1960s, African-Americans such as Rosa Parks and Martin Luther King Jr. led the struggle for equal civil rights in the United States. Algerians in North Africa wanted to be an independent nation, free from France. As they had earlier in the century, **feminists** began to speak out for equal rights for women.

As you read in chapter 10, the United Nations (UN) was formed to encourage peace and human rights. Its Universal Declaration of Human Rights (see p. 135) was translated from English into 250 different languages. It states that all human beings are equal, and that every person in the world has the right to be free and safe from harm. It also states that human beings cannot be discriminated against because of their nationality, gender, religion, race, or culture.

## Canada and Human Rights

After Canada signed the Universal Declaration of Human Rights in 1948, Canadians started to look at injustices in their own country. They found many problems.

For example, Jehovah's Witnesses in Quebec were not allowed to practise their religion. In 1949, Jews and African-Canadians were not allowed to buy land at Beach O'Pines, Ontario.

**Figure 14.2** People demonstrate for civil rights in Montreal, March 1965.

In 1946, an African-Canadian woman named Viola Desmond was arrested in a Nova Scotia movie theatre for sitting in the downstairs seats instead of in the balcony. If a person had dark skin, he or she *had* to sit in the balcony. In 1963, Donald Gordon of the Canadian National Railway (CNR) said that he would never hire French-Canadians for the top jobs at the CNR. He said English Canadians were better employees.

Canada also had to face how it treated Aboriginal peoples. In 1948, people with Indian status were not able to do things that other people could. They could not vote, wear traditional **regalia**, or attend the Calgary Stampede, among other things.

These are only a few of the ways Canadians have treated each other unfairly. How could Canada sign the Universal Declaration of Human Rights without doing something about human rights problems in its own country?

# The Bill of Rights, 1960

Prime Minister John Diefenbaker knew what it was like to face discrimination. People made fun of his name all his life. They did not treat him like a like a true Canadian. When he became prime minister in 1957, Diefenbaker wanted to do something to protect the human rights of Canadians.

In 1960, Diefenbaker introduced the Canadian Bill of Rights. It was like the United Nations' Declaration, but it was for the people of Canada. The bill showed that the Canadian government would stand up for the human rights of *all* Canadians.

Some people worried that the Bill of Rights was not a strong enough law. It was just a **statute.** This meant governments that came after Diefenbaker's could change the Bill of Rights. Other Canadian laws could replace it. The Bill of Rights would only work if it became part of the highest law in the land. That law is a country's constitution.

**Figure 14.3** Prime Minister Diefenbaker shows off Canada's new Bill of Rights in 1960.

## The Bill of Rights could not protect everybody

In the 1960s, Jeannette Lavell, a young Anishinabe (Ojibwa) woman from Manitoulin Island, Ontario, married a man who did not belong to a First Nation. Soon after their wedding, the Department of Indian Affairs took away Lavell's Indian status. The Indian Act stated that a First Nations woman lost her status if she married a man who was not First Nations. So did her children.

**Figure 14.4** Jeanette Lavell

The same law did not apply First Nations men. If a First Nations man married a Norwegian woman, for example, he kept his status. Their children would also be status Indians. The Department of Indian Affairs would view the Norwegian woman as status Indian. Why did First Nations women not have the same rights as First Nations men?

Jeannette Lavell knew this law discriminated against her just because she was a woman. The law went back to a time when women were thought of as their husbands' property. Lavell also knew that the Bill of Rights was supposed to protect her against **gender discrimination**. She took her case to the Supreme Court of Canada. She demanded her status back. The judges, however, ruled that the Bill of Rights was not as strong a law as the Indian Act.

First Nations women who married men who did not have Indian status continued to lose their status until 1985. Although the Bill of Rights might have been created so that Canadians would treat each other fairly, it could not always protect people from discrimination.

# The Charter of Rights and Freedoms

When Pierre Trudeau became prime minister, he realized that Diefenbaker's Bill of Rights did not go far enough. Trudeau wanted a charter of rights that was part of Canada's constitution. That way, Canadians' rights could not easily be changed or taken away in the future.

There was a problem, though. Canadian politicians had never been able to agree on a way to change Canada's constitution, the British North America Act of 1867 (see p. 18). It could only be changed by the British Parliament in London. That meant that Canada still was not completely independent from Britain. Trudeau would have to bring the constitution under Canadian control, or **patriate** it. That would not be an easy job.

Mackenzie King tried to patriate the constitution in 1927. R.B. Bennett tried again in 1931. St. Laurent tried in 1950. So did Diefenbaker in 1960, Pearson in 1964, and Trudeau in 1971. They all failed, because no prime minister could convince the provinces to agree on what should be in the new constitution. The provinces knew the constitution could not be easily changed. They would not agree to a new one unless the provinces' powers were respected.

Trudeau tried to change the constitution again in 1980. By then, some provinces wanted new powers. Newfoundland wanted to control its fishery. Alberta wanted control over its oil. Quebec wanted control over its culture and language. Prime Minister Trudeau, on the other hand, worried Canada would fall apart if the provinces had too much power. He believed Canada must have a strong federal government.

Trudeau decided to push ahead with changes to the constitution, even if all the provinces didn't agree with him. However, the Supreme Court of Canada said that Trudeau had to get most of the provinces to agree. Finally, Trudeau and nine provincial premiers signed the Constitution Act and the Charter of Rights and Freedoms. Premier Lévesque of Quebec did not sign, however. He believed that the old British North America Act was better for Quebec than the proposed new constitution. He thought the new law took powers away from Quebec.

The Constitution Act became law on April 17, 1982. All Canadians now had rights that could not be taken away. The new Charter of Rights and Freedoms was put at the beginning of the Constitution.

**Figure 14.5** Queen Elizabeth II signs Canada's Constitution Act in Ottawa on April 17, 1982. Prime Minister Pierre Trudeau looks on.

# Knowing Your Rights

Has anybody ever said to you, "Hey, it's a free country. I can do what I want!" Have you ever wondered what *free country* means? The Charter of Rights and Freedoms helps to answer this question. The Charter guarantees Canadians many rights, including basic human rights, the right to vote, and the right to go to school in English or French.

Many rights in the Charter and Constitution existed in Canada before 1982. Now, however, they were permanent rights. Below are some of the rights that Canadians have.

## Fundamental freedoms

Fundamental freedoms are the rights that all Canadians have to act, speak, and think freely, without interference from the government. They include

- freedom to follow a religion of one's choice
- freedom to think, believe in, and express one's own opinions
- freedom of the press and other media to report the news
- freedom of peaceful assembly
- freedom of association

Very few countries in the world enjoy such freedoms as these. In some countries, it is against the law to speak against the government (no matter how peacefully) or to organize a protest. Many governments will not let journalists report news that might make the government look bad.

Canadians did not always have these freedoms. They were hard won.

## Equality rights

This part of the Charter states all Canadians are equal. Canadians have the right to be treated equally, no matter their race, national or ethnic origin, religion, gender, age, or mental or physical disability. These rights have also solved problems that some Canadians faced before 1982.

In 1982, the Charter of Rights and Freedoms *was* strong enough to protect Jeannette Lavell (see p. 178). It promised that no Canadian could be discriminated against because of his or her gender. As a result, the part of the Indian Act that took away Jeannette Lavell's status was now made illegal. By 1985, many thousands of First Nations women who had lost their status finally got it back.

## Language rights

Some laws in the Charter have to do with Canada's two official languages. Prime Minister Trudeau hoped that language rights would end the long-standing conflicts between anglophones and francophones. The Charter gives every Canadian the right to communicate with the federal government and courts in either English or French.

Trudeau wanted to protect both languages across Canada. In the past, provincial governments often took language rights away from francophone minorities. Sometimes, they just ignored those rights. Georges Forest had to fight for the French language in Manitoba. So did Acadians in New Brunswick. The new Charter said that no provincial government could take away these rights.

The Charter also includes the right to go to school in French or English. It states that as long as there are enough francophones in a community, they have the right to send their children to French schools. Anglophones in Quebec have the same right to send their children to English schools.

## Aboriginal rights

Aboriginal rights are a collective right protected in the Constitution. These are rights that Aboriginal peoples have because of their traditional use of the land. They include the right to practise Aboriginal ceremonies. Another is the right to hunt and fish in traditional lands. That is because Aboriginal peoples have lived in these places for thousands of years, long before Canada ever became a country.

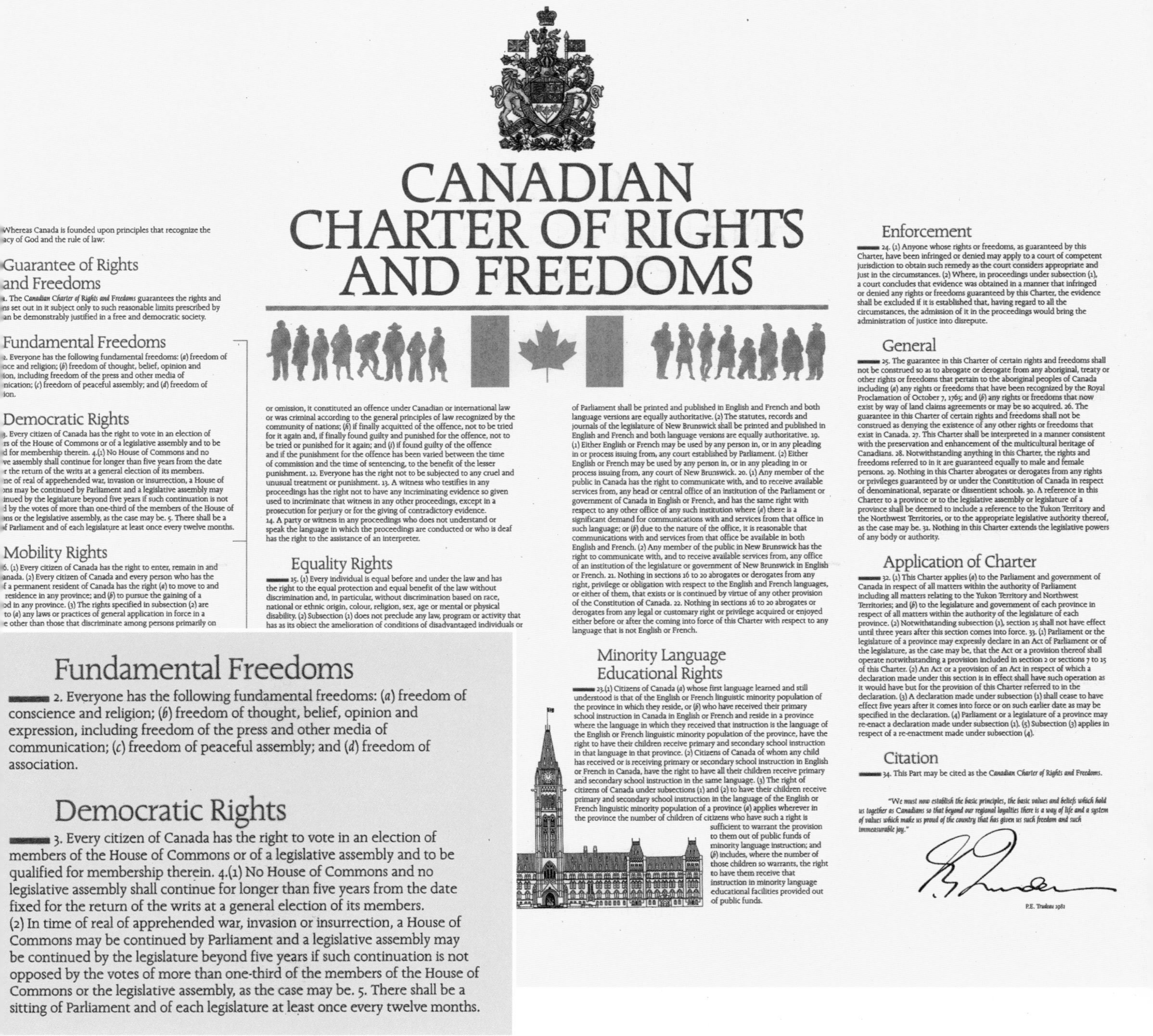

# CANADIAN CHARTER OF RIGHTS AND FREEDOMS

Whereas Canada is founded upon principles that recognize the supremacy of God and the rule of law:

## Guarantee of Rights and Freedoms

1. The *Canadian Charter of Rights and Freedoms* guarantees the rights and freedoms set out in it subject only to such reasonable limits prescribed by law as can be demonstrably justified in a free and democratic society.

## Fundamental Freedoms

2. Everyone has the following fundamental freedoms: (*a*) freedom of conscience and religion; (*b*) freedom of thought, belief, opinion and expression, including freedom of the press and other media of communication; (*c*) freedom of peaceful assembly; and (*d*) freedom of association.

## Democratic Rights

3. Every citizen of Canada has the right to vote in an election of members of the House of Commons or of a legislative assembly and to be qualified for membership therein. 4.(1) No House of Commons and no legislative assembly shall continue for longer than five years from the date fixed for the return of the writs at a general election of its members. (2) In time of real of apprehended war, invasion or insurrection, a House of Commons may be continued by Parliament and a legislative assembly may be continued by the legislature beyond five years if such continuation is not opposed by the votes of more than one-third of the members of the House of Commons or the legislative assembly, as the case may be. 5. There shall be a sitting of Parliament and of each legislature at least once every twelve months.

## Mobility Rights

6. (1) Every citizen of Canada has the right to enter, remain in and leave Canada. (2) Every citizen of Canada and every person who has the status of a permanent resident of Canada has the right (*a*) to move to and take up residence in any province; and (*b*) to pursue the gaining of a livelihood in any province. (3) The rights specified in subsection (2) are subject to (*a*) any laws or practices of general application in force in a province other than those that discriminate among persons primarily on

or omission, it constituted an offence under Canadian or international law or was criminal according to the general principles of law recognized by the community of nations; (*b*) if finally acquitted of the offence, not to be tried for it again and, if finally found guilty and punished for the offence, not to be tried or punished for it again; and (*j*) if found guilty of the offence and if the punishment for the offence has been varied between the time of commission and the time of sentencing, to the benefit of the lesser punishment. 12. Everyone has the right not to be subjected to any cruel and unusual treatment or punishment. 13. A witness who testifies in any proceedings has the right not to have any incriminating evidence so given used to incriminate that witness in any other proceedings, except in a prosecution for perjury or for the giving of contradictory evidence. 14. A party or witness in any proceedings who does not understand or speak the language in which the proceedings are conducted or who is deaf has the right to the assistance of an interpreter.

### Equality Rights

15. (1) Every individual is equal before and under the law and has the right to the equal protection and equal benefit of the law without discrimination and, in particular, without discrimination based on race, national or ethnic origin, colour, religion, sex, age or mental or physical disability. (2) Subsection (1) does not preclude any law, program or activity that has as its object the amelioration of conditions of disadvantaged individuals or

of Parliament shall be printed and published in English and French and both language versions are equally authoritative. (2) The statutes, records and journals of the legislature of New Brunswick shall be printed and published in English and French and both language versions are equally authoritative. 19. (1) Either English or French may be used by any person in, or in any pleading in or process issuing from, any court established by Parliament. (2) Either English or French may be used by any person in, or in any pleading in or process issuing from, any court of New Brunswick. 20. (1) Any member of the public in Canada has the right to communicate with, and to receive available services from, any head or central office of an institution of the Parliament or government of Canada in English or French, and has the same right with respect to any other office of any such institution where (*a*) there is a significant demand for communications with and services from that office in such language; or (*b*) due to the nature of the office, it is reasonable that communications with and services from that office be available in both English and French. (2) Any member of the public in New Brunswick has the right to communicate with, and to receive available services from, any office of an institution of the legislature or government of New Brunswick in English or French. 21. Nothing in sections 16 to 20 abrogates or derogates from any right, privilege or obligation with respect to the English and French languages, or either of them, that exists or is continued by virtue of any other provision of the Constitution of Canada. 22. Nothing in sections 16 to 20 abrogates or derogates from any legal or customary right or privilege acquired or enjoyed either before or after the coming into force of this Charter with respect to any language that is not English or French.

### Minority Language Educational Rights

23.(1) Citizens of Canada (*a*) whose first language learned and still understood is that of the English or French linguistic minority population of the province in which they reside, or (*b*) who have received their primary school instruction in Canada in English or French and reside in a province where the language in which they received that instruction is the language of the English or French linguistic minority population of the province, have the right to have their children receive primary and secondary school instruction in that language in that province. (2) Citizens of Canada of whom any child has received or is receiving primary or secondary school instruction in English or French in Canada, have the right to have all their children receive primary and secondary school instruction in the same language. (3) The right of citizens of Canada under subsections (1) and (2) to have their children receive primary and secondary school instruction in the language of the English or French linguistic minority population of a province (*a*) applies wherever in the province the number of children of citizens who have such a right is sufficient to warrant the provision to them out of public funds of minority language instruction; and (*b*) includes, where the number of those children so warrants, the right to have them receive that instruction in minority language educational facilities provided out of public funds.

## Enforcement

24. (1) Anyone whose rights or freedoms, as guaranteed by this Charter, have been infringed or denied may apply to a court of competent jurisdiction to obtain such remedy as the court considers appropriate and just in the circumstances. (2) Where, in proceedings under subsection (1), a court concludes that evidence was obtained in a manner that infringed or denied any rights or freedoms guaranteed by this Charter, the evidence shall be excluded if it is established that, having regard to all the circumstances, the admission of it in the proceedings would bring the administration of justice into disrepute.

## General

25. The guarantee in this Charter of certain rights and freedoms shall not be construed so as to abrogate or derogate from any aboriginal, treaty or other rights or freedoms that pertain to the aboriginal peoples of Canada including (*a*) any rights or freedoms that have been recognized by the Royal Proclamation of October 7, 1763; and (*b*) any rights or freedoms that now exist by way of land claims agreements or may be so acquired. 26. The guarantee in this Charter of certain rights and freedoms shall not be construed as denying the existence of any other rights or freedoms that exist in Canada. 27. This Charter shall be interpreted in a manner consistent with the preservation and enhancement of the multicultural heritage of Canadians. 28. Notwithstanding anything in this Charter, the rights and freedoms referred to in it are guaranteed equally to male and female persons. 29. Nothing in this Charter abrogates or derogates from any rights or privileges guaranteed by or under the Constitution of Canada in respect of denominational, separate or dissentient schools. 30. A reference in this Charter to a province or to the legislative assembly or legislature of a province shall be deemed to include a reference to the Yukon Territory and the Northwest Territories, or to the appropriate legislative authority thereof, as the case may be. 31. Nothing in this Charter extends the legislative powers of any body or authority.

## Application of Charter

32. (1) This Charter applies (*a*) to the Parliament and government of Canada in respect of all matters within the authority of Parliament including all matters relating to the Yukon Territory and Northwest Territories; and (*b*) to the legislature and government of each province in respect of all matters within the authority of the legislature of each province. (2) Notwithstanding subsection (1), section 15 shall not have effect until three years after this section comes into force. 33. (1) Parliament or the legislature of a province may expressly declare in an Act of Parliament or of the legislature, as the case may be, that the Act or a provision thereof shall operate notwithstanding a provision included in section 2 or sections 7 to 15 of this Charter. (2) An Act or a provision of an Act in respect of which a declaration made under this section is in effect shall have such operation as it would have but for the provision of this Charter referred to in the declaration. (3) A declaration made under subsection (1) shall cease to have effect five years after it comes into force or on such earlier date as may be specified in the declaration. (4) Parliament or a legislature of a province may re-enact a declaration made under subsection (1). (5) Subsection (3) applies in respect of a re-enactment made under subsection (4).

## Citation

34. This Part may be cited as the *Canadian Charter of Rights and Freedoms*.

"We must now establish the basic principles, the basic values and beliefs which hold us together as Canadians so that beyond our regional loyalties there is a way of life and a system of values which make us proud of the country that has given us such freedom and such immeasurable joy."

P.E. Trudeau 1982

---

## Fundamental Freedoms

2. Everyone has the following fundamental freedoms: (*a*) freedom of conscience and religion; (*b*) freedom of thought, belief, opinion and expression, including freedom of the press and other media of communication; (*c*) freedom of peaceful assembly; and (*d*) freedom of association.

## Democratic Rights

3. Every citizen of Canada has the right to vote in an election of members of the House of Commons or of a legislative assembly and to be qualified for membership therein. 4.(1) No House of Commons and no legislative assembly shall continue for longer than five years from the date fixed for the return of the writs at a general election of its members. (2) In time of real of apprehended war, invasion or insurrection, a House of Commons may be continued by Parliament and a legislative assembly may be continued by the legislature beyond five years if such continuation is not opposed by the votes of more than one-third of the members of the House of Commons or the legislative assembly, as the case may be. 5. There shall be a sitting of Parliament and of each legislature at least once every twelve months.

**Figure 14.6** The 34 sections of Canada's Charter of Rights and Freedoms form the first part of the Constitution Act of 1982. Inset, left, are sections 2 and 3 of the Charter.

Treaty rights are a form of Aboriginal rights. These are the rights promised to First Nations by the treaties made with the Canadian government (see p. 50), or earlier, with the British government.

When Prime Minister Trudeau met with the provinces to discuss the new constitution in 1980, Aboriginal leaders were not consulted. The leaders of Aboriginal groups insisted, however, that the rights of Aboriginal peoples in Canada be respected. They won further protections for their rights.

# Mainstream and Minorities

The Charter of Rights and Freedoms is meant to make Canada a fair and just society for all its citizens, whatever their differences. However, racism still exists, censorship can still occur, and people still treat each other unfairly. As a result, citizens still have to insist on the rights they have under the Charter.

Canada is a democracy. In any democracy, governments make decisions based on what most people want. Yet what is to stop a majority from trampling on the will of the minority? The Charter is intended to protect the rights of minorities. No anglo-Canadian province, for example, can take away the Charter rights of a francophone minority.

## The Meech Lake Accord, 1990

Brian Mulroney became prime minister in 1984. He worried that Quebec had never agreed to sign the 1982 Constitution. Mulroney thought that Canada could not work if one province felt left out. He promised to change the Constitution so that Quebeckers would be willing to sign it.

Robert Bourassa, the premier of Quebec, told Mulroney that he would sign the Constitution if it recognized Quebec as a *distinct society.* That meant Quebec would have special powers to protect its language and culture. Mulroney agreed. This agreement became known as the *Meech Lake Accord*, because it was signed at Meech Lake in Quebec.

Canadians had different opinions about the Meech Lake Accord. Some agreed Quebec had different challenges than other provinces and needed different powers to deal with them. Other Canadians thought the Accord was a bad idea. They did not believe any province should get special treatment. Every province should have the same powers.

In the end, Elijah Harper, a First Nations politician from Manitoba, stopped the Meech Lake Accord from becoming law. Harper believed Aboriginal peoples had been ignored in the

**Figure 14.7**   Elijah Harper in the Manitoba Legislature voting against the Meech Lake Accord, June 19, 1990.

constitutional debates. He wanted to send a message that Aboriginal peoples' concerns were as important as those of Quebec. To become law, the Meech Lake Accord needed the vote of every member of the Manitoba legislature. Harper refused to vote for it, however.

The failure of the Meech Lake Accord showed how hard it is to run a country like Canada. It also showed how hard it is to support minority rights while treating everyone as equals.

The Canadian government tried to change the Constitution again with the *Charlottetown Accord* in 1992. This time, there was a referendum to decide on the changes. However, Canadians voted against the Charlottetown Accord by 54 percent.

## Brian Mulroney (1939–)

Brian Mulroney, Canada's 18th prime minister, was born in Baie-Comeau, a small lumber town in northern Quebec. His family was not wealthy. His father was an electrician in the town's paper mill. Young Brian had big dreams, though. Just like his hero, John Diefenbaker, Mulroney wanted to be prime minister when he grew up.

Mulroney joined the Progressive Conservative party when he was still a teenager. As a law student at l'Université Laval in the 1960s, he became renowned for bringing Prime Minister Diefenbaker to his law class.

The Progressive Conservatives chose Mulroney as their new leader in 1983. He was outgoing and confident and spoke both French and English very well. Before Mulroney, no Conservative leader had been bilingual. He was also able to convince different parts of the country to work together. In the 1984 election, Mulroney's Progressive Conservatives won more seats in Parliament than any other party in Canadian history. His popularity would not last, however.

Mulroney made some unpopular decisions as prime minister. He created the Goods and Services Tax (GST) in 1991. It added an additional seven-cent charge to every dollar Canadians spent. His government also helped bring about a free-trade agreement with the United States that many people did not like.

**Figure 14.8** Prime Minister Mulroney in the House of Commons in 1984

When Mulroney retired in 1993, he said, "I always tried to do what I thought would be right for Canada in the long term, not what would be politically popular in the short term." The prime ministers who came after Mulroney have supported many of his most unpopular decisions, including the GST and free trade.

Mulroney also passed laws to reduce pollution and acid rain. He worked to stop apartheid in South Africa.

# Conclusion

People around the world were awakened to new ideas of justice after World War II. Many devoted themselves to creating a fairer world. In Canada, this struggle was led by citizens concerned about discrimination and injustice. The federal government responded by changing the country's law to provide equality and justice for all its citizens. In the next chapter, you will learn how governments work to make laws for its people.

# 15 Our Government

Politicians in the Canadian government make many choices that affect Canadians. The government has the power to make laws, collect taxes, send soldiers to war, or work for peace.

Canada is a democracy. In a democracy, people elect politicians to represent them. That way, all citizens of voting age can play a part in choosing who will lead the country. In Canada, the people who are elected become members of Parliament (MPs).

Citizens have a say in government through their MPs. This does not mean that each time the government passes a new law it has to ask every Canadian for permission. It is up to the MPs to decide what is best. If Canadians do not like a government's decision, they can vote for a new government at election time.

In a democracy, citizens are free to speak out against their government. They can do this in many ways. They can protest outside the House of Commons. They can write letters to newspapers. They can say what they think on radio shows. They can draw political cartoons for newspapers. In a democracy, citizens have

**Figure 15.1** This university student in Toronto votes in the Ontario provincial election.

the right to make their opinions known to the people who represent them.

There are also rules that limit government power. The Charter of Rights and Freedoms says a federal election must be held at least every five years. That way, people have regular opportunities to judge their government. The right to a free vote is important in any democracy. By voting, a citizen can give power to a government or take it away.

## AS YOU READ, THINK ABOUT

- how democracy works in Canada
- the different levels of government, their responsibilities, and how they work
- the roles and responsibilities of our politicians
- what political parties are, and why we need them
- how we elect our representatives
- what you are learning and how it connects to your life

# A Federation

In chapter 1, you learned about *federalism*, which means that power is divided among different levels of government. A country that divides its powers in this way is called a *federation*. In a federation, the central government is called the *federal* or *national* government. The regional governments are often the governments of provinces and territories (as in Canada) or states (as in the United States and Australia). Canada has federal, provincial, and territorial governments. It also has Aboriginal governments and municipal governments for cities and towns.

The federal government in Ottawa controls matters important to all Canadians. Provincial and territorial governments control more local matters. Municipal and Aboriginal governments work within their own communities.

Sometimes, leaders of provincial governments have wanted more power from the federal government. Others have said that Canada needed a "strong, central government" to keep the country united. If the provinces had all the power, they argued, eventually people might see no reason to share the same country. Canada might then separate into smaller countries.

## Changes in democracy

As Canada and the world change, so does democracy. Remember that when Canada was formed in 1867, women could not vote. Neither could men, unless they were rich enough to own property. Asian Canadians could not become citizens until 1947. Status Indians could not vote until 1960.

Today, every Canadian who is 18 years old or older has the right to vote. As a result, they have a say in political decisions that affect them.

**Figure 15.2** This woman unrolls a 25-metre **petition** containing the names of thousands of Canadians who want the federal government to improve child-care programs. Petitions are one way that citizens can tell governments what they want them to do.

**Figure 15.3** In 1913, these women in Swan River, Manitoba, could not take part in Canadian democracy. Now all citizens over the age of 18 can vote to help decide who will represent them in Ottawa.

# The Federal Government

Canada is a *constitutional monarchy*. This means that the king or queen of Great Britain is its head of state. It is also a *parliamentary democracy*. This means that the prime minister is its head of government and a Parliament makes its laws.

The federal government is made up of three parts:

- **The legislative branch.** This branch creates laws. It includes both the House of Commons and the Senate.
- **The executive branch.** This is the main decision-making branch of the government. It includes the governor general, cabinet, prime minister, and government departments.
- **The judicial branch.** This branch applies the laws. It includes the courts and judges.

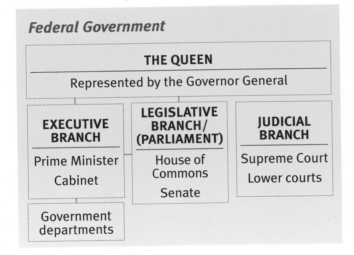

### Federal Government

| THE QUEEN | | |
|---|---|---|
| Represented by the Governor General | | |
| **EXECUTIVE BRANCH** | **LEGISLATIVE BRANCH/ (PARLIAMENT)** | **JUDICIAL BRANCH** |
| Prime Minister Cabinet | House of Commons Senate | Supreme Court Lower courts |
| Government departments | | |

# Parliament, the Legislative Branch

The word *Parliament* comes from the French word *parler,* which means "to speak." A Parliament that is made up of two parts is called *bicameral* [bye-KAM-er-el]. As you read in chapter 1, Canada's Parliament has two parts: the House of Commons and the Senate. The members of the House of Commons are elected by Canadian voters. The members of the Senate are chosen by the prime minister.

**Figure 15.4** In Canadian democracy, opposition parties challenge the government. They suggest improvements to laws. They provide different points of view. This picture shows John Diefenbaker when he was Opposition leader as he spoke against the government, jabbing his finger at the prime minister. A frustrated Mackenzie King once said to him, "You strike me in the heart every time you speak."

## House of Commons

The House of Commons (the *lower house*) is where members of Parliament (MPs) meet. MPs are elected by the citizens of Canada to represent them.

The political party that has the most MPs elected to the House of Commons forms the government. The leader of the party with most seats becomes the prime minister. MPs from other parties form the opposition. The party with the second-largest number of seats forms the official Opposition. Both sides have important roles in Parliament.

Members of Parliament make the country's laws. They also decide on important issues that come up.

## The Speaker of the House

The speaker of the House of Commons sits in the raised speaker's chair at one end of the chamber. He or she manages the debates and keeps order in the House. The speaker must be fair to all members. He or she must give everybody a chance to speak. MPs choose the speaker after an election.

**Figure 15.5**
Speaker of the House in 2007, Honourable Peter Milliken

## Senate

The Senate is the second (or *upper*) house of Parliament. Members of the Senate are called *senators*. They are chosen by the prime minister and appointed by the governor general. Senators represent all parts of the country. They come from different backgrounds and have different ideas. Some have served as MPs in the House of Commons or in their provincial

**Figure 15.6**
Senator Sharon Carstairs is a teacher, politician, and writer. She represents Manitoba in the Senate.

**Figure 15.7** Inside the House of Commons. The speaker sits in the centre, at the end of the room. The government's MPs sit to the left. Opposition members are on the right. Cabinet ministers and party leaders sit in the front seats. Members of Parliament who are not members of the cabinet or spokespeople for the Opposition are known as *backbenchers*.

governments. Others may come from the media, business, or sports communities. They are often chosen because they have helped their communities or their country.

When the government introduces a **bill**, senators review it to make sure it is acceptable to all the different regions and groups in Canada. The Senate has to approve any bills before they become laws.

## How Parliament creates a law

1. An important issue is identified. For example, a species of fish is becoming extinct from overfishing.

2. A member of Parliament writes a bill that will solve the problem. For example, the MP may suggest that there be no more fishing of that species. The MP presents the bill to Parliament. This is called the *first reading*.

3. Members of Parliament debate the bill. If the governing party introduces the bill, its members usually present reasons to support it. Members of the opposition may argue against the bill. This discussion is called the *second reading*.

4. The bill then goes to a committee of 7 to 15 MPs who study the issue further. They may hire experts to provide important information. They may suggest changes to the bill.

5. The bill then goes through a *third reading*. All MPs then vote on it.

6. If the bill gets enough votes to be passed, it goes to the Senate.

7. The bill then goes through three readings in the Senate.

8. Once the bill is passed by both the House of Commons and the Senate, it goes to the governor general for **royal assent**, and the bill becomes a law.

# The Executive Branch

The executive branch of the government puts Canada's laws into action. The executive branch is made up of the governor general (who represents the monarch), the prime minister, the cabinet, and the **administration**.

## Monarch

The monarch is Canada's head of state. Canada is one of many countries in the Commonwealth who have chosen to keep the monarchy as part of its form of government. Because Canada is a former British colony, we share the same monarch as the British.

**Figure 15.8** Queen Elizabeth II in 2007. She became queen in 1952. She is officially known as the Queen of Canada. She is also the queen of other Commonwealth countries.

## Governor general

The governor general acts for the monarch in Canada. The monarch appoints the new governor general based on the prime minister's advice. Like the monarch, the governor general does not make government decisions. He or she has limited powers. In very special cases, however, he or she can refuse to **dissolve Parliament** or to choose a prime minister. The governor general

- has the responsibility to make sure there is always a government in place
- has the power to dissolve Parliament and call an election when the prime minister asks
- swears in a newly elected prime minister
- promotes Canadian culture, and any other causes he or she chooses to take up
- rewards Canadians for their contributions to Canada with honours such as the Governor General's Awards and the Order of Canada.

## Prime minister

The prime minister is leader of the political party that wins the most seats in an election. He or she is the head of government. The prime minister

- leads the federal government, which proposes new laws for the country
- decides with his or her cabinet how to spend the tax money that Canadians pay
- speaks for Canada in other countries
- appoints Supreme Court judges and ambassadors to countries around the world, and suggests appointments to the Senate

**Figure 15.9** Governor general's coat of arms (left); Governor General Michäelle Jean in 2007

**Figure 15.10** Canada's prime minister in 2007, Stephen Harper, in the House of Commons

## Canada's official residences

Many countries have official homes for their political leaders. These include the White House in the United States and 10 Downing Street in Great Britain. Canada has several official homes.

The governor general has two homes. One is Rideau Hall in Ottawa. The other is inside the historic Citadel of Quebec City.

Since 1949, Canada's prime minister has lived in Ottawa at 24 Sussex Drive. The prime minister also has a summer home in Quebec, known as *Harrington Lake* in English and *Lac Mousseau* in French.

The leader of the official Opposition lives in an Ottawa mansion called *Stornoway*. The Reform Party's Preston Manning said he did not like the idea of official homes. He did not think elected politicians should live in mansions while average Canadians could not afford them. He joked about turning Stornoway into a bingo hall. "We could use the proceeds to pay off the national debt!" Manning chuckled. When Manning became Opposition leader in 1997, however, he changed his mind and moved in to the mansion.

**Figure 15.11** Clockwise from top: Rideau Hall, Citadel, 24 Sussex Drive, Harrington Lake, Stornoway

## Cabinet

The cabinet is the prime minister's team. The prime minister chooses a small number of MPs for the cabinet from all the MPs in his or her party. These people serve as ministers. The cabinet

- is in charge of government departments, such as Foreign Affairs, Canadian Heritage, or Indian and Northern Affairs
- runs the government. Members meet in cabinet meetings to talk about what needs to be done and how to do it.

## The Judicial Branch

Once the government creates laws, they need to be **enforced**. Canada's judicial branch, or court system, does this. If someone thinks that a law is not being followed, he or she can take the lawbreaker to court.

The Supreme Court of Canada has nine judges. It is the highest court in the land. There are other courts at the provincial, territorial, and federal level.

Canada's judicial branch is independent. In Canadian democracy, everyone is equal in the eyes of the law. No one – not even the prime minister – is above the law.

**Debate**

Some Canadians think that having a monarch as head of state is undemocratic. They argue that Canada's head of state should be elected by the people. Other Canadians think that Canada's historic link to Britain is worth saving. They say the monarch is part of who we are. Still others think that a monarch as head of state is a symbol of unity in the country. Some Canadians do not care, as the monarch cannot get involved in government decisions.

Australia is also a constitutional monarchy. In 2001, the Australians voted to decide if they should keep the monarchy or get rid of it. By a very narrow margin, Australians voted to keep the Queen as their head of state.

**Figure 15.12** Queen Elizabeth II with Prime Minister Trudeau in 1977. The Queen is fluently bilingual.

# Short-term Prime Ministers

Between 1968 and 2003, three prime ministers stood out in Canadian politics: Pierre Trudeau, Brian Mulroney, and Jean Chrétien (see right). Between each of them, however, were four lesser-known prime ministers, who served for only short terms: Joe Clark (see p. 172), John Turner, Kim Campbell, and Paul Martin.

John Napier Turner was prime minister for only two and a half months in 1984. That is the second-shortest term in Canadian history after Sir Charles Tupper (see p. 85). The Liberals chose Turner as their new leader after Pierre Trudeau retired in 1984. Turner was a lawyer. He joined Pearson's government in 1962. He later served as Pierre Trudeau's minister of justice and of finance. Turner was also a competitive swimmer. Once, in Barbados, he saved John Diefenbaker from drowning.

**Figure 15.13** John Turner

Turner called an election soon after becoming prime minister. He lost to Brian Mulroney, but stayed on as Opposition leader until 1990. He is remembered for fighting against the free trade deal with the United States in 1988.

Kim Campbell took over as prime minister when Mulroney retired in 1993. As the new leader of the Progressive Conservative Party, she became Canada's first female prime minister. She held the job for just over four months. Jean Chrétien's Liberals won in November 1993.

**Figure 15.14** Kim Campbell

Campbell made it easier for Canadian women to join politics. She was the first woman in Canada to serve as minister of justice and then as minister of defence.

Paul Martin became prime minister after Jean Chrétien retired in December 2003.

Martin was a successful businessman who grew up in a political family. His father, Paul Martin Sr., had been an important member of the Liberal governments of King, St. Laurent, and Pearson. Paul Martin Sr. ran to be leader of the Liberal Party three times – in 1948, 1958, and 1968. He failed each time. Martin Jr. was first elected in 1988. He became finance minister in Jean Chrétien's government. As prime minister, Martin won a **minority government** in June 2004. In January 2006, he lost the election to Stephen Harper.

**Figure 15.15** Paul Martin

Politics can involve luck and timing. Turner, Campbell, and Martin took office when their parties were slipping in popularity and Canadians wanted a change. Despite their short terms, however, each contributed to Canada's political history.

# More Prime Ministers of the 21st Century

### Jean Chrétien (1934–)

In the winter of 1934, in the town of Shawinigan, Quebec, Marie and Wellie Chrétien celebrated the birth of their 18th child. Ten of their children had died in infancy. Not only did their newborn, Jean, survive, but 59 years later, he became prime minister of Canada.

**Figure 15.16** Jean Chrétien

Jean Chrétien was a lawyer. He was proud to come from a small town. He called himself "le petit gars de Shawinigan" or "the little guy from Shawinigan." In 1963, barely speaking a word of English, Chrétien went to Ottawa for the first time. He had been elected as an MP to Lester B. Pearson's Liberal government.

Chrétien did many important jobs in government. Under Prime Minister Trudeau, he served as minister of finance. During the Quebec referendum in 1980, Chrétien fought hard for federalism. He was minister of justice when the new Constitution was passed in 1982. Chrétien became leader of the Liberal Party in 1990. Three years later, he was prime minister.

Chrétien won three **majority government**s in a row – in October 1993, June 1997, and November 2000. His government passed laws to make it more difficult for provinces like Quebec to separate from Canada. With his finance minister, Paul Martin, he also balanced Canada's budget. In 2003, when President George W. Bush called on America's allies to join the American-led war in Iraq, Prime Minister Chrétien said that Canada would not take part.

**DID YOU KNOW?** Jean Chrétien was born on the same day as Sir John A. Macdonald, January 11.

### Stephen Harper (1959–)

Stephen Harper was born in Toronto. As a young man, he moved to Alberta for a job in the petroleum industry. He became an economist. He was a member of the Reform Party when it first started. Harper was elected to the House of Commons in 1993, but served only one term.

**Figure 15.17** Stephen Harper

Almost 10 years later, Harper became leader of the Canadian Alliance Party. It had been formed from the Reform Party. In 2003, the Canadian Alliance Party and Progressive Conservative Party joined together to become the *Conservative Party*. Harper was elected as its leader. In the 2006 election, Harper became Canada's 22nd prime minister.

# Provincial and Territorial Governments

Provinces and territories have their own governments. These governments are in charge of such things as running schools, courts, and hospitals. Some provinces, such as Quebec, also have some control over immigration. Territorial governments, however, do not control their land and natural resources as provinces do. Territorial powers are also not part of the Constitution.

Sometimes, provinces do not agree about which powers the federal government should have. This might happen when an important local matter comes under federal control. For example, the federal government controls fisheries and oceans. That may not be a problem for people who live in Saskatchewan. In Newfoundland, however, fisheries are an important local industry.

## Provincial Governments

| THE QUEEN | | |
| --- | --- | --- |
| Represented by the Lieutenant Governor | | |
| **EXECUTIVE BRANCH** | **LEGISLATIVE BRANCH** | **JUDICIAL BRANCH** |
| Premier<br>Cabinet | Legislative Assembly | Provincial Courts |

Canada's provincial governments work in much the same way as the federal government. There are some differences, though. There is only one house – the legislative assembly. There are no provincial senates. Provincial leaders are known as *premiers*. Provinces also use a parliamentary system of government, with cabinets, ministries, and backbenchers.

Instead of a governor general, the provinces have lieutenant [*lef-TEN-ant*] governors who represent the monarch. They are picked by the prime minister. Their role in the province is similar to that of the governor general. They appoint the premier and give royal assent to any laws that are passed. Lieutenant governors represent their provinces and reward their citizens for outstanding achievements.

Territorial governments are like provincial governments. They have an elected legislative assembly and a government leader. Territorial governments have commissioners instead of lieutenant governors, however.

# Municipal Government

Municipal governments run cities, towns, or rural areas. They are responsible for local matters, such as police, fire departments, parks, and roads. They also handle things like snow clearing, garbage collection, public transportation, and water and sewer services.

## The battle of the biffy

**Figure 15.18** Stephen Juba

Municipal and provincial governments sometimes disagree with one another over who has the power to do what. In the 1970s, Winnipeg's mayor, Steve Juba, took on Manitoba's public works minister, Russell Doern. Doern wanted to build a public toilet near the Manitoba legislature in downtown Winnipeg. Juba told him he could not, because it was on city land. Doern said that, as minister of public works for the province, he had the right to build on city land. Doern and Juba argued about which government had the right to build public toilets. Finally, an angry Mayor Juba installed a portable toilet on the legislative grounds. He hung a sign on it that read, "Office of Russ Doern, Minister of Public Works." If the province had a right to install a toilet on city land, then the city had a right to install one on the province's land!

Most municipal governments are made up of councils. Members of a council are known as *councillors*. Councils are headed by a mayor, or in rural areas, by a reeve. Municipal governments pass **bylaw**s. Bylaws apply only in their own communities.

# Aboriginal Government

Just as there are many different Aboriginal groups in Canada, there are different forms of Aboriginal government. Many First Nations run their government by the rules set out in the Indian Act, with a chief and band council elected every two years. Other First Nations choose their governments based on their own traditions, such as rule by hereditary chiefs. The Inuit of Nunavut are the only Aboriginal group who run a public, territorial government.

## Band councils

The most common form of First Nations government is the *band council*. A band council is made up of a chief and a group of councillors. They are all elected by members of their local First Nation. Band councils are like municipal governments. They can pass bylaws to manage reserve affairs, such as traffic control, bridges and roads, and agriculture.

Band councils get their authority from the Indian Act. The Indian Act defines who has Indian status. It states which groups of First Nations people can legally form a band and what powers they have.

Band councils cannot collect taxes from their citizens. This is one way they differ from municipal governments. Instead, band councils are given funds from the Department of Indian Affairs. This means the band council must answer to band members as well as the federal government.

## Self-government

Many First Nations do not to use a band council system. They govern themselves using their own traditions. First Nations people believe self-government is a right they have always had. Long before Europeans arrived in North America, and long before the Indian Act was ever written, First Nations people took care of themselves.

Aboriginal self-government can take many forms. One example is the system used by the Nisga'a of the Nass River Valley in British Columbia. In 1998, the Nisga'a replaced the old band council system with the new Nisga'a Lisims government. The Nisga'a government is led by three officers. They are elected from each village within Nisga'a territory. Representatives are also elected for Nisga'a citizens who live outside their territory. Today, the Indian Act is no longer used within Nisga'a territory. As a result, the Nisga'a pay taxes and govern their own fisheries and natural resources. They run their own education and legal systems, and have control over their language and culture.

Aboriginal self-government does not mean that First Nations are independent of Canada. Self-governing First Nations still use the Canadian Constitution as the highest law in the land.

## The government of Nunavut

The government of Nunavut is the largest system of Aboriginal self-government in Canada. Most of Nunavut's population is Inuit, as are most members of its government.

Nunavut also has many citizens who are not Inuit. This means the government of Nunavut must also be a public government, responsible to all its citizens, regardless of their heritage. That is different from the Nisga'a government, which is only for people of Nisga'a heritage.

Nunavut works in much the same way as other Canadian provincial and territory governments. However, Nunavut's government is different because it uses Inuit values and traditions (see p. 152). Nunavut is an example of how traditional Aboriginal government can work for a population of many different peoples.

# Canada's Political Parties

A political party is a group of people who share the same ideas about how a country should be run. Political parties look at concerns such as health care, climate change, military spending, and taxation. A country with many political parties means that citizens have choices about who will represent them. The three main national political parties in Canada are discussed below.

## Liberal Party

The Liberal Party has governed Canada for most of Canadian history. It led Canada for about 70 years during the 1900s. It was once described as the most successful political party ever in a democratic country.

Political parties change as times change. In the 19th century, for example, the Liberal party wanted more power for the provinces. Today it supports the idea of a strong national government. In the past, the party wanted close ties to the United States. Late in the 20th century, however, it worked to keep Canada's own culture and identity. In 1988 the Liberals opposed the Conservatives' Free Trade Agreement with the United States. In the past, the Liberals supported free trade.

Today, Liberals believe that all Canadians in need should be able to get social services to help them. They also believe that taxes are a fair way to pay for these services. The Liberal Party also supports bilingualism, multiculturalism, civil rights, and equality under the law. In recent years, climate change has became an important concern for the Liberal Party.

## Conservative Party

The Conservative Party was Canada's most successful party from the time of Confederation (1867) until the early 1920s. Many Canadians saw it as the party that created Canada. During that time, Canada faced many problems that might have caused it to break up. The Conservative Party believed in a strong national government. It guided Canada through those early, difficult years.

In its early years, the Conservatives wanted close ties to Great Britain. By the end of the 20th century, however, they grew distant from Britain and became closer to the United States. Conservatives also believed the provinces should have more power. In 1988 they supported free trade with the United States, even though they had been against it in the past.

Since the 1960s, the Conservatives have supported bilingualism and multiculturalism. The Conservative party believes in lower taxes and less public spending. It thinks some services could be taken care of outside the government.

For most of Canadian history, Liberals and Conservatives have agreed on many ideas. They have also traded positions on some important ones.

## New Democratic Party

The New Democratic Party (NDP) began in 1961. It was formed when the Co-operative Commonwealth Federation (CCF) and the Canadian Labour Congress merged. The NDP has never formed a federal government. It has never been the official Opposition in the House of Commons. However, it has formed governments in four provinces.

The CCF, founded in the 1930s, wanted the government to look after industries and services. It wanted to create a **welfare state.**

The NDP sees itself as a party that takes care of average citizens. It supports the idea of a strong central government. It would provide social and educational services to make sure all people are given the same chances in life.

The party supports bilingualism, multiculturalism, and civil rights. It also supports higher taxes to pay for services such as health care and welfare. The NDP has long been concerned with environmental issues.

**Figure 15.19** Left and above: Campaign materials from Canadian political parties

## Lucien Bouchard and the Bloc Québecois

Lucien Bouchard was one of Canada's most well-known sovereignists in the 1990s. He supported an independent Quebec. When Bouchard first entered politics, he was a federalist and believed Quebec should remain within Canada. Bouchard changed his views when the Meech Lake Accord failed in 1990 (see p. 182). He said that if Quebec did not have the right to protect its own distinct culture, then it should become its own country.

**Figure 15.20** Lucien Bouchard

In 1991, Bouchard and some other MPs (both Conservative and Liberal) started a new federal party, the *Bloc Québecois* (BQ), to speak out for the rights of Quebec. Bouchard became its leader. The BQ cannot form a national government, because it only runs candidates in Quebec. Just the same, it has played a significant role in Canadian politics.

In the 1993 federal election, the BQ won enough seats in Quebec to become the official Opposition in Canada's Parliament. This happened even though it ran candidates only in Quebec. Since 2004, the Bloc's strength has made it more difficult for other parties to win a majority in the House of Commons.

# Electing a Government

In a federal election in Canada, voting takes place on only one day. Yet the process leading up to a voting day can take many weeks. Election time starts when the prime minister asks the governor general to dissolve Parliament and to call an election.

Once Parliament is dissolved, political parties have at least 36 days to convince Canadians to vote for their candidates. Candidates try to win seats in the House of Commons. Candidates talk to Canadians and explain their ideas during the campaign, the period leading up to election day.

Campaign time is a busy time for everybody. Politicians work hard to win peoples' votes. Voters choose a candidate who they think will best represent their views. Sometimes the voters choose a candidate because of the party he or she is from. A vote also shows how well or how poorly a voter thinks the government has done its job.

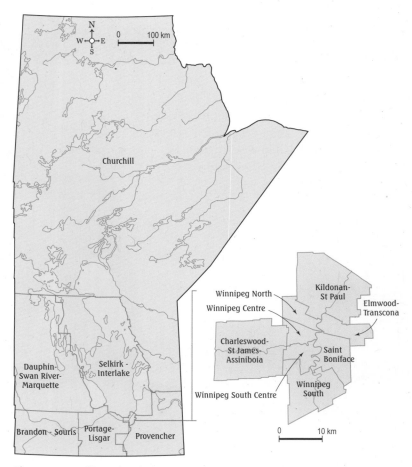

**Figure 15.22** *MANITOBA'S 14 FEDERAL ELECTORAL RIDINGS*

**Figure 15.21** Quebec premier Jean Charest campaigning in 2007

# Please Be Seated!

Canada is divided into ridings. Each riding represents an area of land in Canada. Ridings may differ in size and in the number of people living in them.

Each seat in the House of Commons represents a riding. People who live within the borders of a riding vote for candidates to represent that riding. The candidate who gets the most votes in a riding becomes its member of Parliament (MP). He or she sits in the seat in Parliament that represents the riding.

In this way, every part of Canada has an elected representative. Provinces, territories, and municipalities also use a riding system in their elections. In 2007, there were 308 federal ridings in Canada. That means that 308 members of Parliament sit in the House of Commons.

## Rep by pop

The number of ridings a province or territory has depends on the size of its population. Nunavut, for example, has a small population, so it has only one seat in the federal government. Ontario has a larger population than any other province, so it has the most seats in Parliament, 101. When a province or territory grows in population, it gets more seats in Parliament. This way of assigning seats is called *representation by population* or *rep by pop* for short.

- Before election day, an agency called Elections Canada registers voters. It creates a voters' list.

- When election day arrives, voters go to a **polling station**.

- There, a clerk gives each voter a **ballot**, a piece of paper listing the names of all the candidates.

- The voter takes the ballot behind a private screen. There, the voter marks an *X* next to the name of the candidate of his or her choice.

- The voter then folds the ballot and gives it to the clerk, who places it in a ballot box.
- When the polling station closes, all the ballots are counted.

- The counts from the different polling stations in a riding are then added together.
- The candidate with the most votes wins the seat for that riding.

Elections Canada has laws to make sure elections are fair:

- Voters vote in secret. That is so no one can bully them into voting a certain way. It is also against the law to make somebody tell who they voted for.

- Each person gets one vote. When a voter arrives at the polling station, a clerk crosses his or her name off the voters' list. This shows that a person has voted. He or she is not allowed to vote again.

# Conclusion

Many Canadians have their own ideas about how to improve the way the government works. Some Canadians, for example, think that senators should be elected by the Canadian people instead of picked by the prime minister. Some Canadians think representation by population is unfair, because parts of Canada with smaller populations do not get an equal say in running the country.

Voting is one of the most important rights and responsibilities in a democracy. When people vote, they take an active role in running their country. By voting, citizens judge the decisions their leaders have made in the past. They also decide who should lead them in the future.

**DID YOU KNOW?** In 1970, the voting age in federal elections was lowered from 21 years to 18 years. That also means an 18-year-old can run as a candidate in a federal election.

# Conclusion
## Into the 21st Century

In this book, you have read what people did in the past to make Canada the country it is today. Canada in the 21st century is very different from the Canada of 1867. It is even different from the Canada of 25 or 50 years ago. Change does not just happen, though. It takes the courage of active citizens to bring about change.

When Georges Forest challenged his English-only parking ticket in 1976, he had little political power. He was just a citizen trying to solve a problem that he saw in his community. He was able to make a change. In the same way, Dr. Emily Stowe had to be an active citizen to win the right to practise medicine in Ontario in 1880. She did not have the power to decide on her own. She did not even have the right to vote in her lifetime. However, she found the courage to convince the decision makers that they were unfair. When Elijah Harper stood in the Manitoba legislature in 1990 to stop the Meech Lake Accord, eagle feather in hand, he took a stand for all Aboriginal Canadians. All Canadians have benefited from the actions of these citizens.

Many Canadians are proud of what Canada has become since Confederation: a multicultural, bilingual society, protected by the Charter of Rights and Freedoms. However, many of the challenges Canada faced in the past are still around today. Poverty still exists. So does discrimination. The environment is in danger. There is more work to be done to reach the goal of having a fair and safe place for all Canadians.

We do not yet know how Canadians will deal with these challenges. However, as a citizen of Canada and the world, you can help decide the future.

# Appendix A: Timeline

| | |
|---|---|
| 1858 | Fraser Valley gold rush begins. |
| 1867 | Confederation creates new country of Canada with four provinces: Nova Scotia, New Brunswick, Quebec, and Ontario. |
| 1869 | Red River Resistance begins. |
| 1869 | Canada's first Immigration Act is passed. |
| 1870 | Thomas Scott is executed. |
| 1870 | Manitoba enters Confederation. |
| 1871 | British Columbia enters Confederation. |
| 1871 | The 49th parallel is set as the border between much of Canada and the U.S. |
| 1871 | The first numbered treaty (Treaty 1) is signed. |
| 1872 | Dominion Lands Act is passed. |
| 1873 | Prince Edward Island enters Confederation. |
| 1873 | Cypress Hills Massacre occurs. |
| 1874 | Newly formed North-West Mounted Police make the Great March West. |
| 1875 | Supreme Court of Canada created. |
| 1876 | Indian Act is passed. |
| 1876 | Treaty 6 is signed. |
| 1880 | Emily Stowe becomes the first woman to receive an Ontario medical licence. |
| 1880 | Britain transfers its Arctic lands to Canada. |
| 1881 | New Iceland becomes part of Manitoba. |
| 1883 | Augusta Stowe-Gullen becomes the first female doctor to graduate from a Canadian medical school. |

| | |
|---|---|
| 1885 | Chinese immigrants are forced to pay head tax. |
| 1885 | North-West Resistance begins. |
| 1885 | Canadian Pacific Railway is completed. |
| 1891 | Canada's first prime minister, John A. Macdonald, dies. |
| 1896 | Klondike gold rush begins. |
| 1897 | The British Empire celebrates the Diamond Jubilee (60th year) of Queen Victoria's reign. |
| 1898 | The Yukon becomes a separate territory. |
| 1899 | Boer War begins in South Africa. |
| 1901 | Marconi receives first radio signal from across the Atlantic Ocean at Signal Hill in St. John's, Newfoundland. |
| 1905 | Saskatchewan and Alberta enter Confederation. |
| 1907 | In Vancouver, 10 000 members of the Asian Exclusion League protest Asian immigration. |
| 1907 | Onondaga runner Tom Longboat wins the Boston Marathon. |
| 1910 | Henri Bourassa founds the Montreal newspaper *Le Devoir*. |
| 1910 | The *Naval Service Bill* creates the Royal Canadian Navy. |
| 1913 | The Nisga'a make their first land claim. |
| 1914 | *Empress of Ireland* sinks. |
| 1914 | World War I begins. |
| 1916 | Canadians fight in the Battle of the Somme. |

| 1916 | Berlin, Ontario, is renamed Kitchener. |
| 1916 | Fire destroys most of the Canadian Parliament Buildings. |
| 1916 | Manitoba becomes the first province to give women the right to vote. |
| 1917 | The Halifax Explosion, caused by two ships colliding in Halifax Harbour, kills more than 2000 people. |
| 1917 | Women with family members fighting in Europe are given the right to vote in the federal election. |
| 1917 | Canadian forces claim victory at Vimy Ridge. |
| 1918 | World War I ends. More than 60 000 soldiers are killed. |
| 1918 | Spanish flu reaches Canada. |
| 1919 | Treaty of Versailles is signed, ending World War I. |
| 1919 | Winnipeg General Strike takes place. |
| 1920 | League of Nations is founded. |
| 1920 | Group of Seven artists hold their first show, at the Art Gallery of Toronto. |
| 1920 | First radio broadcast in North America airs from Montreal. |
| 1920 | Royal Canadian Mounted Police is formed. |
| 1921 | Insulin is discovered by Frederick Banting and Charles Best. |
| 1921 | Agnes MacPhail becomes first woman elected to Parliament. |
| 1921 | The last of eleven numbered treaties is signed. |
| 1929 | The New York Stock Exchange crashes. |
| 1929 | The Great Depression begins. |
| 1929 | Britain's Privy Council rules in favour of the Famous Five, declaring women "persons." |

| 1931 | British Parliament passes the Statute of Westminster. |
| 1932 | Cooperative Commonwealth Federation (CCF) is founded in Calgary. |
| 1933 | Adolf Hitler seizes power in Germany. |
| 1935 | Unemployed men board trains for the On-to-Ottawa Trek. |
| 1939 | World War II begins. |
| 1942 | Canadian government begins rationing goods like coffee, tea, butter, sugar, meat, and gas. |
| 1942 | Japanese-Canadians are interned. |
| 1944 | Conscription is introduced. |
| 1944 | On D-Day, June 6, the Allies begin the liberation of France. |
| 1944 | Maurice Duplessis becomes Quebec premier. |
| 1945 | U.S. drops atomic bombs on Hiroshima and Nagasaki in Japan; Japan surrenders. |
| 1945 | World War II ends, with nearly 45 000 Canadians killed. |
| 1945 | United Nations is founded. |
| 1946 | Baby boom begins. |
| 1947 | Oil is discovered in Alberta. |
| 1947 | Canadian Citizenship Act is passed. |
| 1948 | United Nations adopts the Universal Declaration of Human Rights. |
| 1949 | North Atlantic Treaty Organization (NATO) is formed to defend North America and Western Europe against Russia. |
| 1949 | Newfoundland joins Canada. |
| 1950 | National Film Board of Canada (NFB) is created. |
| 1950 | Korean War begins. |

| 1951 | Massey Commission presents its report on Canadian culture. |
| 1951 | Old Age Pension is established in Canada. |
| 1952 | Queen Elizabeth II begins her reign. |
| 1954 | First subway system in Canada opens in Toronto. |
| 1954 | Sixteen-year-old Marilyn Bell swims across Lake Ontario in 21 hours. |
| 1956 | Peacekeepers prevent Middle East war during the Suez Crisis. |
| 1957 | Lester B. Pearson receives the Nobel Peace Prize. |
| 1960 | John Diefenbaker introduces Canadian Bill of Rights. |
| 1960 | Status Indians given the vote in Canadian federal elections. |
| 1961 | NDP created from CCF. |
| 1964 | Canada adopts its own flag. |
| 1966 | Federal medicare program is established. |
| 1967 | Canada celebrates its centennial; Montreal hosts Expo '67. |
| 1968 | Réne Lévesque founds Parti Québécois. |
| 1968 | Canadian Radio-television and Telecommunications Commission (CRTC) is founded. |
| 1969 | French and English are declared official languages of Canada |
| 1970 | The October Crisis occurs in Quebec. |
| 1970 | Voting age for federal elections is lowered from 21 to 18 years of age. |
| 1970 | La Francophonie is founded. |
| 1971 | Greenpeace is founded. |
| 1972 | Canada wins the Canada-USSR hockey series. |

| 1974 | The RCMP begins to hire women. |
| 1975 | The death penalty is abolished. |
| 1976 | René Lévesque becomes premier of Quebec. |
| 1979 | Canadarm is invented. |
| 1980 | Canadian Constitution becomes law. |
| 1980 | Terry Fox begins his Marathon of Hope. |
| 1980 | Quebec holds its first referendum on separation. Quebecers vote to stay in Canada. |
| 1982 | The Canadian Charter of Rights and Freedoms becomes law. |
| 1982 | Assembly of First Nations is founded. |
| 1984 | Marc Garneau becomes the first Canadian in space. |
| 1985 | Bill C31, which amends the Indian Act, is passed. |
| 1986 | Preston Manning creates the Reform Party. |
| 1989 | Canada–United States Free Trade Agreement begins. |
| 1990 | Elijah Harper blocks the Meech Lake Accord. |
| 1990 | Bloc Québécois is established. |
| 1990 | The Oka Crisis takes place in Quebec. |
| 1992 | Roberta Bondar becomes first Canadian woman in space. |
| 1994 | North American Free Trade Act (NAFTA) begins. |
| 1995 | In second referendum, Quebeckers vote to stay in Canada by a narrow margin. |
| 1996 | Last residential school closes in Saskatchewan. |
| 1997 | Canada takes lead in the Mine Ban Treaty. |

| 1998 | Government issues an apology to those abused in residential schools. |
|------|---------|
| 1998 | Nisga'a gain the right to self-government. |
| 1999 | Nunavut, Canada's third territory, is created. |
| 2001 | Canada joins the Afghanistan War. |
| 2002 | Canada signs Kyoto Accord to reduce greenhouse gases. |
| 2004 | Canada wins the Women's World Ice Hockey Championship. |
| 2004 | Montreal Expos play their last baseball game in Montreal. |
| 2006 | Canada's population reaches 31 612 897. |
| 2007 | United Nations passes the Declaration on the Rights of Indigenous Peoples. |
| 2007 | Veterans' Bill of Rights enacted. |

NUNAVUT

Rankin Inlet

Arviat

Hudson Bay

# Appendix B: Prime Ministers of Canada

## Terms of office

| | | |
|---|---|---|
| 1. | John A. Macdonald | 1867–73 1878–91 |
| 2. | Alexander Mackenzie | 1873–78 |
| 3. | John Abbott | 1891–92 |
| 4. | John Thompson | 1892–94 |
| 5. | Mackenzie Bowell | 1894–96 |
| 6. | Charles Tupper | 1896 |
| 7. | Wilfrid Laurier | 1896–1911 |
| 8. | Robert Borden | 1911–17 1917–20 |
| 9. | Arthur Meighen | 1920–21 1926 |
| 10. | William Lyon Mackenzie King | 1921–26 1926–30 1935–48 |
| 11. | Richard Bennett | 1930–35 |
| 12. | Louis St. Laurent | 1948–57 |
| 13. | John Diefenbaker | 1957–63 |
| 14. | Lester B. Pearson | 1963–68 |
| 15. | Pierre Elliott Trudeau | 1968–79 1980–84 |
| 16. | Joseph Clark | 1979–80 |
| 17. | John Turner | 1984 |
| 18. | Brian Mulroney | 1984–93 |
| 19. | Kim Campbell | 1993 |
| 20. | Jean Chrétien | 1993–2003 |
| 21. | Paul Martin | 2003–2006 |
| 22. | Stephen Harper | 2006– |

# Glossary

**administration** government departments, armed forces, and Crown corporations that carry out the business of the government

**advocate** someone who argues in favour of something

**alliance** organization of nations or other groups who join together to achieve certain aims

**Allies** in World War I, the alliance of Great Britain (including Canada), France, and Russia and the other nations that opposed Germany and its partners. In World War II, 26 nations led by Britain, the Soviet Union, the United States, France, China, Canada, and Australia that opposed Germany and the Axis powers.

**amnesty** official release of someone for a crime or for a political offence against a government

**ancestry** nationality or ethnic group that a person is descended from, traced back through parents and generations before them

**anglophone** person whose first language is English

**apartheid** official government policy of the separation of different races in South Africa

**appeal** to take a court case to a higher court for review and possible reversal of a verdict or decision

**artillery** heavy cannons and the explosive shells that they fire

**assimilate** to make something similar to its surroundings. In the case of Aboriginal people, assimilation meant adopting the ways of the larger Euro-Canadian culture

**Axis** name given to the wartime alliance signed on September 27, 1940, between Germany, Italy, and Japan. The Axis was later joined by other countries from Eastern Europe and Asia.

**ballot** piece of paper listing the names of candidates in an election, on which a voter marks his or her choice of candidate

**band** First Nations community, sharing a common ancestral heritage, who control a particular reserve of land under the Indian Act

**biculturalism** policy recognizing two official cultures

**bilingualism** ability to speak two languages. In Canada, *official bilingualism* refers to Canada's two official languages, English and French.

**bill** proposed law, which when passed and signed by the governor general, becomes an Act of Parliament

**Bolsheviks** people who seized power from the Tsar in the Russian Revolution in 1917, then formed the Communist Party

**bomb shelters** room, often underground, that is reinforced against bombs and that contains food and places to sleep

**bushel** unit of measure equal to 35.24 litres, similar in volume to a round laundry basket

**bylaw** law that is made by a municipal or local government

**campaign** time leading up to an election when political parties compete with each other for votes. During the campaign, candidates explain their ideas to voters and try to win their support.

**candidate** person who runs in an election for a seat in government

**centennial** one hundredth anniversary. Canada's centennial refers to the year 1967, when Canada marked its 100th birthday.

**ceremonial** relating to a formal event or occasion

**charter** document that gives an organization or a group of people certain rights

**Christian values** values found in the teachings of Christ, such as charity, love, and forgiveness

**civil liberties** freedoms that protect people from abuse of power by the government. Civil liberties include the right to meet freely, the right to privacy, the right to a fair trial, and the right to be considered innocent until proven guilty.

**claim** in mining, the right to collect minerals (such as gold) in a specific area.

**cohort** supporter

**Cold War** period of tension between the United States and the Soviet Union. The Cold War lasted from 1946 to 1991.

**colony** people who settle in a distant territory that is controlled by the government of their homeland.

**compromise** when each side in a disagreement gives up something they want in order to reach an agreement.

**conquest** takeover of a large territory or country by force.

**conscription** required military service.

**conscript** person called up by the government to serve in the military

**conservationists** people who work to protect (or conserve) the environment

**constitution** basic laws and customs by which a group of people govern themselves

**consumerism** buying things other than the basic necessities of life

**corruption** using a position of trust to get something dishonestly

**D-Day** in World War II, June 6, 1944, the day the Allied forces landed in Normandy, France

**debate** to discuss reasons for and against a plan or idea

**democracy** political system in which citizens have a voice in their own government through their elected representatives

**democratic socialists** people who believe that the government should take control of business and industry for the good of everyone

**depression** a time when people have little money and there are not enough jobs. Trade, investment, and prices drop.

**desperation** having no hope about a situation and not knowing what to do about it

**diabetes** disease in which the body does not produce or properly use insulin, a hormone that converts sugar, starches, and other food into energy

**dictator** ruler with absolute power and authority who is above the laws of the country

**dictatorship** government in which a country is ruled by a single person who has total power over the people in that country

**discrimination** unfair treatment of a person or group

**dissolve Parliament** to end one Parliament so that a new Parliament can be elected

**diversity** variety of people of different ethnic groups, languages, religions, and traditions who make up the population

**division** military unit consisting of 15 to 20 thousand soldiers, commanded by a general

**drought** long period of dry weather that affects agriculture and other human and environmental needs

**dugouts** structures dug deep into the earth at intervals along the trenches. Often reinforced with concrete, they served as command posts and living quarters.

**economy** country's system of production and management of goods and services

**elect** to choose by voting.

**emigrating** leaving from one country to go to another country to live

**emissary** someone who is sent on a mission to represent another person

**enforce** to ensure that laws and rules are followed

**epidemic** widespread outbreak of a disease, with many people in a community infected at the same time

**erosion** the wearing away of land by wind or water.

**ethnic** referring to a group of people with the same race, national background, religion, or culture

**fallow** field left unplanted for a season. This helps to conserve moisture and nutrients in the soil.

**Family Compact** small group of wealthy men who ruled Upper Canada in the early 19th century

**famine** severe shortage of food in a community that causes hunger and starvation

**federalism** system in which political power is divided between different levels of government, such as national, provincial, and municipal

**federalist** person who believes in a strong central national government that shares powers with provincial governments

**feminist** person who believes women should have the same rights and opportunities as men

**foreign policy** government's plans for working with other countries

**forge** to make a copy of something, intending to fool someone with it

**forum** public meeting held to discuss something

**fossil fuels** carbon-rich fuel, such as coal, oil, and natural gas, formed from the remains of ancient animals and plants.

**francophone** person whose first language is French

**free trade** arrangement between countries where tariffs, taxes, and other barriers to trade are eliminated, allowing a free flow of goods across borders

**front** battlefield where opposing sides fight in a war

**gender discrimination** any act that denies people opportunities or privileges because of being male or female

**greenhouse effect** warming of the Earth's atmosphere due to a buildup of carbon dioxide or other gases.

**guerrilla** armed force that does not fight by the same rules as an official army

**harrow** to draw a harrow, a farming implement with teeth designed to break up clods of earth, over plowed land to prepare it for planting

**Holocaust** from the Greek *holo* (whole) and *caustos* (burned). The systematic murder of six million Jews and close to six million others by the Nazis before and during World War II

**home front** nonmilitary Canadian citizens and their activities in support of the war

**homestead** property granted to early settlers to be developed into farms

**immigration** coming to a new country to live

**imperialist** person loyal to a country that rules an empire. In Canada in the 19th century, for example, an imperialist was someone loyal to the mother country of Britain.

**independent** free from outside control

**Indian status** individual's legal standing as a First Nations person under the terms of the Indian Act

**Indians** term first used to describe First Nations people by Christopher Columbus in 1492. Now considered inaccurate and outdated, it is still used in laws and legal documents.

**indigenous peoples** the original peoples of a land and their descendants

**industrialist** someone who owns and operates an industrial business

**industrialization** process of replacing production of items by crafts people, with mass production of goods by paid workers in factories equipped with power-driven machinery

**intellectual** person who uses reason and intelligence rather than emotion when making decisions

**interned** to be kept confined during time of war

**land surveyor** person who takes measurements that define the boundary of an owner's land

**libel** false statement published for the purpose of insulting a living person

**liberation** in World War II, when advancing Allied armies took over German-occupied territory, freeing it from Nazi control

**magistrate** official who enforces laws, but who has less authority than a judge

**majority government** government in which the governing party has more than half the seats in the legislature

**majority** more than half of a group

**manifesto** public declaration of political beliefs and goals

**market** to sell a product to a customer through a system of packaging, promotion, and distribution

**marksman** someone skilled in shooting a gun

**medicare** government insurance system that pays medical costs for all its citizens

**member of Parliament** (MP) person elected to the House of Commons by voters in a riding

**merge** to join together or combine

**militia** part-time army called to service in times of need. In the event of war, the militia is summoned to fight with the regular army. The rest of the time, the members of the militia lead normal lives as civilians. Today, the militia is called the *reserves*.

**minister** politician who heads a government department, such as defence, finance, or immigration

**minority government** government in which the governing party has less than half the seats in the legislature

**minority** less than half of a group

**moderate** to control or lessen the amount of something

**mosaic** many small pieces of coloured stone, glass, or tile arranged to make a design

**multiculturalism** policy of including many different cultures in a society. The Multiculturalism Act (1971) encourages Canadians to practise their different cultures.

**munitions** weapons and equipment used in a war

**nationalist** person who puts the interests of their country first. In Canada in the 19th century, for example, nationalists wanted Canada to be more independent from Britain.

**newsreel** short film of the week's news shown before a movie begins. In the days before television, people often went to the movie theatre to watch the news.

**nucleus** centre or core of something

**occupied** seized and controlled by a foreign country through a military invasion

**oil barons** businesspeople who have become wealthy and powerful from the oil business

**pacifist** opposed to fighting in a war

**patriate** to transfer the power to make laws from one government to another

**pemmican** food made of dried bison meat and fruits or berries

**persecution** mistreatment of an individual or group by another group, usually because of religious belief or ethnic background

**petition** a request to a government, asking it for action on a certain matter, signed by a group of people who agree with the request

**polling station** place where citizens go to vote

**potlatch** ceremony observed by some First Nations of the Northwest Coast of North America

**prejudice** negative opinion about a group of people, based on such things as gender, race, religion, or ethnic background

**proclamation** public announcement of an official act

**prospector** person who searches or explores a region for minerals

**provisional government** temporary government that operates until a permanent government can be formed

**quarantine** to keep sick people away from other people to prevent the spread of contagious diseases

**Quebec nationalism** belief that Quebec is a nation

**Quebec sovereignty** the idea that Quebec should form its own government, independent of Canada, with its own constitution

**rallies** large gatherings of people brought together to arouse enthusiasm

**ransom** payment for the release of a captured person

**ration** to limit the amount of certain goods people could buy in wartime.

**recruit** new soldier.

**referendum** vote that citizens make on important issues

**regalia** fine or decorative clothing, often worn for special ceremonies

**regiment** unit of approximately 800 to 1000 soldiers, commanded by an officer called a colonel

**reign** to rule as a king or queen

**relief** help given to people in times of need, in the form of money, food, clothing, or shelter

**representation by population** system in which the more people that live in a province, the more seats it has in the House of Commons

**reserve** land that is set aside for the use of a particular First Nations group

**Responsible Government** form of government where the executive or cabinet, made up of members of the party with the most seats in the assembly, must answer to the elected representatives of the people

**revolution** overthrow of a government by its citizens

**riding** geographic region of Canada that has one seat in government

**royal assent** last stage that a bill must go through to become a law, when the monarch gives final approval

**royal commission** group of experts who study an issue that the government faces. The experts talk to citizens around the country, conduct research, then write a report and recommendations.

**Rupert's Land** huge area of land, covering much of the north and west of present-day Canada, that was sold by the Hudson's Bay Company to the Canadian government in 1870

**sacred** having a spiritual purpose, or to be treated with utmost respect

**skeptical** to have doubts about something

**seat** chair inside the House of Commons where a member of Parliament sits. Each seat represents a geographical riding. The 308 seats in the House represent 308 ridings across Canada.

**self-government** power of a particular group of people to pass laws and make decisions about their communities and lands, and to create governing structures to do so

**social reformers** people who worked to solve problems in society, such as poverty, hunger, and crime

**sovereignist** person who favours the independence of Quebec from Canada

**space shuttle** spacecraft that carries people and materials into space. It lands like an airplane and can be used again.

**specific land claims** challenges to the government by First Nations about land promised, but never received, through treaties

**speculators** people who buy property in the belief that the value will rise so they can sell it later for more money than they paid for it

**spiritualist** person who believes that the spirits of the dead can communicate with the living

**squadron** group of between ten to eighteen airplanes in the air force

**staple** basic good, such as grain or fuel, that is always needed

**statute** law passed by Parliament

**stocks** share of ownership in a company. Stocks change in value depending on what a company is worth and what it earns.

**strike** refusal to work to protest low pay or bad working conditions

**suffrage** right to vote

**suffragist** someone who promotes the right to vote, often for women

**sustain** to nourish or provide necessities of life

**syndicate** group of people or businesses who join together for a certain reason, such as investing in a new business

**tactics** plans the military uses to fight a battle

**tariff** tax placed on goods brought into the country (imported) from another country. Taxing imported goods discourages people from buying them. This is supposed to encourage people to buy goods made in their own country.

**technology** equipment or techniques that make life easier. Technology can range from something as simple as a pencil to a complicated piece of machinery.

**telegraph** mechanical device, invented in the 1830s, that sends coded messages through a cable

**temperance** belief in the moderate use or avoidance of alcohol

**treason** the crime of being disloyal to one's nation, often by cooperating with an enemy

**treaty** agreement that one nation makes with another. These agreements can concern everything from trade to military defence; also agreements First Nations make with the Canadian government.

**trench** deep ditch dug into the earth

**trestle** braced framework of wood or metal for supporting a road or railroad

**truce** agreement between opponents to stop fighting

**Underground Railway** network of routes and safe houses that could be used by slaves from the southern United States travelling to freedom in the northern states or Canada

**urbanization** process whereby large numbers of people move to cities from rural areas

**utilities** services, such as fuel, electricity, water, sewers, that households use to function

**War Measures Act** federal law that allows the federal cabinet emergency powers to govern when the country is under threat of "war, invasion or insurrection." The act allows the government to take away citizens' civil rights to restore security.

**welfare** money and services given to people in need by the government

**welfare state** government that provides such things as health care, housing, and financial support for citizens who need them.

**Western alienation** feeling that the opinions of Western Canadians are left out or ignored by politicians in Ottawa

**white paper** report that a team of experts prepares for the government on a major issue

**yield** in farming, the amount of a product, such as grain, that is produced within a given time

# Image Credits

*The publisher has made every effort to acknowledge all sources of images that have been used in this book and would be grateful if any errors or omissions were pointed out so they may be corrected in subsequent editions. The following illustrations are identified by figure number.*

## Abbreviations

**AM** Archives of Manitoba
**BCA** British Columbia Archives
**CP** Canadian Press
**CPRA** Canadian Pacific Railway Archives
**CWM** Canadian War Museum
**GA** Glenbow Archives
**LAC** Library and Archives Canada
**TMM** The Manitoba Museum
**MTRL** Metro Toronto Reference Library
**NCC/CCN** National Capital Commission / Commission de la capitale nationale
**NGC** National Gallery of Canada
**NSARM** Nova Scotia Archives and Records Management
**SAB** Saskatchewan Archives Board
**UMASC** University of Manitoba Archives & Special Collections
**YA** Yukon Archives

**About this Book:** 1. 19780702-077/© CWM

**Introduction:** i.1 © CIDA 108-12-18/Roger LeMoyne; i.2 World Vision Canada; i.3 © Jeff Topham; i.4 © CIDA 927-03-04/Carol Hart; i.5 CP/CP (Jeff McIntosh)

**Part I:** I.1 Manitoba Crafts Museum and Library; I.2 LAC/C-0059-812; I.3 © TMM/H9-34-868 A; I.4 © TMM/9-16-4; I.5 RCMP Museum, Regina; I.6 Dawson City Museum (1978.1.807 a-d); I.7 LAC/C-038917; I.8 © TMM/H9.6.307; I.9 © TMM/TFT-93; I.10 Hall & Lowe photographers/Collection of Robert Barrow

**Chapter 1:** 1.1 Queen's University Archives/Kingston Picture Collection, V23; 1.2 LAC/C-021290; 1.4 LAC/C-113885; 1.5 NSARM Photo/Jos. Rogers Coll./1992-412#39 (N-6155); 1.6 LAC/PA-143598; 1.7 LAC/C-009480; 1.8 LAC/C-002500; 1.9 (l to r) Topley Studio/LAC/PA-025459; William James Topley/LAC/PA-027931; Notman Studio/Library and Archives Canada/C-010144; 1.10 MTRL; 1.11 LAC/C-006536

**Chapter 2:** 2.1 GA/NA-710-2; 2.2 AM/N461; 2.4 LAC/C-048653; 2.5 William James Topley/LAC/PA-026300; 2.7 AM/N10484 CT26 P; 2.8 LAC/PA-012854; 2.9 LAC/C-001629; 2.10 AM/N5404; 2.11 Bibaud, M./LAC/PA-074103; 2.12 GA/NA-2839-4; 2. 13 LAC/Acc. No. 1969-3-1

**Chapter 3:** 3.1 GA/NA-3173-9; 3.2 GA/NA-361-2; 3.3 William James Topley/LAC/PA-026308; 3.5 GA/NA-361-22; 3.6 GA/NA-1237-1; 3.7 GA/NA-1444-1; 3.8 Douglas LAC/C-003316; 3.10 LAC/PA-025397; 3.11 LAC/Acc. No. R9266-3470/Peter Winkworth Collection; 3.12 LAC/PA-143155; 3.13 CPRA/NS. 8454; 3.14 MP-0000.25.971/McCord Museum, Montreal; 3.15 Vancouver Public Library/Special Collections/1773; 3.16 YA/H.C. Barley fonds/4832; 3.17 YA/James Albert Johnson fonds/82/341, #2; 3.19 J. Fraser Bryce/LAC/PA-212241; 3.20 E.A. Hegg/LAC/C-005142; inset: LAC/C-004490; 3.21 YA/Gillis family fonds/4533; 3.22 G.D. Clark/LAC/PA-029060; 3.23 LAC/C-009217; 3.24 NFB/LAC/PA-128080

**Part II:** II.1 © TMM/HBC57.53; II.2 GA/NA-720-2; II.3 19930118-034/© CWM; II.4. Le Musée de Saint-Boniface Museum; II.5 AM; II.6 LAC; II.7 © TMM/glee club banner; II.8 LAC/e008303560; II.9 AM/MG8–B34

**Chapter 4:** 4.1 © TMM/plains shirt; 4.2 GA/NA-3351-2; 4.3 AM/N8107; 4.4 GA/NA-1406-165; 4.6 AM/N15364; 4.7 GA/NA-3700-3; 4.8 *Assiniboine Hunting Buffalo*/© NGC; 4.9 GA/NA-2631-2; 4.11 GA/NA-1480-5; 4.12 GA/NA-1315-17; 4.13 GA/NA-1032-3; 4.14 LAC/C-002424; 4.15 GA/NA-2274-21; 4.16 GA/NA-3632-68; 4.17 GA/NA-1081-3; 4.18 GA/NA-3012-4; 4.19 UMASC/A.98-15/Kenneth Hayes Collection; 4.20 GA/NA-1681-4; 4.21 GA/NA-3842-8; 4.22 GA/NA-3241-10

**Chapter 5:** (l to r) LAC/C-030621; Advertising 95/AM/Neg.: CN45; LAC/C-052819; 5.2 LAC/C-075938; 5.3 LAC/PA-116389; 5.4 AM/N4217/Settlement 333; 5.5 William James Topley/LAC/PA-010400; 5.6 Woodruff /LAC/C-004745; 5.7 CPRA/NS.8454; 5.8 LAC/C-081314; 5.9 William James Topley/LAC/PA-010394; 5.10 Courtesy of New Iceland Heritage Museum, Gimli, Manitoba; 5.11 (l to r) CPRA/NS.2365; GA/NA-2878-63; 5.12 GA/NA-3556-1; 5.13 B-03895/Courtesy of British Columbia Archives; 5.14 LAC/PA-117285; 5.15 Isaac Erb/LAC/PA-041785; 5.16 CBC Still Photo Collection; 5.17 LAC/C-010144; 5.18 Yousuf Karsh/LAC/PA-160313/Camera Press London; 5.19 © Jeff Nolte; 5.20 Rideau Hall; 5.21 AP/CP (Ed Reinke); 5.22 Canada's National Ukrainian Festival; 5.23 LAC/C-011030; 5.24 GA/NA 1255-31; 5.25GA/NA-4195-6; 5.26 AM/Urie family fonds; 5.27 GA/NA-3485-2; 5.28 Doukhobors/LAC/C-000678; 5.29 University of Saskatchewan Archives/Saskatchewan Wheat Pool fonds

**Chapter 6:** 6.1 Mayall & Co./LAC/PA-138968; 6.3 © Pedro Gervai; 6.4 19800907-001/© CWM; 6.6 Canada. Patent and Copyright Office/LAC /C-005110; 6. 7 LAC/C-016741; 6.8 LAC; 6.9 Moffett Studio/LAC/C-017335; 6.10 LAC/Acc. No. 1984-4-932/Dominion W. C.T.U; 6.11 Topley Studio/LAC/PA-026320; 6.12 LAC/Acc. No. 1994-315-1; 6.13 Charles Berkeley Powell/LAC/C-001981; 6.14 Elliott and Fry/LAC/C-008549; 6.15 Rudolph Martin Anderson/LAC/PA-172900; 6.17 Notman Studio (Halifax)/LAC/PA-028497

**Part III:** III.1 © TMM/ES 5586/The Prince Medals Committe; III.2 20030058-005/© CWM; 20030096-022a/© CWM; III.3 Robert Barrow; III.4 © CWM; III.5 © TMM/H9-7-251; III.6 © CWM; III.7 © TMM/H9-21-229; III.8 © CWM; III.9 © TMM/H9-36-137; III.10 © TMM/H9-5-356

**Chapter 7:** 7.1 19800283-010/© CWM; 7.3 AM/events 179/3; 7.4 LAC/PA-000262; 7.6 LAC/PA-002084; 7.7 LAC/PA-022654; 7.8 LAC/PA803934; 7.9 LAC/PA-122516; 7.10 LAC/PA-001370; 7.11 AM/Neg. # N480; 7.12 LAC/PA-000074; 7.13 19710261-0389/Beaverbrook Collection of War Art/© CWM; 7.14 Canada. Dept. of National Defence/LAC/PA-001479; 7.15 GA/NA-1959-1; 7.16 LAC/PA-007439; 7.17 © NCC/CCN; 7.18 Archives of Ontario/War Poster Collection/C 233-2-1-0-7; 7.19 19740490-001/George Metcalf Archival Collection/© CWM; 7.20 LAC/C-003624b; 7.21 LAC/C-081360; 7.22 LAC/PA-070057; 7.24 19710261-0770/Beaverbrook Collection of War Art/© CWM; 7.25 Reproduced with the permission of Veterans Affairs Canada, 2007

**Chapter 8:** 8.1 LAC/PA-025025; 8.2 © NGC, Ottawa; 8.3 AM/N12310; 8.4 AM/N12340; 8.5 LAC/C-000691; 8.6 AM/N12296; 8.7 LAC/PA-139947; 8.8 © NCC/CCN; 8.9 LAC/PA-030212; 8.10 Private collection 8.11 © Canada Post Corporation (2007)/LAC/0452 E000008639; 8.12 LAC/C-029468; 8.13 National Inventors Hall of Fame; 8.14 GA/NC-6-12955b; 8.15 LAC/PA-168131; 8.16 University of Saskatchewan Archives/A3412; 8.17 LAC/C-021528; 8.18 National Oceanic and Atmospheric Administration Photo Library; 8.20 LAC/PA-029399; 8.21 LAC/PA 36080; 8.22 Yousuf Karsh/LAC/PA-174051; 8.23 UMASC/*Winnipeg Tribune* fonds

**Chapter 9:** 9.1 1970261-2079/Beaverbrook Collection of War Art/© CWM; 9.3 LAC/PA-145502; 9.4 LAC/PA-175778; 9.5 LAC/PA-803922; 9.6 19750539-007/© CWM; 9.7 BCATP Department of National Defence/PL-3028; 9.9 LAC/PA-108300; 9.10 LAC/C-046350; 9.11 Al Harvey/www.slidefarm.com; 9.12 top: 19920174-003/© CWM; bottom: LAC/C-099610; 9.13 Western Canadian Aviation Museum; 9.14 19930075-001/© CWM; 9.15 Courtesy Graham Broad; 9.16 19750251-008/©CWM; 9.17 LAC/PA-114767; 9.18 LAC/PA 122289; 9.19 AM/Foote 2359/N3000; 9.20 United States Holocaust Memorial Museum/77217; 9.21 Photo by Malak/Courtesy Canadian Tulip Festival

**Part IV:** IV.1 Private Collection; IV.2 © TMM/Cdn Cookbook; IV.3 Le Musée de Saint-Boniface Museum; IV.4 © TMM/H5-3-15;

IV.5 *The Gazette* (Montreal)/LAC/PA-129833; IV.6 Western Development Museum/2005-5-350; IV.7 M965.199.8067/McCord Museum, Montreal; IV.8 © TMM/H9-34-634; IV.9 19780339-003/© CWM; IV.10 Private Collection

**Chapter 10:** 10.1 AP/CP (Virginia Mayo); 10.2 LAC/PA-170294; 10.3 Bill and Jean Newton/LAC/C-008099; 10.4 UN #187335/Eskinder Debebe; 10.5 © NCC/CCN; 10.6 McGill University Archives Photographic Collection; 10.7 CP/CP (Jonathon Hayward); 10.8 AP/CP (Dado Galdieri); 10.9 CP/CP (Fred Chartrand); 10.10 19920107-1-001/Beaverbrook Collection of War Art/© CWM; 10.11 LAC/PA-117107

**Chapter 11:** 11.1 Hulton Getty #2659525; 11.2 Currency Museum, Bank of Canada, Gord Carter; 11.3 Thomas Fisher Library/University of Toronto; 11.4 Walter Curtin/LAC/PA-151722; 11.6 © Amnesty International; 11.7 LAC/PA-093943/By permission Communist Party of Canada; 11.8 GA/NA-789-80; 11.9 UMASC/*Winnipeg Tribune* fonds; 11.10 © TMM/HBC 1480; 11.11 © Portage & Main Press; 11.12 NASA; 11.13 NB/CP (James Forsyth); 11.16 Canada's Sports Hall of Fame; 11.17 STRLEHT/CP; 11.18 CP/CP; 11.19 National Film Board of Canada. Phototèque /LAC/PA-152025; 11.20 Kay & John Einarson family, Flin Flon, c.1955; 11.21 SAB/R-A5739-1; 11.22 SAB/R-B11203-2

**Chapter 12:** 12.1 © Jane Ash Poitras/Courtesy Galerie Vincent, Ottawa; 12.2 LAC/PA-206465; 12.3 Duncan Cameron/LAC/PA-115753; 12.4 Legislative Assembly of Nunavut; 12.6 Government of Nunavut; 12.7 WFP/CP (Wayne Glowacki); 12.8 CP/CP (Marianne Helm); 12.9 Duncan Cameron/LA/PA-115039; 12.10 CP/CP (Chuck Mitchell); 12.11 QBCJ/CP; 12.12 UMASC/*Winnipeg Tribune*/Georges Forest; 12.13 Nova Scotia Communications; 12.14 LAC/PA-047218; 12.15 LAC/PA-124953; 12.16 AP/CP; 12.17 United States Holocaust Memorial Museum/88245; 12.18 NSARM/H.B. Jefferson fonds/1992-304/no. 25 (N-6965); 12.19 Folklorama; 12.20 STRTRSTR/CP (Doug Griffin)

**Part V:** V.1, V.2 Courtesy Doug Whiteway; V.3 Private collection; V.4 Library of Parliament/Mone Cheng; V.5 Courtesy Matthew Rankin; V.6 Private collection; V.7 Robert Barrow; V.8 © TMM/H4-21-87

**Chapter 13:** 13.1 Maltwood Collection/Bequest of Katharine and John Maltwood; 13.3 Chris Lund/National Film Board of Canada. Phototheque/LAC/PA-129262; 13.4 Glenn Bullard photo/Canadian Embassy, Washington, USA; 13.6 Bus Griffiths/Courtenay and District Museum; 13.7 © Frantic World Ltd, 2006/www.thefrantics.com; 13.8 Courtesy Matthew Rankin; 13.9 TRSTR/CP (Frank Lennon); 13.11 (top to bottom) Susan King/LAC / e006610231; Tata, Sam/LAC/ RD-001289; Photo used with permission of the National Film Board of Canada/LAC/PA-184071; 13.12 CBC; 13.13 Courtesy Pierre Perpall; 13.14 House of Commons/Christian Diotte; 13. 15 CP/CP (Fred Chartrand); 13.16 David Buston Photo; 13.17 Department of Canadian Heritage; 13.18 LAC/R7316-606/Courtesy of the Estate of Dr. Naomi Jackson Groves; 13.19 LAC/C-135886; 13.20 LAC/e-001913606; 13.21 Glen Bullard photo/Canadian Embassy, Washington, USA

**Chapter 14:** 14.1 LAC/PA-093833/By permission Communist Party of Canada; 14.2 LAC/PA-093522/By permission Communist Party of Canada; 14.3 LAC/PA-112659; 14.4 Ted Dinsmore/*Toronto Star;* 14.5 CP/CP; 14.6 Department of Canadian Heritage; 14.7 WFP/CP (Wayne Glowacki)

**Chapter 15:** 15.1 CP/CP (Aaron Harris); 15.2 CP/CP (Andrew Vaughan); 15.3 Collection of Robert Barrow; 15.4 Diefenbaker Canada Centre Archives/JGD 4908/Louis Jacques, Canada Wide; 15.5 House of Commons; 15.6 Michael Bedford Photography; 15.7 CP/CP (Andy Shott); 15.8 STRREX/CP (David Hartley/Rex Features); 15.9 (l to r) Rideau Hall; Sgt Eric Jolin/Rideau Hall; 15.10 CP/CP (Tom Hanson); 15.11 (all) © NCC/CCN; 15.12 TRSTR/CP; 15.13 CP/CP (Peter Bregg); 15.14 Denise Grant/LAC/PA-198574; 15.15 Dave Chan; 15.16 WFP/CP (Wayne Glowacki); 15.17 CP/CP (Tom Hanson); 15.18 AM/Collection Juba, Stephen 1; 15.19 Courtesy of Conservative Party, Liberal Party, and New Democratic Party; 15.20 CP/CP (Fred Chartrand); 15.21 CP/CP (Jacques Boissinot)

# Index